READING

the

BIBLE

IN WESLEYAN WAYS

READING

the

BIBLE

IN WESLEYAN WAYS

SOME CONSTRUCTIVE PROPOSALS

EDITED BY

BARRY L. CALLEN & RICHARD P. THOMPSON

Beacon Hill Press of Kansas City
Kansas City, Missouri

Copyright 2004
by Beacon Hill Press of Kansas City

ISBN 083-412-0488

Printed in the
United States of America

Cover Design: Ted Ferguson

Citations from texts of John Wesley that are abbreviated as *Works* (Bicentennial ed.) refer to *The Bicentennial Edition of the Works of John Wesley,* published under the general editorship of Frank Baker and Richard Heitzenrater, first by Oxford University Press and then (since 1984) Abingdon Press (still in the course of publication).

Citations from texts of John Wesley that are abbreviated as *Works* (Jackson ed.) refer to *The Works of John Wesley,* published under the editorship of Thomas Jackson by the Wesleyan Methodist Conference Office in 1872 and reprinted by Zondervan Publishing House in 1958-59.

Citations from John Wesley's letters that are abbreviated as *Letters* (Telford ed.) refer to *The Letters of the Rev. John Wesley* (8 vols.), edited by John Telford and published by Epworth Press (1931).

Citations from John Wesley's journal that are abbreviated as *Journal* (Curnock ed.) refer to *The Journal of the Rev. John Wesley,* edited by Nehemiah Curnock and published by Epworth Press (1909-16).

Library of Congress Cataloging-in-Publication Data

Reading the Bible in Wesleyan ways : some constructive proposals / editors, Barry L. Callen, Richard P. Thompson.
    p. cm.
   Includes bibliographical references.
   ISBN 0-8341-2048-8
   1. Bible—Reading. 2. Bible—Hermeneutics. 3. Wesley, John, 1703-1791. I. Callen, Barry L. II. Thompson, Richard P.

   BS617.R42 2004
   220.6'088'287—dc22

2003018223

10 9 8 7 6 5 4 3 2 1

In grateful memory of John Wesley (1703-91), on the occasion of his 300th birthday. Man of one book, he sought to know it above all else and to be truly transformed by the Spirit who inspired its writing and continues to inspire its current significance.

Contents

INTRODUCTION

The development of this volume was prompted by a series of questions. Should the Bible remain as the central authority for the contemporary Christian community? If the Bible's authority does remain central, how should a believer go about interpreting it? How should the church as a whole undertake the task of interpreting the Bible? In the process of seeking a responsible interpretation of the Bible, are there within the Wesleyan theological tradition important resources for appropriate and currently relevant interpretation? Put otherwise, are there distinctly Wesleyan ways of reading the Bible? If there are, what are they and are they worthy of clarification for a new generation of Wesleyans and for the ongoing life of the whole church? The essays presented in this book explore the possibility of distinctively Wesleyan ways of reading and interpreting the Scriptures. The reader will find in this book answers to the above questions given cautiously, thoughtfully, and in a nonsectarian spirit by a group of scholars and theologians who represent and address the concerns of the Wesleyan communities of faith.

THE NORMING NORM

Often one encounters the phrase "the norming norm" when persons from the Wesleyan and some other Christian traditions refer to the special authority of the Bible and how it is to be read for the sake of proper Christian belief and practice. Typically this phrase means that one should recognize multiple ways of "knowing" (there is more than one norm) and affirm that in their midst the Bible holds a privileged place (the norm of the norms). This present volume is intended to explore such a crucial affirmation and to inquire whether the Wesleyan theological tradition can and should claim that the Bible is to be read and interpreted in particular ways, indeed, in Wesleyan ways.

The idea of a "quadrilateral" often is said to be a particularly helpful way of graphically imaging the interplay of biblical revelation, human reason, spiritual experience, and church tradition in understanding the present significance of the biblical text. While appreciated in various Christian traditions, it typically is called the "Wesleyan quadrilateral." This four-part image is explained well by Donald Thorsen, who views the quadrilateral concept as a carefully balanced affirmation that properly integrates all historic authority claimants for Christians. Biblical authority is said to be primary, although not exclusive and independent among such claimants. Joining biblical revelation are (1) the interpretive church tradition extending back to classical Christian orthodoxy, (2) rational methods of inquiry, and (3) spiritual experience.[1]

To protect such quadrilateral thinking from a loss of intended Wesleyan balance and thus from serious distortion, Randy Maddox offers the view that this matrix of interacting ways of Christian knowing may be described best as "a unilateral *rule* of Scripture within a trilateral *hermeneutic* of reason, tradition, and experience."[2] As Scott Jones demonstrates in his landmark study,[3] John Wesley held to the authority of Scripture alone, although Scripture never stands alone but always is read and understood in an interpretive tension with reason, Christian antiquity, the Church of England, and experience. So, one might say that we have a single but complex locus of authority, the one authority (the Bible) infused with multiple reading contexts and interpretive aids.[4]

Two things, then, appear necessary to say. First, the Bible is the norming norm that plays a central role in directing Christian wisdom. Second, the Bible does not play its central role in isolation from what inevitably impacts how the biblical text is read and interpreted. While the Bible may be preeminent in its authoritative significance, it necessarily interfaces with worlds that keep it from being a wholly isolated and independent authority source. In fact, there are interactive aids to biblical understanding, aids graciously provided by God and ignored at the reader's peril. God's revelation, to be received and interpreted properly, necessarily includes a written apostolic witness (the Bible), a faithful remembering community (the traditions), a process of existential appropriation (spiritual experience), a way to test for internal consistency (reason), and a commitment of readers to be open to the biblical text in this multiple and interactive manner. For Wesleyans, then,

> Scripture has been understood as the means by which the Holy Spirit dynamically communicates the Word of God, rather than as a collection of codified divine propositions whose authority is dogmatically and rationally asserted by philosophical argumentation. In-

1. Donald A. D. Thorsen, *The Wesleyan Quadrilateral: Scripture, Reason, Tradition, and Experience as Model for Evangelical Theology* (Grand Rapids: Zondervan, 1990; reprint, Indianapolis: Light and Life Communications, 1997), 251.

2. Randy L. Maddox, *Responsible Grace: John Wesley's Practical Theology* (Nashville: Abingdon/Kingswood, 1994), 46.

3. Scott J. Jones, *Wesley's Conception and Use of Scripture* (Nashville: Abingdon/Kingswood, 1995).

4. For additional perspective and a bibliography of related articles found in the publishing history of the *Wesleyan Theological Journal,* see Barry L. Callen and William C. Kostlevy, compilers and editors, *Heart of the Heritage* (Salem, Ohio: Schmul, 2001), 81-83.

stead, Wesleyans have seen Scripture as a "means of grace" through which the Spirit functions to carry on the life-giving ministry of Christ.[5]

The fundamental conviction of Christian faith is that God is self-revealed through particular historical events, notably the life of Israel culminating in the Christ-event. Hence, Christianity is less a philosophy or system of theological ideas and more a commitment to a given set of historical occurrences as the clue to the meaning of God and human existence. This historical authority ground is Christ-centered and biblically conveyed. Reading the Bible appropriately is essential.

FOUNDATIONS FOR READING THE BIBLE IN WESLEYAN WAYS

A pivotal historical event in the distant past obviously requires for the contemporary person a medium of conveyance, a dependable report and interpretation, and thus the necessity of the Bible for Christians. It can be said that Scripture is the appointed means by which a believer, in faith, enters into a life-transforming conversation with and then relation to the God who is intentionally disclosed in the events to which the Bible bears witness. Since the divine intent of the historical Christ-event and its faithful conveyance in Scripture is present transformation of life (a key Wesleyan assumption), the Bible should be read soteriologically. Seeing Scripture in this salvation way leads to Wesleyan reading strategies that (1) focus on the ministry of the Spirit of Christ to illumine the present significance of the text, (2) privilege the role of the faith community as the crucial location of Scripture's meaning and present significance, and (3) highlight the interpretive importance of a Bible reader who is both spiritually mature and united with other believers in the pursuit of God's love realized in the heart and in the world. William M. Greathouse and H. Ray Dunning rightly affirm that the Bible (1) *is* the written Word of God in the sense that it fulfills the necessary function of mediating God's self-disclosure to humankind, (2) *contains* the Living Word of God in that in it one finds Christ, the Living Word, and (3) may *become* God's personal Word when it is read in faith and illumined by the Spirit to reveal the identity and vocation of the people of God.[6]

Robert W. Wall explains why the professional guilds of biblical scholarship often lead readers away from the crucial roles that should be

---

5. R. Larry Shelton, "A Wesleyan/Holiness Agenda for the Twenty-First Century," *Wesleyan Theological Journal* 33/2 (Fall 1998): 91.

6. William M. Greathouse and H. Ray Dunning, *An Introduction to Wesleyan Theology*, rev. ed. (Kansas City: Beacon Hill Press of Kansas City, 1989), 9-15.

played by the church and spiritual maturity in proper biblical reading and understanding.[7] He also argues that the attempt to approach Scripture in distinctively Wesleyan ways can and should be more than a defensive parochialism. In fact, if praxis is the church's goal in biblical interpretation, "then a model of interpretation that features a Wesleyan theological reading of biblical texts must help to shape the theological understanding and spiritual vitality of its Wesleyan constituency. Only then will the Wesleyan voice be preserved into the next generation for the church catholic."[8] This call to "retribalize" Wesleyan hermeneutics for the sake of real life and the whole church is affirmed by the compilers and editors of this present volume.

As the "assured results" of modern scholarship have become *less* assured in the rubble of the Enlightenment experiment, we affirm that it is possible and important to pursue at least the general contours of a distinctively Wesleyan hermeneutic of Scripture. We gladly join Joel Green in the call "to loosen our grips on the tradition of modern biblical scholarship, and to loosen its grip on us, in order that we might participate in forms of biblical study that take with utmost seriousness our location within the church, and more particularly within the Wesleyan tradition of the church."[9] The challenge now being presented to the church by postmodernity may actually be an open door with fresh possibilities for Wesleyan-oriented Christians. Richard Thompson suggests one such possibility of reading the Bible, which accounts for the text, the reader, and the reader's context.[10]

Bible reading in Wesleyan ways, to be true to the Wesleyan tradition, will include giving careful attention to the Bible-Spirit relationship. The Holy Spirit is key to the illumination needed for discovering the current significance of Scripture for Christian belief and life. God, the original divine inspirer of the biblical story, surely is in the best position to assist with its contemporary understanding and application. The Spirit was given to lead believers into all truth, that is, "to help us to see the meaning of what Jesus

---

7. Robert W. Wall, "The Future of Wesleyan Biblical Studies," *Wesleyan Theological Journal* 33/2 (Fall 1998): 102. Included in this volume.

8. Robert W. Wall, "Toward a Wesleyan Hermeneutic of Scripture," *Wesleyan Theological Journal* 30/2 (Fall 1995): 56. Included in this volume.

9. Joel B. Green, "Reading the Bible As Wesleyans," *Wesleyan Theological Journal* 33/2 (Fall 1998): 129. A revision of this article is included in this volume.

10. Richard P. Thompson, "Community in Conversation: Multiple Readings of Scripture and a Wesleyan Understanding of the Church," *Wesleyan Theological Journal* 35/1 (Spring 2000): 206-7. Included in this volume.

said in the new contexts that would arise afterwards."[11] We hear Christ say, "Let anyone who has an ear listen to what the Spirit is saying to the churches" (Rev. 3:22, NRSV). The biblical text is basic. The ongoing Spirit-illumination of the text is essential in relation to the particular world of each Bible reader.[12] Illumined and disciplined human reason is not optional but essential. In addition, the Wesleyan reading of the Bible should be informed by the teaching tradition of the whole church and should function in humble openness to God's present transformational intent. The biblical text is read best as a crucial servant to the salvation process.

APPROACHING THIS PRESENT VOLUME

This present volume intends to serve the Spirit-listening resolve and skill of pastors and of students and teachers in colleges and seminaries. This intention is much like John Wesley's prefatory comment to his *Explanatory Notes upon the Old Testament:* "But it is not part of my design, to save either learned or unlearned men from the trouble of thinking. . . . On the contrary, my intention is, to make them think, and assist them in thinking. This is the way to understand the things of God." To assist the present generation of Bible readers with the necessary thinking, we have assembled a group of significant essays by outstanding biblical scholars and theologians who both represent and address the Wesleyan theological tradition in particular and convey insights vital for today's Bible readers who are formed in any tradition of the faith.

The essays that follow are grouped under two categories, Foundations for Interpretation and Frontiers for Interpretation. Within the first category, the reader will encounter essays addressing issues such as the Scripture principle, a trinitarian perspective, a call to "retribalize," a concept of inspired imagination, and a suggested pattern of interpretative balance. Each of these essays supplements the others and helps to form broad perspective on Wesleyan ways of Bible reading.

Because of the relational character involved in the foundations of biblical interpretation, there are vital frontiers of such foundations that are still taking shape. With the "enlightenment experiment" in serious decay

---

11. Clark H. Pinnock, *The Scripture Principle* (San Francisco: Harper and Row, 1984), 171.

12. Thus we read this in Greathouse and Dunning, *Introduction to Wesleyan Theology,* 14: "The proper attitude to assume, therefore, in reading the Bible is that of the child Samuel who was instructed by Eli to answer, 'Speak, Lord; for thy servant heareth' (1 Sam. 3:9). . . . To pray as we read, and read as we pray—this is the proper approach to Holy Scripture. Suddenly a familiar verse flames with new meaning as the Spirit illuminates it to our hearts!"

and a major struggle now going on in the evangelical community over issues of biblical interpretation, how can Scripture's central role among Wesleyan and other Bible readers be clarified and enhanced in a postmodern time? Adequate reading strategies require that the church commit to serious conversation involving the biblical text. Gender exclusion from any dimensions of this process must cease. All voices are to be included in the conversation as both the past and future meanings of God's revelation are pursued in our time. This volume is dedicated to informing and furthering this conversation.

FOUNDATIONS
FOR
INTERPRETATION

Geoffrey Wainwright has had a distinguished career as professor and systematic theologian. He is best known for his significant work on the doctrine of the Trinity. This chapter focuses on an aspect of John Wesley's work that has often gone unnoticed: his trinitarian hermeneutics. Although trinitarian vocabulary is relatively sparse in Wesley's writings, this study accentuates the thoroughly trinitarian dimension of Wesley's understanding of the nature of Scripture and his reading of these texts.

What Professor Wainwright offers here is an important study that provides insights into the theological thought of Wesley that informed his practice of reading and interpreting Scripture. While it has been often noted that Wesley's thought centered on the pastoral or soteriological, here one finds that such soteriological emphases come from Wesley's understanding of the Trinity. This relation between Wesley's trinitarian thought and his soteriological reading of Scripture is a crucial dimension of ongoing readings of the biblical texts in the Wesleyan tradition.

1

THE TRINITARIAN
HERMENEUTIC OF JOHN WESLEY[1]

Geoffrey Wainwright

◆

If one consults the entry "Trinity" in the index of an edition of John Wesley's works or in a book on Wesley's theology, the pickings are likely to be slim. The superficial impression might be formed that Wesley undervalued the reality and the doctrine of the Trinity. Or else, from another corner, the paucity of references might happily be taken as confirmation that "the Trinity" belonged to that "orthodoxy" by which Wesley seemed to set such little store in comparison with "the religion of the heart." Thus Wesley could indeed say, in his sermon "The Way to the Kingdom":

> A man may be orthodox in every point; he may not only espouse right opinions, but zealously defend them against all opposers; he may think justly concerning the incarnation of our Lord, concerning the ever blessed Trinity, and every other doctrine contained in the oracles of God. He may assent to all three creeds—that called the Apostles', the Nicene, and the Athanasian—and yet 'tis possible he may have no religion at all, no more than a Jew, Turk, or pagan. He may be almost as orthodox as the devil (though indeed not altogether; for every man errs in something, whereas we can't well conceive him [the devil] to hold any erroneous opinion) and may all the while be as great a stranger as he to the religion of the heart.[2]

However, two things need to be noted. First, when Wesley appears in his writings to demean orthodoxy, it is *dead* orthodoxy he is aiming at; he is well aware that *living* faith has classic Christian doctrine as the intellectual formulation of its content. Second, it will be observed in the very passage just quoted that Wesley includes "the ever blessed Trinity" among the "doctrines" that are "contained in the oracles of God." This point should itself suffice to give initial plausibility to looking for the trinitarian dimension in Wesley's hermeneutics of the Bible.

There is a further reason why people may miss the trinitarian dimension in Wesley: he himself does not often use the term "Trinity" in his writ-

---

1. Appeared originally in the *Wesleyan Theological Journal* 36/1 (Spring 2001). Used by permission.

2. "The Way to the Kingdom" (1746), I.6, Sermon 7, in *Works* (Bicentennial ed.), 1:220-21.

ings. In the sermon that bears by way of exception the title "On the Trinity," Wesley writes:

> I dare not insist upon anyone's using the word "Trinity" or "Person." I use them myself without any scruple, because I know of none better. But if any man has scruple concerning them, who shall constrain him to use them? I cannot; much less would I burn a man alive —and that with moist, green wood—for saying, "Though I believe the Father is God, the Son is God, and the Holy Ghost is God, yet I scruple using the words 'Trinity' and 'Persons' because I do not find those terms in the Bible." These are the words which merciful John Calvin cites as wrote by Servetus in a letter to himself. I would insist only on the direct words unexplained, just as they lie in the text: "There are three that bear record in heaven, the Father, the Word, and the Holy Ghost; and these three are one."[3]

We shall return to that sermon of Wesley's and to the problematic character of the scriptural text on which it is based, but meanwhile a passage may be quoted from the conclusion of the sermon that puts us on the right track toward Wesley's trinitarian hermeneutics. Listen for the soteriological and doxological thrusts in this paragraph:

> The knowledge of the Three-One God is interwoven with all true Christian faith, with all vital religion. . . . I know not how anyone can be a Christian believer till "he hath" (as St. John speaks) "the witness in himself" [1 John 5:10]; till "the Spirit of God witnesses with his spirit that he is a child of God" [cf. Rom. 8:16]—that is, in effect, till God the Holy Ghost witnesses that God the Father has accepted him through the merits of God the Son—and having this witness he honours the Son and the blessed Spirit "even as he honours the Father" [cf. John 5:23].[4]

Incidentally, that same passage uses the other term that Wesley sometimes used in place of "Trinity," namely "the Three-One God."

Fortified by the passage from the sermon "On the Trinity," I shall now seek to expound Wesley's trinitarian hermeneutics, sometimes picking up what may be considered mere hints but at other times drawing on quite explicit statements of his. My argument will be that Wesley was thoroughly trinitarian in his understanding of the composition of the Scriptures, in

---

3. "On the Trinity" (1775), 4, Sermon 55, in *Works* (Bicentennial ed.), 2:377-78. Wesley's ironic reference to Calvin is perhaps not surprising. Outler shows, however, that Wesley's account both of Servetus' teaching and of Calvin's part in the affair is somewhat garbled.

4. Ibid., 17, 385.

his ways of proceeding with the Scriptures and in his reading of the content of the Scriptures.

How the Scriptures Came to Be

In the preface to his *Explanatory Notes upon the New Testament,* Wesley gives the following succinct account of the historical origins of the Scriptures:

> Concerning the Scriptures in general, it may be observed, the word of the living God, which directed the first Patriarchs also, was, in the time of Moses, committed to writing. To this were added, in several succeeding generations, the inspired writings of the other Prophets. Afterwards, what the Son of God preached, and the Holy Ghost spake by the Apostles, the Apostles and Evangelists wrote. This is what we now style the Holy Scripture: This is that "word of God which remaineth for ever"; of which, though "heaven and earth pass away, one jot or tittle shall not pass away." The Scripture, therefore, of the Old and New Testament is a most solid and precious system of divine truth.[5]

A human role of various kinds, differing according to historical circumstances, is clearly recognized by Wesley in the writing down of God's word by Moses and his successors, and by the apostles and evangelists. For present purposes we do not need to go into the question of Wesley's oscillation in other discussions between a dictation theory—whereby certain parts of Scripture were given to the human writer by "particular revelation"—and the allowance that the human writers used their human judgment in a more general accordance with "the divine light which abode with them, the standing treasure of the Spirit of God."[6] What is clear from the passage in the preface to the *Explanatory Notes upon the New Testament* and remains consistently so in Wesley's thought, is that Scripture is *God's* word all through, including now Gospels and Epistles as well as the Law and the Prophets. The God of Israel, who directed the patriarchs and inspired the prophets, is (as we shall later see) the Holy Trinity, who has now been revealed as such in the incarnation of the Son, the Word made flesh, and in the Holy Spirit who was seen to rest upon Jesus and heard to speak through the apostles at Pentecost and beyond.

---

5. Preface to *Explanatory Notes upon the New Testament* (1754-55), 10, in *Works* (Jackson ed.), 14:238.

6. See Scott J. Jones, *John Wesley's Conception and Use of Scripture* (Nashville: Abingdon/Kingswood, 1995), 18-21.

This trinitarian origin of the Scriptures is to be matched, according to Wesley, in our appropriation of them.

SEARCHING THE SCRIPTURES

Searching the Scriptures is, in Wesley's view, an "ordinance of God," a "means of grace," and a "work of piety." Thus in the General Rules, the "ordinances of God" include both "searching the Scriptures," apparently understood as a family or private exercise, and "the ministry of the Word, either read or expounded" as part of "the public worship of God."[7] In the sermon titled "The Means of Grace," the list contains "searching the Scriptures (which implies reading, hearing, and meditating thereon)."[8] In the sermon "On Working Out Our Own Salvation," the exhortation to "works of piety" embraces "Search the Scriptures: hear them in public, read them in private, and meditate therein."[9]

The guidance that Wesley gives for proceeding with the Scriptures is trinitarian in shape. He begins pneumatologically. In the preface to the *Explanatory Notes upon the Old Testament,* Wesley declares that "Scripture can only be understood through the same Spirit whereby it was given."[10] Similarly in the lengthy letter to William Warburton, bishop of Gloucester: "I do firmly believe (and what serious man does not?), *omnis scriptura legi debet eo Spiritu quo scripta est:* 'We need the same Spirit to understand the Scripture, which enabled the holy men of old to write it.'"[11] The Latin tag comes from Thomas à Kempis's *Imitation of Christ* (I.5) and was taken up by the Second Vatican Council's constitution on Divine Revelation, *Dei Verbum* (12), and quoted in turn by the new universal *Catechism of the Catholic Church* (sec. 111) as "a principle of correct interpretation": "Sacred Scripture must be read and interpreted in the light of the same Spirit by whom it was written."

For John Wesley, this pneumatological principle entailed in practice that the study of Scripture be surrounded by prayer. That is explicitly stated in the same paragraph 18 of the preface to the *Explanatory Notes upon the Old Testament:* "Serious and earnest prayer should be constantly used

---

7. "Nature, Design, and General Rules of the United Societies" (1743), 6, in *Works* (Bicentennial ed.), 9:73.

8. "The Means of Grace" (1746), II.1, Sermon 16, in *Works* (Bicentennial ed.), 1:381.

9. "On Working Out Our Own Salvation" (1785), II.4, Sermon 85, in *Works* (Bicentennial ed.), 3:205.

10. Preface to the *Explanatory Notes upon the Old Testament* (1765), 18, in *Works* (Jackson ed.), 14:253.

11. "A Letter to the Right Reverend the Lord Bishop of Gloucester, occasioned by his tract 'On the Office and Operations of the Holy Spirit'" (1762), in *Works* (Jackson ed.), 9:154.

before we consult the oracles of God; seeing 'Scripture can only be understood through the same Spirit whereby it was given.' Our reading should likewise be closed with prayer, that what we read may be written on our hearts."[12] In his counsel to the reader of his edition of the English New Testament, Wesley provides a sample prayer whose phraseology we have already heard him echo:

> I advise every one, before he reads the Scripture, to use this or the like prayer: "Blessed Lord, who hast caused all holy Scriptures to be written for our learning, grant that we may in such wise hear them, read, mark, learn, and inwardly digest them, that by patience and comfort of thy holy word, we may embrace, and ever hold fast, the blessed hope of everlasting life, which thou hast given us in our Saviour Jesus Christ."[13]

That is a collect from the Book of Common Prayer, located in the 1662 Prayer Book at the second Sunday in Advent. It carries a subtle trinitarian watermark: the "Lord" of the opening address may be either the First Person or the entire Trinity; "patience" and "comfort" are characteristically in the Scriptures the result of the Holy Spirit's operation; the work of redemption is Christ's.

So we may now proceed christologically. Throughout the Church's history, Christ has been taken as the key to the Scriptures. Again, the *Catechism of the Catholic Church* sums up the entire tradition thus: "Different as the books which comprise it may be, Scripture is a unity by reason of the unity of God's plan, of which Christ Jesus is the center and heart, open since his Passover" (sec. 112). In line with the Christian tradition, beginning from the writers of the New Testament, the Old Testament is interpreted by Wesley in a broadly prophetic way, as the preparation for the coming of Christ. The point is put in a nutshell when Wesley recalls Jesus' instruction to Jewish controversialists to "search the Scriptures, for they testify of me" (John 5:39): "For this very end did he direct them to search the Scriptures, that they might believe in him."[14] Then, in the preface to his *Explanatory Notes upon the New Testament*, Wesley delineates the contents of the New Testament—Gospels, Acts, Epistles, Revelation—christocentrically:

> The New Testament is all those sacred writings in which the new testament or covenant is described. The former part of this contains the writings of the Evangelists and Apostles; the latter, the Revelation of Jesus Christ. In the former is, first, the history of Jesus Christ, from

---

12. *Works* (Jackson ed.), 14:253.
13. Ibid., 307.
14. "The Means of Grace," III.7, Sermon 16, in *Works* (Bicentennial ed.), 1:387.

his coming in the flesh to his ascension into heaven; then, the institution and history of the Christian Church, from the time of his ascension. The Revelation delivers what is to be, with regard to Christ, the Church, and the universe, till the consummation of all things.[15]

Christ himself is our way to the Father. For Wesley, according to the preface of his *Explanatory Notes upon the Old Testament,* the purpose of reading the Scriptures is "to understand the things of God":

> "Meditate thereon day and night" [cf. Josh. 1:8; Ps. 1:2]. So shall you attain the best knowledge, even to "know the only true God, and Jesus Christ whom He hath sent" [John 17:3]. And this knowledge will lead you "to love Him, because He hath first loved us" [1 John 4:19]; yea, "to love the Lord your God with all your heart, and with all your soul, and with all your mind, and with all your strength" [cf. Deut. 6:5; Matt. 22:37; Mark 12:30; Luke 12:27]. Will there not then be all "that mind in you which was also in Christ Jesus" [Phil. 2:5]? And in consequence of this, while you joyfully experience all the holy tempers described in this book, you will likewise be outwardly "holy as He that hath called you is holy, in all manner of conversation" [1 Pet. 1:15].[16]

Thus this particular hermeneutical circle—the trinitarian one—is complete. Study of the Scriptures in the Spirit, by whom they were divinely written, conveys the incarnate Christ, who gives us knowledge of the Father who sent him, so that we may love the Father and thus be conformed to the Son and enjoy the holiness which the Holy Spirit gives. The dynamic pattern described by Wesley matches well the movement which St. Basil of Caesarea sets forth in one of the most important treatises in the history of trinitarian doctrine, his work *On the Holy Spirit:* the Father's blessings reach us through the Son in the Holy Spirit, in whom then our thanks and prayers ascend through the Son to the Father. Wesley traces the function of the Scriptures in this soteriological and doxological process. With that, we come to what may be called the scope of the Scriptures.

THE SCOPE OF THE SCRIPTURES

John Wesley characteristically spoke of the "general tenor of Scripture" or "the whole scope of Scripture."[17] As a Greek scholar, he would know that *skopos* connotes both goal and range.

---

15. Preface to the *Explanatory Notes upon the New Testament,* 13, in *Works* (Jackson ed.), 14:239.

16. Preface to the *Explanatory Notes upon the Old Testament,* 17, in *Works* (Jackson ed.), 14:252.

17. See Jones, *John Wesley's Conception and Use of Scripture,* 43-53.

The salvific purpose of the Scriptures is graphically rendered in the celebrated passage of Wesley's preface to the *Sermons on Several Occasions* that appears indebted, perhaps via William Law's *Christian Perfection,* to the arrow and the sparrow of Wisdom 5:9-13 and Bede's story from the court of King Edwin:

> To candid, reasonable men I am not afraid to lay open what have been the inmost thoughts of my heart. I have thought, I am a creature of a day, passing through life as an arrow through the air. I am a spirit come from God and returning to God; just hovering over the great gulf, till a few moments hence I am no more seen—I drop into an unchangeable eternity! I want to know one thing, the way to heaven—how to land safe on that happy shore. God himself has condescended to teach the way: for this very end he came from heaven. He hath written it down in a book. O give me that book! At any price give me the Book of God! I have it. Here is knowledge enough for me. Let me be *homo unius libri.* Here then I am, far from the busy ways of men. I sit down alone: only God is here. In his presence I open, I read his Book; for this end, to find the way to heaven. Is there a doubt concerning the meaning of what I read? Does anything appear dark or intricate? I lift up my heart to the Father of lights: "Lord, is it not thy Word, 'If any man lack wisdom, let him ask of God'? Thou 'givest liberally and upbraidest not' [cf. James 1:5]. Thou hast said, 'If any be willing to do thy will, he shall know' [cf. John 7:17]. I am willing to do, let me know thy will." I then search after and consider parallel passages of Scripture, "comparing spiritual things with spiritual" [1 Cor. 2:13]. I meditate thereon, with all the attention and earnestness of which my mind is capable. If any doubt still remains, I consult those who are experienced in the things of God, and then the writings whereby, being dead, they yet speak. And what I thus learn, that I teach.[18]

Having been sensitized by the passages already read from Wesley on the subject, we shall perhaps be ready to catch the trinitarian hints here: God's "condescension" in the incarnation of the Son and in the Spirit's writing of the Scriptures; the "Father of lights" [James 1:17], who works by his "Word of truth" [James 1:18] and "reveals deep things by his Spirit" [cf. 1 Cor. 2:10-16].

Moreover, when Wesley speaks of "the way to heaven," the road is intrinsically related to the destination. The pilgrim's encounter with the tri-

---

18. Preface to the *Sermons on Several Occasions* (1746), 5, in *Works* (Bicentennial ed.), 1:104-5.

une God is a foretaste of the complete achievement of "man's chief end," which Wesley likes to quote from the Westminster Catechism, "to glorify God and enjoy Him for ever"[19]—and which Wesley himself describes in a trinitarian way in the peroration to his sermon "The New Creation": "And to crown all, there will be a deep, an intimate, an uninterrupted union with God; a constant communion with the Father and his Son Jesus Christ, through the Spirit; a continual enjoyment of the Three-One God, and of all the creatures in him!"[20]

That universal vision of the end allows us to treat also the range of the Scriptures in their testimony to God's purpose in the beginning; and it emerges that not only the new creation but also the first creation is presented by Wesley in trinitarian fashion. To interpret "The End of Christ's Coming," in a sermon under that title, Wesley backtracked to Genesis.[21] Without the benefit of Wellhausen's source criticism, Wesley obviously considered the first three chapters as a single story; whether in "P" or in "J(E)," it was the same Holy Trinity who said, "Let us make man in our image" (Gen. 1:26-27), and who "formed the man from the dust of the ground and breathed into his nostrils the breath of life" (2:7): "To take the matter from the beginning, 'the Lord God' (literally 'Jehovah, the Gods'; that is, One and Three) 'created man in his own image.'" That meant not only in God's "natural" image (endowment with understanding, will, and "a measure of liberty") but also in God's "moral" image, that is, "he created him not only in knowledge, but also in righteousness and true holiness":

> As his understanding was without blemish, perfect in its kind, so were all his affections. They were all set right, and duly exercised on their proper objects. And as a free agent he steadily chose whatever was good, according to the direction of his understanding. In so doing he was unspeakably happy, dwelling in God and God in him, having an uninterrupted fellowship with the Father and the Son through the eternal Spirit.

But, as is told in Genesis 3, humankind fell; and that is why, for the reestablishment of that communion with the triune God (indeed "a holiness and happiness far superior to that which Adam enjoyed in Paradise"), the entire trek from Genesis to Revelation had to occur, and "for this pur-

---

19. "The Unity of the Divine Being" (1789), 10, Sermon 120, in *Works* (Bicentennial ed.), 4:64; cf. "What Is Man? Psalm 8:4" (1788), 13-15, Sermon 116, ibid., 25-26.

20. "The New Creation" (1785), 18, Sermon 64, in *Works* (Bicentennial ed.), 2:510.

21. "The End of Christ's Coming" (1781), I.3-7, Sermon 62, in *Works* (Bicentennial ed.), 2:474-76, in particular for the following quotations.

pose the Son of God was manifested, that he might destroy the works of the devil" (1 John 3:8 [KJV], the text of Wesley's sermon on "The End of Christ's Coming").

It is this need for redemption that makes it necessary for the Bible, as it tells the intervening story, to be interpreted according to what Wesley calls "the analogy of faith."

THE ANALOGY OF FAITH

Drawn from Romans 12:6, which the RSV translates with a subjective slant as "in proportion to our faith," the "analogy of faith" bears in the older theology the objective meaning of "the proportion of the faith." Still in that line, the 1992-94 *Catechism of the Catholic Church* gives as its third hermeneutical rule "attention to the analogy of faith" and defines the *analogia fidei* as "the coherence of the truths of faith among themselves and within the whole plan of Revelation" (sec. 114). That corresponds exactly to the advice given by John Wesley in the preface to his *Explanatory Notes upon the Old Testament:* "Have a constant eye to the analogy of faith, the connexion and harmony there is between those grand, fundamental doctrines, original sin, justification by faith, the new birth, inward and outward holiness."[22] True, Wesley here considers Scriptures and the faith under the aspect of the human appropriation of salvation; but this rests, as Wesley makes amply clear throughout his sermons, upon the self-revelation of the triune God, the redemptive work of Christ, and the sanctifying work of the Spirit.[23]

We must note also that Wesley varies slightly, but not substantively, in his listings of the elements in the doctrinal scheme or the links in what he calls, in the sermon on "The End of Christ's Coming," the "connected chain" that "runs through the Bible from the beginning to the end."[24] Thus, in *The Principles of a Methodist Farther Explained,* he writes: "Our main doctrines, which include all the rest are three, that of repentance, of faith, and of holiness"; and he likens them to "the porch of religion," "the door,"

---

22. Preface to the *Explanatory Notes upon the Old Testament,* 18, in *Works* (Jackson ed.), 14:253.

23. Note also this from the treatise *The Doctrine of Original Sin* (1757), in *Works* (Jackson ed.), 9:429: "A denial of original sin contradicts the main design of the gospel, which is to humble vain man, and to ascribe to God's free grace, not man's free will, the whole of his salvation. Nor, indeed, can we let this doctrine go without giving up, at the same time, the greatest part, if not all, of the essential articles of the Christian faith. If we give up this, we cannot defend either justification by the merits of Christ, or the renewal of our natures by his Spirit."

24. "The End of Christ's Coming" (1781), III.5, Sermon 62, in *Works* (Bicentennial ed.), 2:483.

and "religion itself."[25] In his commentary on 1 Peter 4:11, Wesley writes this about speaking according to Scripture: "The oracles of God teach that men should repent, believe, obey. He that treats of faith and leaves out repentance, or does not enjoin practical holiness to believers, does not speak as the oracles of God."[26] In commenting on Romans 12:6, Wesley takes up the point from 1 Peter 4:11 about "the oracles of God" and then gives his fullest definition of prophesying "according to the analogy of faith," that is:

> According to the general tenor of them [the oracles of God]; according to that grand scheme of doctrine which is delivered therein, touching original sin, justification by faith, and present, inward salvation. There is a wonderful analogy between all these; and a close and intimate connexion between the chief heads of that faith "which was once delivered to the saints." Every article, therefore, concerning which there is any question should be determined by this rule; every doubtful scripture interpreted according to the grand truths which run through the whole.[27]

For present purposes, I will now demonstrate the trinitarian character of the "analogy of faith" by which Wesley interprets Scripture. A convenient text is Wesley's sermon "The Scripture Way of Salvation." Take first what Wesley says here about "preventing grace" or "the first dawning of grace in the soul," sometimes identified with "conscience," though Wesley will not allow that it is merely "natural." In the bringing of persons to repentance and the conviction of sin, Wesley can ascribe a role to each of the three Persons of the Trinity, seen in Johannine terms as the Father who "draws" (John 6:44), the Son who "enlightens" (1:9), and the Holy Spirit who "convicts" (16:8). Thus, prevenient grace comprises

> all the "drawings" of "the Father," the desires after God, which, if we yield to them, increase more and more; all that "light" wherewith the Son of God "enlighteneth everyone that cometh into the world," showing every man "to do justly, to love mercy, and to walk humbly with his God"; all the convictions which his Spirit from time to time works in every child of man; although, it is true, the generality of men stifle them as soon as possible, and after a while, forget, or at least deny, that ever they had them at all.[28]

---

25. *The Principles of a Methodist Farther Explained* (1746), VI.4, in *Works* (Bicentennial ed.), 9:227.

26. *Explanatory Notes upon the New Testament,* ad loc. (1 Pet. 4:11).

27. *Explanatory Notes upon the New Testament,* ad loc. (Rom. 12:6).

28. "The Scripture Way of Salvation" (1765), I.2, Sermon 43, in *Works* (Bicentennial ed.), 2:156-57.

Then "The Scripture Way of Salvation" takes us to justification and sanctification. Here the emphases are respectively christological and pneumatological. The Father forgives the believer for the sake of Christ, thereby setting us in a new relationship to himself (a "relative" change), and at the same time begins to make us holy (a "real" change) by regenerating us through the Holy Spirit, whereby we start to be conformed to Christ:

> Justification is another word for pardon. It is the forgiveness of all our sins, and (what is necessarily implied therein) our acceptance with God. The price whereby this hath been procured for us (commonly termed the "meritorious cause" of our justification) is the blood and righteousness of Christ, or (to express it a little more clearly) all that Christ hath done and suffered for us till "he poured out his soul for the transgressors" [cf. Isa. 53:12]. The immediate effects of justification are, the peace of God, a "peace that passeth all understanding" [Phil. 4:7], and a "rejoicing in hope of the glory of God" [Rom. 5:2], "with joy unspeakable and full of glory" [1 Pet. 1:8].
>
> And at the same time that we are justified, yea, in that very moment, sanctification begins. In that instant we are "born again," "born from above," "born of the Spirit" [John 3:3-8; cf. Titus 3:4-7]. There is a real as well as a relative change. We are inwardly renewed by the power of God. We feel "the love of God shed abroad in our heart by the Holy Ghost which is given unto us" [Rom. 5:5], producing love to all mankind, and more especially to the children of God; expelling the love of the world, the love of pleasure, of ease, of honour, of money; together with pride, anger, self-will, and every other evil temper—in a word, changing the "earthly, sensual, devilish" mind [James 3:15] into "the mind which was in Christ Jesus" [Phil. 2:5].[29]

When "The Scripture Way of Salvation" moves on to treat assurance, the trinitarian structure of the Godhead, of God's dealings with the world, and of the Christian life in relation to God is made abundantly clear on the basis of Ephesians 4:4-6, Galatians 2:20, 1 John 5:6-12, Romans 8:14-17, and Galatians 4:4-6:

> The Apostle says: "There is one faith, and one hope of our calling," one Christian, saving faith, as "there is one Lord" in whom we believe, and "one God and Father of us all." And it is certain this faith necessarily implies an assurance (which is here only another word for evidence, it being hard to tell the difference between them) that "Christ loved me, and gave himself for me." For "he that be-

---

29. Ibid., I.3-4, 157-58.

lieveth" with the true, living faith, "hath the witness in himself." "The Spirit witnesseth with his spirit that he is a child of God." "Because he is a son, God hath sent forth the Spirit of his Son into his heart, crying, Abba, Father"; giving him an assurance that he is so, and a childlike confidence in him.[30]

Given what Wesley describes as "the Scripture way of salvation," it is hardly surprising that he should declare in his sermon "On the Trinity" that "the knowledge of the Three-One God is interwoven with all true Christian faith, with all vital religion."

THE TRINITY REVEALED AND BELIEVED

In Wesley's sermon "On the Trinity," the trinitarian experience of the believer confirms the doctrine of the Trinity, while the doctrine rests on the "fact" that "God has revealed" that "God is Three and One." As things stand, Wesley appears to find a divine revelation of the Trinity in propositional form in the sentence he takes as the text of his sermon, namely the so-called Johannine comma at 1 John 5:7-8: "There are three that bear record in heaven, the Father, the Word, and the Holy Ghost: and these three are one" (KJV). The apologetic thrust of his argument is that, as with the creation of light or with the incarnation of the Word, one may believe the fact, which has been revealed, without understanding the manner, which has not been revealed and therefore remains mysterious:

I believe this *fact* also (if I may use the expression)—that God is Three and One. But the *manner, how,* I do not comprehend; and I do not believe it. Now in this, in the *manner,* lies the mystery. And so it may; I have no concern with it. It is no object of my faith; I believe just so much as God has revealed and no more. But this, the *manner,* he has not revealed; therefore I believe nothing about it. But would it not be absurd in me to deny the fact because I do not understand the manner? That is, to reject *what God has revealed* because I do not comprehend *what he has not revealed?*

This is a point much to be observed. There are many things which "eye hath not seen, nor ear heard, neither hath it entered into the heart of man to conceive" [1 Cor. 2:9]. Part of these God hath "revealed to us by his Spirit" [1 Cor. 2:10]—*revealed,* that is, unveiled, uncovered. That part he requires us to believe. Part of them he has not revealed. That we need not, and indeed cannot, believe; it is far above, out of our sight. Now where is the wisdom of rejecting what is revealed because we do not understand what is not re-

30. Ibid., II.3, 161-62.

vealed? Of denying the *fact* which God has unveiled because we cannot see the *manner,* which is veiled still?[31]

Wesley was aware of the question about whether the text of the Johannine comma was "genuine": "Was it originally written by the Apostle or inserted in later ages?" He was persuaded of its authenticity by Bengel's arguments.[32] Had Wesley not been persuaded of the verse's canonical authenticity, it is unlikely that he would have preached on it orally 23 times.[33]

I hope a personal intrusion may be allowed at this point. While I believe, in line with teachings of the councils of Nicea (325) and Constantinople (381), that the contested verse is an accurate summary of the scriptural witness to the triune God, and while I have no objection of principle to the notion of propositional revelation, I am nevertheless grateful that Wesley should also have provided other trinitarian confessions of faith that rely on a broader range of Scripture and on a more complex understanding of how the self-revelation of the triune God has taken place in the words and events and authorized interpretations that Scripture records. Note this example from the sermon "On the Discoveries of Faith":

> I know by faith that above all these [the spirits of angels and men] is the Lord Jehovah, he that is, that was, and that is to come [Rev. 1:4; 4:8], that is God from everlasting and world without end [cf. Ps. 41:13; 90:2; 103:17; 106:48]; he that filleth heaven and earth [Jer. 23:24; cf. Eph. 1:23]; he that is infinite in power, in wisdom, in justice, in mercy, and holiness; he that created all things, visible and invisible [Col. 1:16], by the breath of his mouth [Ps. 33:6], and still "upholds" them all, preserves them in being, "by the word of his power" [Heb. 1:3]; and that governs all things that are in heaven above, in earth beneath, and under the earth [cf. Exod. 20:4; Deut. 5:8]. By faith I know "there are three that bear record in heaven, the

---

31. "On the Trinity" (1775), 15-16, Sermon 55, in *Works* (Bicentennial ed.), 2:384.

32. Ibid., 5, in *Works* (Bicentennial ed.), 2:378-79.

33. That figure is given by editor Albert C. Outler, ibid., 373. In his *Explanatory Notes upon the New Testament,* Wesley offers quite a detailed exegesis of the passage. Concerning the divine witnesses to Jesus Christ as "the complete, the only Saviour of the world," Wesley's exegesis reads in part: *"The Father*—Who clearly testified of the Son, both at His baptism and at His transfiguration. *The Word*—Who testified of Himself on many occasions, while He was on earth; and again, with still greater solemnity, after His ascension into heaven (Rev. 1:5; 19:13). *And the Spirit*—Whose testimony was added chiefly after His glorification (1 John 2:27; John 15:26; Acts 5:32; Rom. 8:16). *And these three are one*—even as those two, the Father and the Son, are one (John 10:30). Nothing can separate the Spirit from the Father and the Son. If He were not one with the Father and the Son, the apostle ought to have said, 'The Father and the Word,' who are one, 'and the Spirit are two.' But this is contrary to the whole tenor of revelation. It remains that *these three are one.* They are one in essence, in knowledge, in will, and in their testimony."

Father, the Word, and the Holy Spirit," and that "these three are one" [1 John 5:7]; that "the word," God the Son, "was made flesh" [John 1:14], lived, and died for our salvation, rose again, ascended into heaven, and now sitteth at the right hand of the Father. By faith I know that the Holy Spirit is the giver of all spiritual life; of righteousness, peace, and joy in the Holy Ghost [Rom. 14:17]; of holiness and happiness, by the restoration of that image of God wherein we are created [cf. Col. 3:10]. Of all these things faith is the evidence, the sole evidence to the children of men.[34]

The plaiting of scriptural and creedal phraseology is not surprising, given that the ancient creeds offer a summary of what is told in Scripture and traditionally provide a grid for reading it. And the creeds, it is known, grew up around the practice of "baptizing . . . in the name of the Father and of the Son and of the Holy Spirit" (Matt. 28:19).[35]

Another writing in which Wesley brings together the trinitarian creeds and the Scriptures is the "Letter to a Roman Catholic." In setting out the content of what "a true Protestant believes," Wesley weaves into the trinitarian structures and language of Nicea, Constantinople, and Chalcedon such further threads as the classical doctrine concerning the *munus triplex* of Christ as prophet, priest, and king and his own scripturally based teaching concerning the Holy Spirit as "not only perfectly holy in himself, but the immediate cause of all holiness in us": "enlightening our understandings, rectifying our wills and affections, renewing our natures, uniting our persons to Christ, assuring us of the adoption of sons, leading us in our actions; purifying and sanctifying our souls and bodies to a full and eternal enjoyment of God."[36] Then, when Wesley comes to set out the matching practice of a true Protestant, he again follows a broadly trinitarian pattern, with scriptural echoes throughout:

A true Protestant believes in God, has a full confidence in his mercy, fears him with a filial fear, and loves him with all his soul. He

---

34. "On the Discoveries of Faith" (1788), 7, Sermon 117, in *Works* (Bicentennial ed.), 4:31-32.

35. In his *Explanatory Notes upon the New Testament,* Wesley makes no comment on the threefold name at Matt. 28:19, but he refers to it obliquely in his explanation of the instruction at Acts 10:48 that Cornelius and his household be baptized "in the name of the Lord": *"In the name of the Lord*—Which implies the Father who anointed Him, and the Spirit with which He was anointed, to His office. But as these Gentiles had before believed in God the Father, and could not but now believe in the Holy Ghost, under whose powerful influence they were at this very time, there was less need of taking notice that they were baptized into the belief and profession of the sacred Three; though doubtless the apostle administered the ordinance in that very form which Christ Himself had prescribed."

36. "Letter to a Roman Catholic" (1749), in *Works* (Jackson ed.), 10:81-82.

worships God in spirit and in truth [John 4:23-24], in everything gives him thanks [1 Thess. 5:18]; calls upon him with his heart as well as his lips [cf. Rom. 10:9-13], at all times and in all places; honours his holy name and his word, and serves him truly all the days of his life. . . .

A true Protestant loves his neighbour, that is, every man, friend or enemy, good or bad, as himself, as he loves his own soul, as Christ loved us. And as Christ laid down his life for us, so he is ready to lay down his life for his brethren [cf. John 15:12-13; Eph. 5:2]. . . . Knowing his body to be the temple of the Holy Ghost [1 Cor. 6:19], he keeps it in sobriety, temperance, and chastity.[37]

As a final example, we may take the passage in the sermon "Catholic Spirit" in which Wesley spells out what is implied in the question "Is thine heart right?" Again the structure is trinitarian (provided one remember that the source of love in the Christian is the Holy Spirit who, according to Romans 5:5, has been poured into our hearts), and the text is a tissue of scriptural phrases:

The first thing implied is this: Is thy heart right with God? Does thou believe his being, and his perfections? His eternity, immensity, wisdom, power; his justice, mercy and truth? Dost thou believe that he now "upholdeth all things by the word of his power" [Heb. 1:3]? And that he governs even the most minute, even the most noxious, to his own glory and the good of them that love him [cf. Rom. 8:28]? Hast thou a divine evidence, a supernatural conviction of the things of God [cf. Heb. 11:1]? Dost thou "walk by faith, not by sight" [2 Cor. 5:7], looking not at temporal things but things eternal [cf. 2 Cor. 4:18]?

Dost thou believe in the Lord Jesus Christ, "God over all, blessed for ever" [Rom. 9:5]? Is he "revealed in" thy soul [cf. Gal. 1:16]? Dost thou "know Jesus Christ and him crucified" [1 Cor. 2:2]? Does he "dwell in thee and thou in him" [cf. John 6:56]? Is he "formed in thy heart by faith" [cf. Gal. 4:19; Eph. 3:17]? Having absolutely disclaimed all thy own works, thy own righteousness, hast thou "submitted thyself unto the righteousness of God" [Rom. 10:3], which is by faith in Christ Jesus [cf. Rom. 3:22]? Art thou "found in him, not having thy own righteousness, but the righteousness which is by faith" [Phil. 3:9]? And art thou, through him, "fighting the good fight of faith, and laying hold of eternal life" [1 Tim. 6:12]?

Is thy faith *energoumenê di' agapês*, "filled with the energy of love" [Gal. 5:6]? Dost thou love God? I do not say "above all things",

---

37. Ibid., 83-84.

for it is both an unscriptural and an ambiguous expression, but "with all thy heart, and with all thy mind, and with all thy soul, and with all thy strength" [Luke 10:27]? . . . Dost thou love as thyself all mankind without exception? . . . Do you show your love by your works? While you have time, as you have opportunity, do you in fact "do good to all men" [Gal. 6:10], neighbours or strangers, friends or enemies, good or bad?[38]

Our emphasis in the last few pages has fallen on the soteriological and the doctrinal, but the passage from Wesley's "Letter to a Roman Catholic" brought back a dimension that I earlier asked you to notice toward the end of the sermon "On the Trinity," namely the doxological. Christians worship God in spirit and in truth; they honor the Son and the Spirit even as they honor the Father.

WORSHIP IN SPIRIT AND IN TRUTH

In a score or so of passages in his sermons, Wesley quotes or alludes to John 4:23-24: "The hour cometh, and now is, when the true worshippers shall worship the Father in spirit and in truth: for the Father seeketh such to worship him. God is a Spirit: and they that worship him must worship him in spirit and in truth" (KJV).[39] In the words "spirit" and "truth," trinitarianly attuned ears will pick up christological and pneumatological resonances, echoing such texts as John 1:14 and 17; 8:31-32; 14:6 and 17; 15:26; 16:7 and 13-15; 17:17-19. In a sermon titled "Spiritual Worship," Wesley sums up his theme as "the happy and holy communion which the faithful have with God the Father, Son, and Holy Ghost"; and it is to that sermon that we shall turn, since it offers one of the most sustained examples of trinitarian hermeneutics in Wesley's works.

The text of the sermon "Spiritual Worship" was 1 John 5:20: "This is the true God, and eternal life" (KJV).[40] As a preliminary, let it be noted how highly Wesley regarded the First Letter of John. At Dublin he wrote in his *Journal* for July 18, 1765: "In the evening, I began expounding the deepest part of the Holy Scripture, namely the First Epistle of St. John, by which, above all other even inspired writings, I advise every young preacher to form his style. Here are sublimity and simplicity together, the strongest sense and the plainest language! How can anyone that would 'speak as the oracles of God' use harder words than are found there?"[41]

38. "Catholic Spirit" (1750), I.12-18, Sermon 39, in *Works* (Bicentennial ed.), 2:87-89.
39. For Wesley's uses of that text, see Geoffrey Wainwright, "Worship According to Wesley," *Australian Journal of Liturgy* 13/1 (May 1991), 5-20, especially 7-9.
40. "Spiritual Worship" (1780), Sermon 77, in *Works* (Bicentennial ed.), 3:88-102.
41. *Works* (Bicentennial ed.), 22:13.

In the prelude to his sermon "Spiritual Worship," Wesley analyzes the structure of what he calls St. John's "tract." Between the opening statement of apostolic authority and purpose (1:1-4) and the final recapitulation (5:18-21), the bulk of the Epistle is seen by Wesley to fall into a trinitarian pattern, treating first communion with the Father (1:5-10), next communion with the Son (2:1—3:24), then communion with the Spirit (4:1-21), and finally the testimony of the entire Trinity on which Christian faith and life depend (5:1-12).

Wesley spends the first part of his own sermon in establishing from Scripture that Christ is indeed "the true God," which he takes his text to declare.[42] Not only do the Scriptures directly attribute divinity to him (John 1:1-2; Rom. 9:5; Phil. 2:6) and "give him all the titles of the most high God," including "the incommunicable name, Jehovah, never given to any creature"; they also "ascribe to him all the attributes and all the works of God": he is of all things the Creator (Col. 1:16; John 1:3; Heb. 1:10), the Supporter (Heb. 1:3), the Preserver (Col. 1:17), the Author or Mover, the Governor (Ps. 103:19; Isa. 9:6), and the End (Rom. 11:36), and he is "the Redeemer of all the children of men" (with appeal to Isa. 53:6). Then, in the second part of his sermon, Wesley shows how, according to his text, Christ is "eternal life." Christ is "the author of eternal salvation to all them that obey Him" (Heb. 5:9), "the purchaser of that 'crown of life' which will be given to all that are 'faithful unto death' [Rev. 2:10]." This does not apply only to the future resurrection (John 11:25; 1 Cor. 15:22; 1 Pet. 1:3-4), but begins now (1 John 5:11-12). Here Wesley's description is thoroughly trinitarian:

> This eternal life then commences when it pleases the Father to reveal his Son in our hearts; when we first know Christ, being enabled to "call him Lord by the Holy Ghost" [1 Cor. 12:3]; when we can testify, our conscience bearing us witness in the Holy Ghost [cf. Rom. 8:16; 1 John 5:10], "the life which I now live, I live by faith in the Son of God, who loved me, and gave himself for me" [Gal. 2:20]. And then it is that happiness begins—happiness real, solid, substantial. Then it is that heaven is opened in the soul, that the proper, heavenly state commences, while the love of God, as loving us, is shed abroad in the heart [Rom. 5:5], instantly producing love

---

42. It must be admitted that some exegetes take the *houtos* of 1 John 5:20 to refer to the Father, not to the Son. Wesley does not even consider this possibility but proceeds immediately to demonstrate the deity of Christ from Scripture. Among recent scholars, the distinguished Raymond E. Brown favors Wesley's exegetical option at 1 John 5:20; see his commentary, *The Epistles of John*, Anchor Bible 30 (Garden City, N.Y.: Doubleday, 1982), 639-40. Brown, by the way, does not support the textual authenticity of the Johannine comma, to which he devotes an informative appendix (775-87).

to all mankind: general, pure benevolence, together with its genuine fruits, lowliness, meekness, patience [Eph. 4:2; Col. 3:12], contentedness in every state; an entire, clear, full acquiescence in the whole will of God, enabling us to "rejoice evermore, and in everything to give thanks" [1 Thess. 5:16-18].[43]

That euchological ending encourages me to turn, for one final demonstration of Wesley's trinitarian hermeneutics, to his exposition of the Lord's Prayer.

THE LORD'S PRAYER

Wesley expounds the Lord's Prayer as part of his Sixth Discourse on Our Lord's Sermon on the Mount. This is what he there says concerning the name that is to be hallowed:

The name of God is God himself—the nature of God so far as it can be discovered to man. It means, therefore, together with his existence, all his attributes or perfections—his eternity, particularly signified by his great and incommunicable name Jehovah, as the Apostle John translates it, "the Alpha and Omega, the Beginning and the End; he which is, and which was, and which is to come" [Rev. 1:8; 21:6]. His "fullness of being" [cf. Eph. 3:19; Col. 2:9], denoted by his other great name, "I am that I am" [Exod. 3:14]; his omnipresence; his omnipotence—who is indeed the only agent in the material world, all matter being essentially dull and inactive, and moving only as it is moved by the finger of God [cf. Exod. 8:19; Luke 11:20]. And he is the spring of action in every creature, visible and invisible, which could neither act nor exist without the continued influx and agency of his almighty power; —his wisdom, clearly deduced from the things that are seen [cf. Rom. 1:20], from the goodly order of the universe; his Trinity in Unity and Unity in Trinity, discovered to us in the very first line of his Written Word, bara' elohim, literally "the Gods created," a plural noun joined with a verb of the singular number, as well as in every part of his subsequent revelations, given by the mouth of all his holy prophets and apostles; his essential purity and holiness; and above all his love, which is the very brightness of his glory [cf. Heb. 1:3].[44]

There stands Wesley's deliberate statement that God is self-disclosed as Trinity throughout Scripture.[45] It forms the justification for the remark-

---

43. "Spiritual Worship," II.5, in *Works* (Bicentennial ed.), 3:96.
44. "Upon Our Lord's Sermon on the Mount, Discourse the Sixth" (1748), III.7, Sermon 26, in *Works* (Bicentennial ed.), 1:580-81.
45. To the point about the plural form Elohim being used with singular verbs may be

able hymn that Wesley appends to the sermon under consideration.[46] The text begins with three stanzas developing "Our Father, who art in heaven, hallowed be thy Name." The next two stanzas develop the next two petitions—"Thy kingdom come," "Thy will be done on earth as it is in heaven"—with a christological and a pneumatological address respectively: "Son of thy Sire's eternal love" and "Spirit of grace, and health, and power." The sixth, seventh, and eighth stanzas take the remaining petitions of the Lord's Prayer according to a trinitarian sequence: the prayer for bread (addressed to the Father), the prayer for forgiveness (addressed to the "eternal, spotless Lamb of God"), and the prayer for preservation from temptation and deliverance from evil (addressed to the "Giver and Lord of life"). The concluding doxological stanza is addressed conjointly to the Triune God. The stanzas follow.

I

Father of all, whose powerful voice
Called forth this universal frame,
Whose mercies over all rejoice,
Through endless ages still the same:
Thou by Thy word upholdest all;
Thy bounteous love to all is showed;
Thou hear'st Thy every creature's call,
And fillest every mouth with good.

II

In heaven Thou reign'st enthroned in light,
Nature's expanse beneath Thee spread;

---

added the point noticed earlier about the composite name Jehovah Elohim—which, incidentally, is frequently taken as designating the Trinity in Charles Wesley's "Hymns on the Trinity" (1767), in *The Poetical Works of John and Charles Wesley,* ed. George Osborn (London: Wesleyan-Methodist Conference Office, 1868-72), 7:201-348. Another indication of Wesley's perception of the pervasive presence of the Trinity in Scripture is found in his comment in the *Explanatory Notes upon the New Testament* on the words of Jesus at Luke 4:18: "How is the doctrine of the ever-blessed Trinity interwoven even in those scriptures where one would least expect it! How clear a declaration of the great Three-One is there in those very words, The *Spirit* of the *Lord* is upon *me!*"

46. "A Paraphrase on the Lord's Prayer," in *Works* (Bicentennial ed.), 1:589-91. The hymn had first appeared in *Hymns and Sacred Poems* (Bristol, 1742), published under the joint names of John and Charles Wesley. In the 1780 *Collection of Hymns for the Use of the People Called Methodists,* it figured in three equal parts—numbers 225, 226, and 227—among the section "For Believers Rejoicing." Doubtless adjudged too long for regular liturgical use, the hymn was retained in abbreviated form—with loss of the trinitarian structures and disturbance of the sequence of petitions—as hymn 47 in the British *Methodist Hymn Book* of 1933.

Earth, air, and sea, before Thy sight,
And hell's deep gloom are open laid.
Wisdom, and might, and love are Thine;
Prostrate before Thy face we fall,
Confess Thine attributes divine,
And hail the sovereign Lord of all.

III

Thee, sovereign Lord, let all confess
That moves in earth, or air, or sky,
Revere Thy power, Thy goodness bless,
Tremble before Thy piercing eye;
All ye who owe to Him your birth,
In praise your every hour employ;
Jehovah reigns! Be glad, O earth,
And shout, ye morning stars, for joy.

IV

Son of Thy Sire's eternal love,
Take to Thyself Thy mighty power;
Let all earth's sons Thy mercy prove,
Let all Thy bleeding grace adore.
The triumphs of Thy love display,
In every heart reign Thou alone,
Till all Thy foes confess Thy sway,
And glory ends what grace begun.

V

Spirit of grace, and health, and power,
Fountain of light and love below,
Abroad Thy healing influence shower,
O'er all the nations let it flow.
Inflame our hearts with perfect love,
In us the work of faith fulfil,
So not heaven's host shall swifter move
Than we on earth to do Thy will.

VI

Father, 'tis Thine each day to yield
Thy children's wants a fresh supply;
Thou cloth'st the lilies of the field,
And hearest the young ravens cry.
On Thee we cast our care; we live
Through Thee, who know'st our every need;

O feed us with Thy grace, and give
Our souls this day the living bread.

VII

Eternal, spotless Lamb of God,
Before the world's foundation slain,
Sprinkle us ever with Thy blood;
O cleanse, and keep us ever clean!
To every soul (all praise to Thee)
Our bowels of compassion move,
And all mankind by this may see
God is in us—for God is love.

VIII

Giver and Lord of life, whose power
And guardian care for all are free,
To Thee, in fierce temptation's hour,
From sin and Satan let us flee;
Thine, Lord, we are, and ours Thou art;
In us be all Thy goodness showed,
Renew, enlarge, and fill our heart
With peace, and joy, and heaven, and God.

IX

Blessing, and honour, praise, and love,
Co-equal, co-eternal Three,
In earth below, and heaven above,
By all Thy works be paid to Thee.
Thrice holy, Thine the kingdom is,
The power omnipotent is Thine;
And when created nature dies,
Thy never-ceasing glories shine.[47]

---

47. This paper has deliberately been kept almost exclusively at the historical level. It will achieve its purpose if it encourages exegetes, historians, and theologians in the Wesleyan tradition to develop a trinitarian hermeneutic in their work. My own systematic developments on the Trinity are found elsewhere, chiefly in "The Doctrine of the Trinity: Where the Church Stands or Falls," *Interpretation* 45 (1991): 117-32; "Renewal as a Trinitarian and Traditional Event," *Lexington Theological Quarterly* 25 (1991): 117-24; "Trinitarian Worship," in my *Worship with One Accord: Where Liturgy and Ecumenism Embrace* (New York: Oxford University Press, 1997), 237-50; and "The Ecumenical Rediscovery of the Trinity," *One in Christ* 34 (1998): 95-124. Note also my "Psalm 33 Interpreted of the Triune God," *Ex Auditu* 16 (2000): 101-20. A fully systematic proposal of a trinitarian approach to Scripture, by an author in the Pentecostal tradition, is found in my pupil Telford Work's book, *Living and Active: Scripture in the Economy of Salvation* (Grand Rapids: Eerdmans, 2002).

Robert Wall is a professor and biblical scholar who has contributed significantly within both the Wesleyan-Holiness tradition and the larger field of biblical scholarship. This point should not go unnoticed, as he openly laments over the chasm that often exists between biblical scholarship and broader theological conversations within the church. Among his purposes is a reminder of the critical place and role of the biblical canon within the continuing life, practice, and theological conversations of the contemporary church.

Professor Wall suggests that all readers listen to the Bible from their theological context, Wesleyans included. That being the case, he offers several distinctive features of a Wesleyan understanding of Scripture that may potentially shape Wesleyan readings of these sacred texts. Such ways of reading the Bible should contribute to but not dominate the ongoing theological discussions within the broader church. However, what may be most important is not merely the distinctiveness of these Wesleyan readings of the Bible but the ways that such readings shape the life and practices of the church for faithfulness to God and for holy living.

2

TOWARD A WESLEYAN HERMENEUTIC OF SCRIPTURE[1]

Robert W. Wall

◆

Not long ago, I asked another Wesleyan biblical scholar, Professor Richard Hays of Duke Divinity School, whether he thought it possible to construct a Wesleyan hermeneutic of Scripture. He responded only by wishing me "good luck," adding that once he was asked to read a paper on this very topic, only to give up in complete frustration. Even though Hays did allow that the possibility exists in theory, one may well wonder with Stanley Fish whether "theory's day is dying and the hour is late."[2]

Indeed, I suspect this essay will be read by postmodern pragmatists like Fish as yet another last-minute attempt to build yet another theoretical model, this one supposing the possibility and importance of a distinctively Wesleyan approach to Scripture. They may wonder why I make the effort, which seems to them too parochial and anachronistic. For justification, they may even appeal to Frank Spina's survey of those biblical scholars serving Wesleyan communions, which shows that scant connection apparently exists between the core convictions of their Wesleyan heritage and their actual exegetical conclusions.[3] By this evidence, one is tempted to agree that no interpretation of Scripture is or can be distinctively Wesleyan in either methodological or theological interest.[4]

Before responding to such a pessimistic analysis, let me note that this nonrelationship between Wesleyan theology and Wesleyan biblical inter-

---

1. Appeared originally in the *Wesleyan Theological Journal* 30/2 (Fall 1995). Used by permission.

2. Stanley Fish, "Consequences," in *Against Theory: Literary Studies and the New Pragmatism*, ed. W. J. T. Mitchell (Chicago: University of Chicago Press, 1985), 128. But see Allan David Bloom's biting response to Fish's point in *Giants and Dwarfs* (New York: Simon and Schuster, 1990), 13-31.

3. Frank A. Spina, "Wesleyan Faith Seeking Biblical Understanding," *Wesleyan Theological Journal* 30/2 (Fall 1995): 26-49.

4. I appreciate the keen insight and civil ecumenism reflected by George Lyons' important essay, "Hermeneutical Bases of Theology," *Wesleyan Theological Journal* 18/1 (Spring 1983): 63-78. I join his efforts in encouraging holiness scholars to become more current and "critical" in their hermeneutical methods. My proposal, however, is grounded in the hope that these same scholars become more self-critically Wesleyan in their reading of biblical texts.

pretation is characteristic of the entire modern academy. Most Scripture scholars are still engaged in a variety of descriptive tasks, while theologians are left to settle the normative claims of faith and witness. At issue is whether theological reflection is any longer a methodological interest of modern biblical scholarship, or whether the subject matter of biblical teaching is even useful for theological discourse. In my view, most biblical scholars remain largely disenchanted with human relations and current audiences, and seem more concerned with disciplinary tasks that seem relevant to the text qua text rather than with the ultimate issues of life that are of a theological sort. It comes as no small surprise, then, that the results of modern biblical scholarship are not very conducive to theological reflection.[5]

Yet, especially the recent emergence in the postcritical milieu of canon as a heuristic category of biblical-theological reflection challenges this status quo on at least two different fronts.[6] On the first, an emphasis on the canonicity of Scripture concentrates its subject matter and final shape as normative for every Christian confession of and witness to God (as *norma normata*): the whole of Scripture constitutes a certain compass for a biblical people. By the very nature of its subject matter as God's Word, then, Scripture helps draw the church's theological boundaries and supply the language and grammar of normative Christian faith.[7] This pre-

---

5. Sandra Marie Schneiders begins her work, *The Revelatory Text: Interpreting the New Testament as Sacred Scripture* (San Francisco: Harper Collins, 1991), with a similar critique of guild protocol. Following the lead of Hans-Georg Gadamer, she argues that most scholars are primarily interested in historical "information" rather than in interpersonal "transformation," in particular methods leading to data-collection rather than in understanding leading to universal truth. The full meaning of a biblical text pursues the information it may yield, but as a means to its more existential aspect—meaning that explains "self" in relation to God and neighbor, community, and creation. I stand with Dr. Schneiders in these criticisms.

6. See Robert W. Wall, "Reading the New Testament in Canonical Context," in *Hearing the New Testament: Strategies for Interpretation,* ed. Joel B. Green (Grand Rapids: Eerdmans, 1995). Also, my introduction to Robert W. Wall and Eugene E. Lemcio, *The New Testament as Canon: A Reader in Canonical Criticism,* JSNT Supplemental Series 76 (Sheffield: JSOT Press, 1992), 15-26.

7. This point concentrates the canonical approach to biblical interpretation pioneered by Bernard S. Childs, already in his programmatic "Interpretation in Faith," *Interpretation* 18 (1964): 432-49, but then brilliantly introduced in his commentary on Exodus (Old Testament Library; Philadelphia: Westminster, 1974) and *Introduction to the Old Testament as Scripture* (Philadelphia: Fortress, 1979). In his work Childs addresses the question: which form of the biblical text bears witness to the truth about God and God's salvation most acutely and accurately for Christian readers? While Childs would deny that the text in its final, canonical form has a monopoly on the gospel truth, he would contend that this particular placement of the gospel truth has been privileged by the church to be normative or canonical for its faith and life. The biblical text in its final, canonical form is the primary medium, then, of Christian theological interpretation and reflection (following Karl Barth).

cious conviction about Scripture's authority as a written "rule of Christian faith" asserts that the church's collection(s) of sacred writings bear(s) trustworthy witness to the Sacred One and accordingly must receive our most devoted attention. In this sense, we continually move toward and position ourselves before the canonical texts as sacred ground where we expect to hear the "voice" of the Lord God Almighty.[8]

Yet, to posit an "objective" witness to God in the whole of the canonical texts says nothing about how the faith community retrieves it in order to nurture its theological understanding. In fact, Scripture's timeless and trustworthy truths find their way into the community's life only by every new effort to reinterpret their meaning for today—"discoveries of original meaning hitherto hidden."[9] It is, in fact, the canonicity of Scripture that both justifies and requires its interpretation for believers today (as *norma normans*).[10] Sometimes faithful interpretation merely confirms the

---

For a balanced critique of Childs' canonical approach, see John Barton, *Reading the Old Testament: Method in Biblical Study* (Philadelphia: Westminster, 1984), 77-103. The more polemical objection raised by James Barr in his *Holy Scripture: Canon, Authority, Criticism* (Philadelphia: Westminster, 1983) that the canonical form is not necessarily "superior" (at least in a historical sense) has since been nicely handled by Mark G. Brett in his *Biblical Criticism in Crisis?* (Cambridge: Cambridge University Press, 1991).

8. I am aware that this particular aspect of a canon's importance, as the authoritative and distinctive deposit of divine revelation, is currently under sharp attack. Most of this criticism is concentrated by the claim of a canon's special character and unique importance on its readers. Typically there are two observations made: (1) Each canon shares certain qualities with other canons, which seems to undermine the claim of its special character. Therefore, to place confidence in one canon but not in another requires an act of nonrational faith. For this reason, Childs underscores the canonical role of Scripture to bear witness to Jesus Christ, whose particular life and vocation justifies the "special character" of the Christian canon. (2) Especially M. Foucault argues that every canon privileges and legitimizes a particular ideology (whether sociopolitical or intellectual). Further, canons of various disciplines and groups are used by those "priests" in charge to maintain their power over the rank-and-file by controlling which texts are used and by determining the rules by which the "official" meaning of these texts is discerned. For this reason, Childs also underscores the importance of a holistic reading of Scripture, which provides ample illustration and justification for ideological diversity among its diverse Christian readership. Scripture bears witness to, in J. A. Sanders' apt phrase, a "pluralizing monotheism." It delineates a debating ground on which self-correcting and mutually informing conversations take place, which promise even greater clarity in the church's hearing and obedience to God's Word.

9. Frank Kermode, *Forms of Attention* (Chicago: University of Chicago Press, 1985), 75.

10. Throughout the history of forming the Christian Scriptures (as well as the Jewish Scriptures), the idea of a biblical canon was concerned not only with the question of a normative literature but also with the question of its proper interpretation. To accept the canonicity of the Christian Bible is to insist that interpretation must be done again and again on it in search of God's will and word for each and every new situation. While Scripture's multivalency and the interpretive situation's fluidity allow for great freedom, methodological and

faith of our foreparents. More often, however, the talented interpreter of Scripture responds to a hermeneutical crisis, when Scripture itself fails to exercise its canonical authority because its community of faithful readers finds its teaching either incomprehensible or irrelevant.[11] But "there's the rub." While the Christian Bible is an authorized medium of divine revelation for the church, it nevertheless comprises texts that remain severely gapped in two different ways.

1. Many biblical texts are intertexts, composed with other biblical texts in mind and heart, and still other texts, unknown or unintended by the author, that come to the interpreter's mind in canonical context.[12] The talented interpreter listens for echoes of other biblical texts, however low their volume, and looks for allusions, however dim their reflection, that link biblical texts together, the one glossing and thickening the meaning of the other.[13]

2. There remain other gaps of the full meaning of biblical texts that the interpreter slips into in order to complete the meaning of the text for the current faith community. Therefore, the plain sense of every canonical text unfolds throughout its history as every talented interpreter adapts its meaning to ever-changing social locations. Biblical interpretation always revises the meaning of Scripture, as well as the faith tradition of its readers, with the authority to transform the terms of present faith and witness under the aegis of the Spirit. For this reason, interpretation is a necessary but disturbing activity, which presumes that the talented interpreter makes the timeless ever timely for a particular community of Scripture's faithful but skeptical readers.

---

theological controls do exist that limit and even rank the possible meanings made of a canonical text. Certainly only a few interpreters have requisite authority or talent to find God's will and word in Scripture. More importantly, the subject matter of interpretation must never disagree with the subject matter of Scripture, which bears witness to the God made flesh in Christ Jesus.

11. See Michael A. Fishbane's brilliant analysis of this point in "Inner-biblical Exegesis," in *The Garments of Torah: Essays in Biblical Hermeneutics* (Bloomington, Ind.: Indiana University Press, 1989), 3-18.

12. I suspect that most NT writers wrote their compositions with their Scriptures in mind. The writings of the NT are christological midrashim on the OT. However, the case that biblical texts are intertexts can be made quite apart from authorial intentions. That is, whether or not biblical texts were composed with other biblical texts in mind, the simultaneity of Scripture commends its intertextuality and is a canonical rather than authorial property.

13. The intertextuality of Scripture only underscores the fundamental importance of what Childs commends as the "holistic reading of Scripture," where Scripture's final shape as well as the entirety of its subject matter lead us in edifying conversation with God's Word—*Biblical Theology of the Old and New Testaments* (Minneapolis: Fortress, 1992), 717-27.

Note the importance of theological location as a tacit but critical feature of the interpreter's social context: the talented hermeneut is also a faithful tradent.[14] If the interpreter's faith is keenly Wesleyan, the rendering of Scripture's full meaning should necessarily underscore and embellish the (especially soteriological) accents of the Wesleyan theological tradition. This is the particular gap of Scripture's meaning that is filled by a Wesleyan's interpretation of Scripture. This affirmation of a particular theological perspective, embodied and conveyed in privileged interpretations of Scripture, should intend to form and even transform the faith of believers who not only belong to that same faith tradition but are enabled to preserve its theological perspective. Rather than discrediting privileged interpretations as lacking sufficient "objectivity," then, the church should celebrate and advance them as an aspect of the interpreter's vocation.[15]

Of course, we must recognize that every faith tradition is inherently gapped. Therefore, the scholar's search for the Wesleyan meaning and significance of biblical texts should not be marked by a triumphalism, which has discredited some of our work in the past. Nor should we fall prey to the romanticism that fails the critical task. A Wesleyan interpretation of Scripture must allow for countervailing accents that are also well-supported by the plain sense of canonical Scripture, as well as by other non-Wesleyan interpretive traditions.[16] To presume the simultaneity between every faith tradition of the whole, without also adequately discerning the impor-

---

14. In his important book *The Soul of the American University* (New York: Oxford University Press, 1994), George Marsden well notes that, while the postmodernist challenge to the myth of objectivity in the academy has concerned social class and gender, this same line of inquiry could be applied to religious commitments and values as well (433-35). That is, the interpreter's core convictions about God also lead to a particular understanding of the subject matter of one's inquiry. Marsden argues, of course, that the public academy, especially that which upholds a democratic people, ought to tolerate and provide a forum for different religious commitments even as it supports the diversity of social class and gender.

15. In this sense, I continue to unpack the thesis illustrated by "Law and Gospel, Church and Canon," *Wesleyan Theological Journal* 22/1 (Spring 1987): 38-70. From a Pentecostal perspective, the very same point is made nicely by J. C. Thomas, "Women, Pentecostals and the Bible: An Experiment in Pentecostal Interpretation," *Journal of Pentecostal Theology* 5 (1994), 41-56. In his essay, Thomas argues that faithful interpretation of God's Word occurs only when the discrete roles/experiences of Spirit, community, Scripture, and teacher are properly integrated. When one of these authoritative "voices" lacks volume, a distortion of meaning will result.

16. According to Paul Ricoeur, the sense of a text is ascertained by properly arranged words and logically developed ideas. Critical exegesis arrives at this sense on which all (ideally) might agree. Only on this basis of what a text actually says can readers then determine its full meaning—both its truthfulness and contemporary significance—for their more particular and differentiated lives and faiths. See Paul Ricoeur, *Interpretation Theory* (Fort Worth: Texas Christian University Press, 1976), 8-22.

tance of each in turn, undermines the integral nature of the "one holy, catholic, and apostolic church," thereby distorting its full witness to God.

That is, while Scripture's message for the whole church will surely be distorted without its Wesleyan meaning, so also will its message be distorted if understood only in Wesleyan terms. The mutual criticism that engages and learns from other interpretive traditions and from the full witness of Scripture only deepens the significance of each part that makes up the whole church and its biblical canon. We are all scholars of the church of God, who should embrace the catholic task of nurturing the theological understanding of those believers in our care "for building up the whole body of Christ, until we all attain to the unity of the faith and knowledge of the Son of God" (Eph. 4:12-13).

My concern is the prospect of a Wesleyan approach to Scripture, and I seek to proffer a theoretical frame of reference that guides in the formation of Christian faith and belongs in a privileged way to the Wesleyan tradition. In my view, such is needed in response to the practical failure among most Wesleyan scholars to produce a vital scholarship from and for the Wesleyan church community. Sharply put, we have been too easily domesticated by the influences of the modern academy (theological methods) and of evangelical Protestantism (theological convictions). If the goal of biblical interpretation for the church is praxis, then a model of interpretation that features a Wesleyan theological reading of biblical texts must help to shape the theological understanding and spiritual vitality of its Wesleyan constituency. Only then will the Wesleyan voice be preserved into the next generation for the church catholic.

A WESLEYAN CONCEPTION OF SCRIPTURE

I propose one such model of a Wesleyan interpretation of Scripture in order to continue our conversation together.[17] Because theoretical models have a certain structure, which then insures the transmission of the in-

---

17. Much of what follows agrees, in different words and methodology, with John Stanley's "postmodern" scheme recently introduced in his "Postmodern Holiness." One of the more intriguing features of his essay is Stanley's extended autobiographical introduction, which is characteristic of postmodern commentary. Autobiography underscores the contextual cast of interpretation and helps to frame meaning as—at least in part—subjective, self-critical, and provisional. As Stanley clearly indicates, the postcritical interpreter does consider the literary and historical "evidence" of critical exegesis in determining the meaning and significance of a biblical text. There is a sense in which the "full" or objective meaning of a biblical text is the integral collection of the interpretive community's various subjectivities, including those belonging to holiness interpreters like Stanley. See John E. Stanley, "Elements of a Postmodern Holiness Hermeneutic Illustrated by Way of the Book of Revelation," *Wesleyan Theological Journal* 28/1-2 (Spring-Fall 1993): 23-43.

terpreter's theological and methodological interests, what follows is an attempt to reconceive select features that constitute a Wesleyan approach to biblical interpretation.

Recall my earlier observation that hermeneuts are tradents.[18] That is, interpreters of Scripture participate in particular histories of interpretation consisting of methodological and theological interests, whose intention is to preserve the identity of a particular people within and for the wider interpretive community. I proceed from the conservative assumption that Wesleyan interpretation participates in an interpretive history inaugurated by the Wesleys. The programmatic model of Wesleyan hermeneutics, which continues to support this particular history, was forged especially by John Wesley—by his conception and use of the Scriptures.

Before I stand on the shoulders of others to find my way in this matter,[19] let me agree with my colleagues in Wesleyan studies that the founder and framer of our particular history was himself an early modern interpreter of Christian traditions, canonical and ecclesial (esp. patristic and Anglican), whose interpretations were informed by his own intellectual culture and personal experience.[20] It seems wrongheaded for us to as-

---

18. Of course, Gadamer also links the interpreter with the history of a tradition. Yet, rather than the deposit of core convictions and moral values found in "classic" texts, which the interpreter then translates for the "next generation," a tradition is itself hermeneutical. That is, there exist certain hermeneutical presumptions and protocols that also belong to a tradition that must guide the interpreter when translating a tradition in and for a new context.

19. Since I am not a scholar of Wesley nor the son of one, my evaluation of recent studies of Wesley's view of Scripture is more "instinctive" than academic. Forgive me if my "instinct" is to select only those features that agree with my hermeneutical assumptions. With that qualification, my consideration of several recent studies of Wesley's idea of Scripture and its interpretation has found most helpful for this discussion the fine study by Scott S. Jones, "John Wesley's Conception and Use of Scripture" (Ph.D. diss., Southern Methodist University, 1992), which promises to set the standard for this topic in Wesley studies. Also useful is Donald A. D. Thorsen's *The Wesleyan Quadrilateral: Scripture, Tradition, Reason and Experience as a Model of Evangelical Theology* (Grand Rapids: Zondervan, 1990; reprint, Indianapolis: Light and Life Communications, 1997), 125-50, whose discussion of this topic is more theologically interested; William M. Arnett, "John Wesley—Man of One Book" (Th.D. diss., Drew University, 1954); and most recently, Randy L. Maddox, *Responsible Grace: John Wesley's Practical Theology* (Nashville: Abingdon/Kingswood, 1994), esp. 36-47.

20. Too much has been made of the well-documented inconsistency between Wesley's conception of Scripture and its interpretation, and his actual use of Scripture. What seems clear is that Wesley's Scripture is a "means of grace" and must always be subordinated to the ministry of salvation. Therefore, while pressing in theory for the authority of its "literal meaning," and even for the oracular character of its very words, Wesley's interpretation of Scripture is really midrashic—and follows therefore the Bible's own unwritten rules of interpretation!—often adding or subtracting from the biblical text in order to find its theological

sume, then, that the subject matter of Wesley's interpretation of Scripture is somehow normative for current Wesleyan interpreters, fixed in his time for our time. Rather, what remains from Wesley in retrospect is the core conception of biblical interpretation, however vague and sometimes muddled in practice, which continues to "filter" a Wesleyan meaning of Scripture down to those whose contingent crises, cultural and theological, threaten to undermine a distinctively Wesleyan confession and incarnation of the Bible's normative witness to God for today. In what follows, I want to sketch four features of Wesley's conception and use of Scripture that are of decisive importance in my mind for a Wesleyan approach to biblical interpretation today.

1. The Sacrament of Scripture. Every perspective of Scripture's authority decisively shapes how the text is interpreted. Wesley's view of Scripture is no exception. As is well known, he claimed to be *homo unius libri*—a claim justified by even a cursory reading of his sermons and other works, where the primacy and sufficiency of Scripture is clear and certain. Wesley understood true Christianity to be a biblical religion. Yet, surely Outler is right in distinguishing Wesley's conception of biblical authority from the *sola Scriptura* tradition of the magisterial Reformation.[21] Hence, for example, nowhere does Wesley appeal to Scripture as "infallible" nor posit divine revelation exclusively in the propositions of Scripture, verbally inspired by God.[22] The Wesleyan objection to the fundamentalist Protestant formulation of biblical authority is not so much that it lacks empirical evidence but that it lacks theological perspicacity. Not only does it seem to follow the errors of christological docetism, but it also fails to understand adequately the

---

address in meanings that indicate the "way into heaven." I believe this is the case even though Wesley himself considered the "original" meaning an important feature of sound exegesis.

21. "Methodists in Search of Consensus," in *What Should Methodists Teach? Wesleyan Tradition and Modern Diversity,* ed. M. Douglas Meeks (Nashville: Abingdon/Kingswood, 1990), 37.

22. So Robert E. Cushman, *John Wesley's Experimental Divinity* (Nashville: Abingdon/Kingswood, 1989), 81. I caution us not to import back into Wesley's age those terms (e.g., "infallibility" or "inerrancy"), which have taken on a more recent connotation during the "modernist vs. fundamentalist" debates of the 20th century. Surely Wesley did not think Scripture fallible in its witness to God or anything less than an "infallible test" (his words) of faith and life. Rather, it is simply to contend that in consideration of Wesley's actual use of Scripture, especially in his preaching ministry, its authority is always posited in and proven by its redemptive performance rather than in its "inerrant" propositions. Thus, Jones argues that Wesley's appeal to the Bible's infallibility envisages Scripture's reliability as a source and norm for Christian doctrine, not the assured result of empirical analysis of its scientific or historical statements ("John Wesley's Conception and Use of Scripture," 26-35).

canonicity of Scripture. Let me explain this observation from a Wesleyan perspective, which views Scripture as a sacrament of divine revelation and is to be linked to Wesley's robust vision of divine grace.[23]

First, the revivalist ethos shaped by Wesley's ministry shifted emphasis from the "faith which is believed" *(fides quae creditur)* to the "faith which believes" *(fides qua creditur)*. The result was hardly to set aside the sacramental cast of true religion inherited from the Church of England, but rather to qualify it. Rather than merely a confession or a confirmation of the believer's placement among the people of God, sacraments are the via media of the sacred that issue in the transforming experience of salvation. In this sense, then, Wesley viewed Scripture as the privileged medium of God's self-disclosure. The reading and hearing of the biblical word in evangelistic preaching and pastoral teaching create the context wherein the word of God is heard and understood as the instrument of prevenient grace, thereby restoring human freedom and enabling the Spirit to bring people freely to saving faith in and fervent love for God. This is the primary role that Scripture performs, then, and on this basis its authority depends. God "authors" Scripture not to warrant some grand system of theological ideas to guide people in orthodox confession, but rather to lead sinful people into thankful worship of a forgiving Lord.

Despite his rhetoric to the contrary, there is ample reason, envisaged especially by his homiletical use of Scripture (see below), that Wesley did not think Scripture's authority to be unilateral and absolute but rather conversational and relational.[24] Rather than coercing faith, Scripture restores the human capacity to respond to God freely. Scripture's appeal is not primarily intellectual but affective and moral, and the ethics of its interpretation are therefore consequentialist. That is, Scripture invites the lost to be found: the poor to be rich in faith; the suffering to experience compassion; the marginal to find a caring community; and the one who hears and is enlightened by Scripture's invitation to new life is made responsible to accept it.

While the biblical promise of transformation is certain, it is also possible to resist. Scripture does not force compliance, even though its actual effect is more convincing than if issued as an edict. Since Scripture bears witness to a God who invites assent by loving concern and not by power

---

23. R. Larry Shelton, "John Wesley's Approach to Scripture in Historical Perspective," *Wesleyan Theological Journal* 16/1 (Spring 1981): 23-50; and followed by Thorsen, *The Wesleyan Quadrilateral*, 136-37.

24. For the difference between these two classes of authority, see Schneiders, *Revelatory Text*, 55-59. An argument for a similar point is made by Bryan P. Stone, "Wesleyan Theology, Scriptural Authority, and Homosexuality," *Wesleyan Theological Journal* 30/2 (Fall 1995): 111-20.

plays, its canonicity as a sacrament of divine revelation is understood finally in a profoundly relational way: Scripture discloses God by inviting faith in a God-for-us, who is then confirmed by our concrete experience of God's grace.

Second, even as sacraments require priestly agency for their gracious effect, so also Scripture requires human mediation under the aegis of Spirit and in proper consideration of other religious authorities.[25] Neither can Scripture interpret itself nor stand alone. The act of interpretation is therefore a collaborative enterprise, which looks above, around, and within in prayerful devotion, and reaches far behind to older Christian wisdom still available. A theological reflection upon Scripture takes place within a pluriformed whole, which includes the whole of Scripture and the history of its interpretation as well as the interpreter's own situation before God and among the community of neighbors.

While the role of the strong interpreter should be underscored according to this model, Wesley's sacramental view of Scripture is not sacerdotal—a point even more fully embodied in the populism of the American Methodist experience. In this limited sense, Wesley's hermeneutics are indeed more Protestant than Catholic. The authority of the interpreter is granted as "gift" rather than as "office"; the vocation is for ministry within a community of disciples who are also gifted, rather than for maintenance of a priestly hierarchy that then manages the spiritual and theological formation of the rank-and-file faithful. The interpreter's real credentials are those of vital piety imbued by learning, which are then recognized by the congregation that alone grants authority for the interpreter to guide them into biblical understanding.

2. The Simultaneity of Scripture. In my opinion, the essential characteristic of the Bible for Wesley is its simultaneity. According to Wesley, to presume the simultaneity between every part of the whole, without also ad-

---

25. Cf. Albert C. Outler, "The Wesleyan Quadrilateral—in John Wesley," in *Doctrine and Theology in the United Methodist Church,* ed. Thomas Langford (Nashville: Abingdon/ Kingswood, 1991), 75-88. In the same volume, T. Campbell demonstrates that the idea of a "quadrilateral" of religious authorities was conceived by Outler rather than by Wesley ("The Wesleyan Quadrilateral," 155-61). According to Jones, Wesley actually appealed to five: Scripture, reason, Christian antiquity, Church of England, and human experience ("John Wesley's Conception and Use of Scripture," 80-136). While united and integral in witness to a single Godhead, when properly understood, only Scripture is competent to "norm" all aspects of the Christian's life. Reason and the Fathers collaborate with Scripture in matters of theological understanding, whereas experience collaborates with Scripture in matters of life. I find most interesting Wesley's appeals to the Church of England, which help to draw the boundaries of that context of faith and life that Scripture then interprets.

equately discerning the plain sense of each in turn, undermines the integral nature of Scripture and distorts its full witness to God. On this basis, one might well contend that the critical aim of exegesis, which successfully exposes the pluriformity of Scripture, is "to put the text back together in a way that makes it available in the present and in its (biblical) entirety—not merely in the past and in the form of historically contextualized fragments."[26]

In this sense, then, the plain sense of individual biblical texts (e.g., Rom. 3:23) or of whole biblical traditions (e.g., Pauline), although foundational for scriptural interpretation, has value only in relation to this more holistic end. We should note and celebrate the fact that much of Wesley's theological innovation appealed to the non-Pauline writings for its biblical justification. Indeed, especially his soteriology is possible only by the creative integration of the deeper logic of Pauline teaching (which emphasizes justification by faith) and the non-Pauline teaching (which emphasizes sanctification by faithfulness), which are found together in the New Testament.[27]

Perhaps Wesley presses for a more holistic reading of Scripture to correct the regrettable tendency of Protestant hermeneutics to prioritize the New Testament generally and the Pauline corpus specifically over the rest of the biblical canon. The pitfall of the Protestant hermeneutical tradition is its tendency toward a "canon within the Canon," a reductionism that in its worst form approaches Scripture much like a church potluck supper, where one can eventually find something edible if one is hungry enough. Biblical interpretation takes from Scripture whatever appeals to the reader's taste. Wesley clearly believed that every scripture in every case embodied a straightforward meaning (plain sense) that complied with the rest of Scripture (wholeness). Thus, "the Scripture of the Old and New Testaments is a most solid and precious system of divine truth. Every part is worthy of God, and all together are one entire body" ("Preface" to Notes, par. 10).

Wesley certainly agreed that the Christian Bible is the church's "rule of faith" (or "analogy of faith") by which authorized theological and moral boundaries are marked off around the confessing community. The theological subject matter of the proper interpretation of Scripture will never disagree with the subject matter that believers have always witnessed and confessed to be true about the God made flesh in Christ Jesus our Lord. Even though this point is a cardinal article of catholic hermeneutics, which comes to us from Irenaeus through Calvin to Wesley, the particular content of this confessed "faith," which reflects biblical teaching, differs in impor-

26. So Jon D. Levenson, *The Hebrew Bible, the Old Testament, and Historical Criticism* (Louisville, Ky.: Westminster/John Knox Press, 1993), 79.

27. So Wall, "Law and Gospel."

tant ways between faith traditions. Biblical interpreters whose faith is shaped by the accents of differing theological traditions will (and should) find different analogical meanings apropos to their particular theological and ecclesial locations.

It therefore seems crucial for us to describe the core convictions of this "divine truth" that unifies the whole of Scripture. In Wesley's case, the grand themes that make up this "system of divine truth" are those that frame the *ordo salutis*—justification and sanctification, divine grace by human faith and works, love for God/neighbor and holiness of life.[28] Perhaps it is even more apropos to our tradition to call this a "way of salvation," since, more than a "system of divine truth," it is an experience of divine grace that issues in a way of holy living. In any case, every part of Scripture, studied independently from the whole, bears witness to this same soteriological reality whether as promise (OT) or fulfillment (NT). That is, a Wesleyan approach to biblical interpretation will seek after and recover those meanings from every biblical passage that either calls (priestly task) or corrects (prophetic task) a proper understanding of salvation among Wesleyan believers.[29]

One final point. D. Jacobsen contends that different hermeneutical programs are shaped by different religious sociologies and epistemologies, which result from fundamentally different views of Scripture's authority and character that are deeply ingrained in a faith tradition and passed on to its interpreters. He argues that the socioreligious shaping of the Wesleyan tradition naturally inclines its biblical interpreters toward viewing their task as "open-ended and conversational." Meanings made of Scripture are more fluid and contextual. Jacobsen believes this is so because Arminius (whom Wesley follows at this point) understood Scripture's authority in functional terms, whether to confirm the actual experience of conversion or to interpret the holiness of life for a particular setting. In effect, the simultaneity of Scripture bears witness not only to the simultane-

---

28. So S. Jones, "John Wesley's Conception and Use of Scripture," 60, with many others. I have tried to summarize this same theological core in "The Relevance of the Book of Revelation for the Wesleyan Tradition," under the rubric "A Wesleyan Location for Hermeneutics" (paper presented to the Wesleyan Theological Society, Oklahoma City, 1993).

29. Childs defends the wholeness of Scripture by arguing that while the OT and NT sound different notes—one by Israel and the other by the Church—both bear witness to the same God and salvation. While the prophetic voices of Israel, congregated in the OT, issue God's promise of salvation, the apostolic voices of the Church, congregated in the NT, claim that God's promised salvation has been fulfilled through the messianic ministry of the risen Jesus and has been made present in his Spirit. See *Biblical Theology of Old and New Testaments* (Minneapolis: Fortress, 1992), 721-22. This seems right to me.

ity of the church catholic but also to every experience under heaven that is transformed by the grace of God. Those of Calvinist traditions, on the other hand, tend to press for a uniform interpretation of Scripture and its single meaning that justifies a creedal and uniform "orthodoxy"—one book, one faith. Scripture's authority is viewed in propositional terms to confirm the written text as the *vox Dei* (itself the Word of God).[30]

3. The Soteriological Use of Scripture. According to Wesley, the proper interpretation of Scripture should lead people into the way and experience of salvation. In this sense, not only is the Wesleyan analogy of faith soteriological in theological content, so that the meaning made of every scripture articulates the salvific purposes of God but the intended effect of Scripture's performance is also soteriological, so that the beneficiaries of sound interpretation will be liberated from their sin and its destructive results. The soteriological cast of Wesleyan hermeneutics is both theological and practical. In this light, Scripture's functional role is to facilitate saving faith, both its transformed life and transforming practice. For Wesley, the best evidence of Scripture's authority is the experience of a transformed life, since the deeper logic of his theological conception is that sound doctrine follows from and supplies an interpretation of the experience of divine grace. In this sense, then, Scripture nurtures not only theological understanding but also the sort of person who knows and responds to God's Word.

Again, the revivalist ethos that helped shape Wesley's conception of salvation also helped shape this presumption of Scripture's usefulness. The idea of scriptural holiness presumes that Scripture functions to inspire an understanding of holiness that allows grace to form a new capacity for a holy life in the world rather than as the legal arrangement with God that only cheapens grace and allows sin and selfishness to persist. The God of Wesley's Bible is no nominalist: God's grace results in public and historical proof of God's saving activity. Holiness is the primary characteristic of the trans-

---

30. Douglas Jacobsen, "The Calvinist-Arminian Dialectic in Evangelical Hermeneutics," *Christian Scholar's Review* 23/1 (1993): 72-89. Jacobsen's intriguing conclusion is that Reformed hermeneutics is better suited for the mind-set of modern interpreting, while Wesleyan hermeneutics is better suited for postmodern interpretation. Indeed, the methodological interests of many conservative Reformed interpreters seem positivistic. Their approach to a text is to capture the fixed meaning—perhaps from the mind of its author—for all time. Such positivism has utterly failed to convince or compel. On this basis, he predicts the ascendancy of Wesleyan interpretation within the postmodern evangelical subculture! The dialectical cast of postmodern hermeneutics, which moves in a controlled yet creative way between text and reader to locate its current meaning, seems better equipped to correct the pitfalls of modern interpretation.

formed life that does not retire from the world but resides as light in the midst of darkness. Nor does Scripture teach that holiness is a capacity of grace given only to a privileged few; rather, grace finds all, no matter their class or rank. Nor does Scripture bear witness to a quiet holiness that remains the inward evidence of personal salvation. Scripture forms an understanding of divine grace that is practical and participatory, empowering the believer's ministry toward others in opposition toward everything and anyone that opposes the Creator's good intentions for everything and anyone.

In making these observations, I am separating Wesley's conventional rhetoric about Scripture's importance from his core convictions about its practical usefulness, which were primarily pastoral and evangelical. Biblical interpretation is concerned with awakening a faithful commitment to God in the present rather than in researching the past in order to warrant an orthodox creedalism. It is this emphasis in Wesley, as several have noted, that agrees theologically and methodologically with the postmodern interest in human liberation.[31] I suspect there is a fairly robust hermeneutical agreement here as well, especially in understanding the interpreter's role in facilitating the dynamic dialogue between text and context, where the word of God is located and where the preferred meaning of the biblical text effects saving faith in those who hear and respond to it.[32] The conservative Protestant objection to the contextual cast of liberation exegesis, which moves from external referents in need of liberation to the biblical text for hope and direction, is rooted in the tacit positivism of the magisterial Reformation and its *sola Scriptura* principle (see above), which more naturally moves from biblical texts to their author's intended meaning and only then to external referents.[33] This seems similar to Wesley's tacit objection to Protestant hermeneutics as practiced by the mainstream clergy of the Church of England.

4. The Sermonic Midrash of Scripture. Let me start this final point with an impression, sharply stated. Wesley's hermeneutics are more mid-

---

31. Esp. Theodore Runyon, "Introduction: Wesley and the Theologies of Liberation," in *Sanctification and Liberation: Liberation Theologies in Light of the Wesleyan Tradition,* ed. Theodore Runyon (Nashville: Abingdon, 1981), 9-48.

32. See Christopher Rowland and Mark Corner, *Liberating Exegesis* (Louisville, Ky.: Westminster/John Knox, 1989).

33. My observation is similar to the criticism of Elizabeth Schüssler Fiorenza that an imperialist reading of Scripture seeks to establish timeless patterns and rules, whereas a liberationist reading of Scripture is "critically open to the possibility of its own transformation," *In Memory of Her* (New York: Crossroad, 1983), 34. That is, the meaning of Scripture is itself transformed by the interpreter's attempts to understand the will and Word of God for the current people of God.

CONCLUSION

I conclude feeling even more tentative about the project of Wesleyan hermeneutics than when I began. Am I correct, however, to presume that we possess from Wesley a particular perspective on Scripture and that this perspective forges in turn those presuppositions of biblical interpretation that help shape in a decisive way what it means for Wesleyans to be the church and to act like the church should for the glory of God? Am I right to sponsor a hermeneutics whose agenda is to retribalize Wesleyanism in order to nurture, even to reform the theological understanding and praxis of the whole church? I think so. Moreover, the Wesleyan interpreter has primary loyalty to Wesleyan communions of believers, as prophet or priest. In this regard, the Wesleyan interpreter should cast biblical meaning/theology in a way that enables our particular cloud of Christian witnesses to understand and embody more fully a distinctively Wesleyan form of saving faith and holy life. What I am less certain of is how best to do this.

Richard Thompson is a Wesleyan biblical scholar with specialized studies in New Testament and, more specifically, the Synoptic Gospels and Acts. He has particular interest in the application of literary-critical methods to the reading and interpretation of the Bible. In this chapter, he offers this approach as a viable alternative for Wesleyan biblical hermeneutics by suggesting some possible correlations between John Wesley's understanding of the Bible and literary-critical approaches to reading such sacred texts.

Literary-critical approaches to reading and interpreting the Bible are among the more recent developments in biblical studies. Among other things, such approaches focus on the rhetorical and affective features of the biblical text as well as on the reading process itself, which other more traditional approaches often ignore in the task of interpretation. This does not mean that the attention given to these literary matters excludes the historical-critical concerns that have dominated biblical studies for over two centuries. Indeed, literary-critical readings of the Bible typically give significant attention to the historical dimensions of the biblical text. However, such dimensions are considered within a broader interpretive paradigm where the literary features and reading process (including how one interprets, what happens to the reader, etc.) take center stage, not the historical factors surrounding the writing of the text. In other words, Professor Thompson's goal is not to reject other critical methods of reading the Bible as invalid or not compatible with a Wesleyan context. Rather, he suggests that literary-critical approaches to reading the Bible are both compatible with the Wesleyan tradition and offer potentially significant contributions to the reading and interpretation of the Bible within that tradition.

3

INSPIRED IMAGINATION: JOHN WESLEY'S CONCEPT OF BIBLICAL INSPIRATION AND LITERARY-CRITICAL STUDIES[1]

Richard P. Thompson

❖

The undergraduate class that I was leading on the Synoptic Gospels was using Mary Ann Tolbert's work *Sowing the Gospel: Mark's World in Literary-Historical Perspective* as one of its textbooks.[2] Admittedly, some students were having difficulty with the introductory concepts found there. The following statement, however, provoked more than a few questions and even hostile reactions: "Literary criticism understands the biblical text as *fiction,* the result of literary imagination, not of photographic recall."[3] After the smoke from the ensuing vigorous debate had cleared, it was quite apparent that, in the minds of some of these young women and men, a literary-critical approach to Scripture is incompatible with the understanding(s)[4] of Scripture that their Wesleyan-Holiness upbringing had instilled in them.[5]

The question that inquires about the compatibility of certain methodological approaches in biblical studies with Wesleyan conceptions of Scripture is an appropriate one. Many, among them pastors and scholars, have raised such questions about other recent trends in biblical studies; a few have even sought (either directly or indirectly) to answer them![6] As

---

1. Appeared originally in the *Wesleyan Theological Journal* 34/1 (Spring 1999). Used by permission.

2. Mary Ann Tolbert, *Sowing the Gospel: Mark's World in Literary-Historical Perspective* (Minneapolis: Fortress, 1989).

3. Ibid., 25.

4. The reference to "understanding(s)" is an assumption based on my observation that a univocal understanding or view of the Bible for the Wesleyan-Holiness movement does not exist.

5. See Paul M. Bassett, "The Fundamentalist Leavening of the Holiness Movement, 1914-1940. The Church of the Nazarene: A Case Study," *Wesleyan Theological Journal* 13/1 (Spring 1978): 65-91. His argument identifies a "fundamentalist leavening" within Wesleyan-Holiness circles. This fundamentalist element may be a primary factor in such student reactions, but the identification of such influences is not the focus of this paper.

6. See, e.g., George Lyons, "Hermeneutical Bases for Theology: Higher Criticism and the Wesleyan Interpreter," *Wesleyan Theological Journal* 18/1 (Spring 1983): 63-78; Frank A.

scholars increasingly appropriate interdisciplinary methods in working with biblical texts, new questions naturally arise concerning such trends and their potential impact on biblical studies. Literary-critical approaches[7] are, because of their recent emergence within biblical studies, among the adolescents[8] within the methodological family of biblical studies. Like adolescents, they are often misunderstood by the older, wiser members of that family, and yet have unique and potentially significant contributions to make to that family. Thus, just as scholars have deliberated about the potential role that literary-critical methods may have in biblical studies,[9] such inquiry and dialogue, particularly from a Wesleyan perspective, are natural and necessary developments as persons within the Wesleyan tradition seek, with John Wesley, to affirm Scripture as the primary source of authority for the church.[10]

Thus, the purpose of this essay is to explore the plausible contributions of literary-critical methodology to biblical studies in the Wesleyan-Holiness tradition. What is posited for consideration is the hypothesis that John Wesley's views concerning inspiration may provide a conceptual link between the Wesleyan tradition and the appropriation of literary-critical methodology in biblical interpretation. This essay consists of three parts. First, the writings of John Wesley and his interpreters are examined to delineate Wesley's concept of inspiration. Second, basic issues in the use of literary-critical methods in biblical studies are considered, with particular

---

Spina, "Wesleyan Faith Seeking Biblical Understanding," *Wesleyan Theological Journal* 30/2 (Fall 1995): 26-49; and Robert W. Wall, "Toward a Wesleyan Hermeneutic of Scripture," *Wesleyan Theological Journal* 30/2 (Fall 1995): 50-67 (included in this volume).

7. "Literary-critical approaches" refers very generally here to those methods of biblical study that focus on the rhetorical and affective features of the literary text and/or the reading process in the interpretation of the biblical text. Such a reference includes, for instance, narrative criticism and reader-response criticism.

8. Another recent, developing approach to biblical studies that has yielded fruitful results appropriates social-scientific models and principles in working with the biblical texts.

9. See, e.g., John R. Donahue, "The Changing Shape of New Testament Theology," *Theological Studies* 50 (1989): 314-35; and Pheme Perkins, "Crisis in Jerusalem? Narrative Criticism in New Testament Studies," *Theological Studies* 50 (June 1989): 296-313.

10. See Donald A. D. Thorsen, *The Wesleyan Quadrilateral: Scripture, Tradition, Reason and Experience as a Model of Evangelical Theology* (Grand Rapids: Zondervan, 1990; reprint, Indianapolis: Light and Life Communications, 1997), 71: "If one insists on choosing a geometric figure as a paradigm for Wesley . . . a tetrahedral pyramid . . . would be more appropriate. Scripture would serve as the foundation of the pyramid, with the three sides labeled tradition, reason, and experience as complementary but not primary sources of religious authority." See also Timothy L. Smith, "John Wesley and the Wholeness of Scripture," *Interpretation* 39 (July 1985): 248, who suggests that Scripture provided the "solid foundation" for a hermeneutical "three-legged stool" of experience, reason, and Christian faith.

attention to two general issues that relate to Wesley's concept of inspiration. Third, the idea of "inspired imagination"[11] is offered as one vital point of compatibility and intersection between the Wesleyan tradition and literary-critical approaches to Scripture.

JOHN WESLEY'S CONCEPT OF INSPIRATION

John Wesley regarded the Bible as the primary authoritative source for Christian teachings and doctrine. He stated: "The written Word is the whole and sole rule of their [the Protestants'] faith, as well as practice."[12] Such confidence in the sufficiency of the Bible in these matters came from Wesley's views on divine inspiration of the Bible. The problems do not arise, however, in the identification of Wesley's view that the writing of the biblical texts was, in some way, divinely inspired. Rather, the problems arise in sorting out Wesley's scattered comments about the Bible and inspiration, since his pastoral concern did not lend itself to a systematic presentation of his theological views.[13] However, by examining what Wesley stated throughout his writings, three emphases may be highlighted as particularly significant to his concept of inspiration.

1. Product of Divine Inspiration. One emphasis in Wesley's writings is that the Bible is the product of the inspiration or "assistance"[14] of the Holy

---

11. I am indebted to my former colleague at Olivet Nazarene University, Dr. Russell Lovett, who suggested "inspired imagination" as a possible designation for my initial observations about the possible correlation of divine inspiration and literary imagination/creativity in the Wesleyan tradition.

12. Wesley, "On Faith (Hebrews 11:6)," in *Works* (Bicentennial ed.), 3:496. See also Wesley, "Preface" to *Sermons,* in *Works* (Bicentennial ed.), 1:105, where the famous "man of one book" statement is found: "O give me that book! . . . let me be *homo unius libri . . .*"; and Wesley, "Popery Calmly Considered," in *Works* (Jackson ed.), 10:141.

13. See Randy L. Maddox, *Responsible Grace: John Wesley's Practical Theology* (Nashville: Abingdon/Kingswood, 1994), who identifies the pastoral concern of being responsive to the grace of God. Cf. Thorsen, *Wesleyan Quadrilateral,* 77, who states: "Although he sensed the need to elaborate on his view, Wesley generally cared less about the theory of divine inspiration than he cared about the content of the gospel message concerning salvation and how that message might best be experienced and communicated." Cf. also Scott J. Jones, *John Wesley's Conception and Use of Scripture* (Nashville: Abingdon/Kingswood, 1995), 17, who also notes that Wesley would have been aware of prior discussions concerning the Bible within Protestant theology, and so he does not repeat it; and R. Larry Shelton, "John Wesley's Approach to Scripture in Historical Perspective," *Wesleyan Theological Journal* 16/1 (Spring 1981): 23-50. It should be noted that Wesley did focus on the issue of divine inspiration and the Bible in "A Clear and Concise Demonstration of the Divine Inspiration of the Holy Scriptures" (*Works* [Jackson ed.], 11:484), but this is merely a brief statement that adds little to our understanding of his views.

14. See Wesley, "A Farther Appeal to Men of Reason and Religion," in *Works* (Bicen-

Spirit that occurred when the human authors wrote the respective texts.[15] He stated: "The Scripture, therefore, being delivered by men divinely inspired, is a rule sufficient of itself."[16] Wesley recognized the human participation in the writing of the respective texts; however, he identified Scripture as teachings or words that had come directly from God. Two prefatory remarks for different publications both reflect Wesley's conviction. In the preface to *Sermons*, he wrote: "I want to know one thing, the way to heaven. . . . [God] hath written it down in a book."[17] Wesley also wrote the following, in the preface to *Explanatory Notes upon the New Testament:*

> In the language of the sacred writings we may observe the utmost depth, together with the utmost ease. All the elegancies of human composures sink into nothing before it: God speaks, not as man, but as God. His thoughts are very deep, and thence His words are of inexhaustible virtue. And the language of His messengers, also, is exact in the highest degree: for the words which were given them accurately answered the impression made upon their minds.[18]

Wesley identified God as the source for all that the Bible contains, so that the entire collection of biblical texts *together* provides God's revelation for humanity.[19] Thus, he stated:

> Concerning the Scriptures in general, it may be observed, the word of the living God, which directed the first patriarchs also, was, in the time of Moses, committed to writing. To this were added, in several succeeding generations, the inspired writings of the other prophets. Afterwards, what the Son of God preached, and the Holy Ghost spake by the apostles, the apostles and evangelists wrote. . . . The Scripture, therefore, of the Old and New Testament is a most solid and precious

---

tennial ed.), 11:171-72, where he defined inspiration as the "immediate assistance" of the Holy Spirit, which he also equates with what "the apostles felt when they were first 'filled with the Holy Ghost.'"

15. See Wesley's frequently cited statement on 2 Tim. 3:16 in *Explanatory Notes upon the New Testament* (London: Epworth, 1958), 794.

16. Wesley, "Popery Calmly Considered," in *Works* (Jackson ed.), 10:141.

17. Wesley, "Preface" to *Sermons*, in *Works* (Bicentennial ed.), 1:105.

18. Wesley, *Explanatory Notes upon the New Testament*, 9. See also "A Clear and Concise Demonstration of the Divine Inspiration of the Holy Scripture," in *Works* (Jackson ed.), 11:484, where Wesley sought to prove that "[the] Bible must be the invention either of good men or angels, bad men or devils, or of God."

19. Thus, Wesley consistently interpreted one biblical text in light of other similar texts or the "whole of Scripture," which he understood to be unified by the "analogy of faith." Wesley asked, "Have I a full and clear view of the analogy of faith, which is the clue to guide me through the whole?" ("An Address to the Clergy," in *Works* [Jackson ed.], 10:490). See Smith, "John Wesley and the Wholeness of Scripture," 246-62; Jones, *John Wesley's Conception and Use of Scripture*, 43-53; and Maddox, *Responsible Grace*, 38-39

system of divine truth. Every part thereof is worthy of God; and all together are one entire body, wherein is no defect, no excess.[20]
Other references make it clear that Wesley understood the Bible as the direct words of God that, although given to human beings as conduits of
God's message, were faithfully transmitted by those writers.[21] Thus, Wesley's understanding of the divine participation in the writing of the biblical
texts, not matters of inerrancy, is the point of emphasis in his assertion
that, "if there be any mistakes in the Bible, there may as well be a thousand. If there is one falsehood in that book, it did not come from the God
of truth."[22] It should be cautioned, then, that these matters of inerrancy
must not be read in light of contemporary inerrancy debates within fundamentalist circles.[23] Rather, one should keep in focus the primary emphasis
of Wesley himself—that God reveals God's will through the Bible.

While Wesley underscored the divine element of inspiration in his
comments on the Bible, he did not ignore the human side of the equation.
Comments reflecting some of Wesley's thoughts about the role of the human author provide some degree of balance to his statements about God's
"dictation" to those writers. In his notes on 1 Corinthians 7:25, Wesley
distinguished between two texts stimulated by divine inspiration: that
which was written because of "a particular revelation" from God, and that
which was written "from the divine light which abode with them, the
standing treasure of the Spirit of God."[24] While Wesley suggested that,
through the inspiration of the biblical writers, "their knowledge transcend-
ed what could be known by empirical experience or inference alone,"[25]
he also affirmed that normal human judgments were left intact.[26] Wesley
noted in his comments on 1 Corinthians 14:32 that the inspired person
was left to employ personal judgment in matters such as when, what, and

---

20. Wesley, *Explanatory Notes upon the New Testament*, 8-9.

21. Jones, *John Wesley's Conception and Use of Scripture*, 18. See Wesley, *Explanatory Notes upon the New Testament*, 938-39 (Rev. 1:11), 942 (Rev. 1:20).

22. Wesley, *Journal* (24 July 1776), in *Works* (Bicentennial ed.), 23:25. See Troy W. Martin, "John Wesley's Exegetical Orientation: East or West?" *Wesleyan Theological Journal* 26/1 (Spring 1991): 114, 131 n57.

23. Cf. Shelton, "John Wesley's Approach to Scripture," 36-40; Maddox, *Responsible Grace*, 269 n96; and Rob L. Staples, "John Wesley's Doctrine of the Holy Spirit," *Wesleyan Theological Journal* 21 (Spring-Fall 1986), 98-99.

24. Wesley, *Explanatory Notes upon the New Testament*, 605. It should be noted that Wesley emphatically stated here that "the apostles wrote *nothing* [emphasis added] which was not divinely inspired" before making this distinction. See Jones, *John Wesley's Conception and Use of Scripture*, 19.

25. Maddox, *Responsible Grace*, 31.

26. Jones, *John Wesley's Conception and Use of Scripture*, 20-21.

how long to speak, as well as how best to communicate that message.[27] That is to say, there was nothing inconsistent or incompatible, in Wesley's mind, between divine inspiration and the appropriation of human judgment; the message came from God, but its expression often came from the inspired person's discernment and creativity.[28]

One comment in particular highlights what seems to be Wesley's perception of both the divine and human elements in the inspired writing of the biblical texts. In the preface to *Explanatory Notes upon the Old Testament*, Wesley stated:

> These books [Joshua to Esther] . . . [were written] by prophets, men divinely inspired. Indeed it is probable they were collectors of the authentic records of the nation, which some of the prophets were divinely directed and assisted to put together. It seems the substance of several histories was written under divine direction, when the events had just happened, and long after put into the form wherein they stand now, perhaps all by the same hand.[29]

Here Wesley identifies the role of divine inspiration or direction in more than one level of the writing process. That is to say, Wesley did not limit his understanding of inspiration to verbal dictation.[30] He recognized that the biblical texts were products of collaboration by both God and the human authors. As a result, Wesley perceived Scripture as the accurate communication of the message of God; the written text both reveals that inspired message and reflects the judgments and expressions of the human author.[31]

2. Writing and Reading Events. A second emphasis in Wesley's writings was that inspiration included not only the "writing event" of the biblical texts but also the "reading event" of those texts. Wesley stressed that the inspiring activity of the Spirit was not limited to the time of writing; the

---

27. Wesley, *Explanatory Notes upon the New Testament*, 631: "The impulses of the Holy Spirit, even in men really inspired, so suit themselves to their rational faculties, as not to divest them of the government of themselves. . . . But the Spirit of God left His prophets the clear use of their judgment, when, and how long, it was fit for them to speak, and never hurried them into any improprieties either as to the matter, manner, or time of their speaking." See Jones, *John Wesley's Conception and Use of Scripture*, 20.

28. Maddox, *Responsible Grace*, 269 n95, cites several of Wesley's notes in *Explanatory Notes upon the New Testament* as indicating this human participation: Matt. 1:1 (15); 2:6 (19); John 19:24 (383); and Acts 15:7 (453).

29. John Wesley, *Explanatory Notes upon the Old Testament*, 3 vols. (Bristol: William Pine, 1765), 1:701.

30. See John B. Cobb, Jr., *Grace and Responsibility: A Wesleyan Theology for Today* (Nashville: Abingdon, 1995), 172.

31. Cf. Jones, *John Wesley's Conception and Use of Scripture*, 21.

Spirit was also active to inspire the believer's reading of the Bible.[32] His comment on 2 Timothy 3:16 in *Explanatory Notes upon the New Testament* provides the most explicit statement of this dual understanding of inspiration: "The Spirit of God not only once inspired those who wrote it, but continually inspires, supernaturally assists, *those that read it with earnest prayer*" [emphasis added].[33] This inspiring activity of the Holy Spirit was not for Wesley an optional element in the task of biblical interpretation. He stressed that the reader could only interpret the divinely inspired message of the biblical text through the continuing inspirational activity of the Holy Spirit. Wesley insisted that readers "need the same Spirit to *understand* the Scripture which enabled the holy men of old to *write* it."[34]

In Wesley's opinion, the inspiring work of the Spirit was essential for one to read and understand Scripture, and it was unprofitable for one to read or listen to those texts without that work.[35] His rationale was that one could not discern spiritual or divine matters only with one's natural sens-

---

32. Cf. Maddox, *Responsible Grace*, 119-40, who thoroughly articulates Wesley's view of the Holy Spirit and, more specifically, Wesley's concept of "inspiration" by defining it broadly as "the restored influence of the Holy Spirit that enables persons to love and serve God" (121).

33. Wesley, *Explanatory Notes upon the New Testament*, 794. See also the following hymn (number 247) in *Works* (Bicentennial ed.), 7:388-89 (also quoted by Staples, "John Wesley's Doctrine of the Holy Spirit," 99):

> Spirit of Truth, essential God,
>   Who didst thy ancient saints inspire,
> Shed in their hearts thy love abroad,
>   And touch their hallowed lips with fire;
> Our God from all eternity,
> World without end, we worship thee.
>
> Still we believe, almighty Lord,
>   Whose presence fills both earth and heaven,
> The meaning of the written Word
>   Is by thy inspiration given;
> Thou only dost thyself explain
> The secret mind of God to man.
>
> Come then, divine Interpreter,
>   The scriptures to our hearts apply;
> And taught by thee we God revere,
>   Him in Three Persons magnify;
> In each the Triune God adore,
> Who was, and is for evermore.

34. Wesley, "A Letter to the Right Reverend the Lord Bishop of Gloucester," in *Works* (Bicentennial ed.), 11:509. See also *Explanatory Notes upon the Old Testament*, 1:ix.

35. Wesley, "The Means of Grace," in *Works* (Bicentennial ed.), 1:382. Cf. Staples, "John Wesley's Doctrine of the Holy Spirit," 99.

es; rather, Wesley concluded that one must also possess spiritual senses so that one has "the *hearing* ear and the *seeing* eye."[36] Of course, this understanding of inspiration was no substitute for one's reasoning capabilities.[37] Wesley contended that the Spirit's inspiring activity complemented or enlightened one's rational capacities, so that the reader, through the Spirit's inspiring assistance in the reading process, could explore and understand in some measure "the deep things of God."[38] Thus, as Randy Maddox states: "The definitive revelation of God may come to us through Scripture but still be immediate because the Spirit who originally addressed the spiritual senses of the writers will also open our spiritual senses to perceive and attest to the truth they expressed."[39]

This conception of the Spirit's activity of inspiration in the reading process suggests that, in Wesley's mind, the biblical text *alone* does not convey the message of God that the human reader can fully comprehend. What is required is the inspiration of the Spirit of God, an activity that stimulates the capacities of human reason to think about the will of God as revealed through the Bible.[40] The reader, in this understanding, does not participate passively in the reading event by functioning as a sponge that merely soaks up the words and facts of the biblical texts. Nor did Wesley believe that the biblical texts alone could dictate the response of its readers. Wesley stated: "We know there is no inherent power in the words that are spoken in prayer, in the letter of Scripture read, the sound thereof heard . . . but that it is God alone who is the giver of every good gift, the author of all grace."[41] Rather, the faithful reader intersects with the biblical text as enabled by the Spirit, thus discovering the potential message of that text.[42] Wesley's prefatory comment to his *Explanatory Notes upon the Old*

---

36. Wesley, "An Earnest Appeal to Men of Reason and Religion," in *Works* (Bicentennial ed.), 11:56-57.

37. See Jones, *John Wesley's Conception and Use of Scripture,* 106-8, who argues that, although Wesley's insistence on the inspiration of the Spirit for proper biblical interpretation draws on the Reformed tradition, Wesley's unique contribution was his understanding of the Spirit's influence on human reasoning powers.

38. Wesley, "An Earnest Appeal to Men of Reason and Religion," in *Works* (Bicentennial ed.), 11:57. See also Wesley, "The Case of Reason Impartially Considered," in *Works* (Bicentennial ed.), 2:592.

39. Maddox, *Responsible Grace,* 31.

40. See Wesley, "Letter to Miss March" (July 5, 1768), in *Letters* (Telford ed.), 5:96, where he states: "By enlightening our reason to see the meaning of the Scriptures, the Holy Spirit makes our way plain before us."

41. Wesley, "The Means of Grace," in *Works* (Bicentennial ed.), 1:382. Cf. Shelton, "John Wesley's Approach to Scripture in Historical Perspective," 39.

42. The "faithful reader" is not a specific designation by Wesley but is an attempt to refer to the interpreter who seeks to apply what the text reveals to one's life. See Wesley, *Ex-*

Testament implies such an understanding: "But it is not part of my design, to save either learned or unlearned men from the trouble of thinking. . . . On the contrary, my intention is, to make them think, and assist them in thinking. This is the way to understand the things of God."[43] Thus, Wesley clearly emphasized the necessity of the Spirit's activity of inspiration in reading the Bible, but understood that activity as the potential inducement of the faithful reader to discover the will of God through the biblical texts.

3. The Salvation Purpose. A third emphasis in Wesley's writings concerning inspiration and Scripture focused on the purpose of these texts. Wesley understood Scripture to have a soteriological purpose, as scholars within the Wesleyan tradition have already noted.[44] Wesley stated simply: "In his presence I open, I read his book; for this end to find the way to heaven."[45] He considered faith and salvation as the substance or "the marrow . . . of the whole Scripture."[46] Wesley's comments throughout *Explanatory Notes upon the New Testament* reveal his confidence in the soteriological purpose of the biblical texts.[47] This purpose depended on the response of the reader to the grace mediated by God through the biblical text. The focus of Wesley's thoughts was on the "spiritually transforming intent"[48] of Scripture, which he understood both as trust in God and as ethical living.[49]

The assumed soteriological purpose of Scripture framed Wesley's approach to other questions that might be raised about theology or the biblical message. In Wesley's mind, other matters were of lesser importance. Thus, as Maddox notes, "When Wesley took up questions in Christology, his focus was definitely not on the 'Jesus of history.' . . . It was in Jesus as the Christ, the Saviour of the world."[50] Answers to questions about science and the physical world, which were of interest to Wesley, were not sought

planatory Notes upon the New Testament, 332: "He that is *thoroughly willing* to do it, shall certainly know what the will of God is" [emphasis added].

43. Wesley, *Explanatory Notes upon the Old Testament,* 1:ix.
44. See, e.g., Lyons, "Hermeneutical Bases for Theology," 71; Maddox, *Responsible Grace,* 15-25; Martin, "John Wesley's Exegetical Orientation," 112; and Shelton, "John Wesley's Approach to Scripture in Historical Perspective," 38-39.
45. Wesley, "Preface" to *Sermons,* in *Works,* 1:105.
46. Wesley, "The Scripture Way of Salvation," in *Works,* 2:156.
47. See, e.g., Wesley, *Explanatory Notes upon the New Testament,* 368 (John 15:3), 420-21 (Acts 7:38), and 819 (Heb. 4:12).
48. Lyons, "Hermeneutical Bases for Theology," 71.
49. See Maddox, *Responsible Grace,* 230-53, who stresses the role of ethics in Wesley's eschatology.
50. Maddox, *Responsible Grace,* 94-95. Cf. Luke Timothy Johnson, *The Real Jesus: The Misguided Quest for the Historical Jesus and the Truth of the Traditional Gospels* (San Fran-

from the biblical texts.[51] Answering theological questions on the basis of biblical texts was not as significant to Wesley as his concern about salvation.[52] Even in noting the discrepancies between the genealogies found in Matthew and Luke, Wesley emphasized the respective purpose of those accounts rather than the potential problems of historical accuracy. He stated:

> If there were any difficulties in this genealogy, or that given by St. Luke, which would not easily be removed, they would rather affect the Jewish table than the credit of the evangelists; for they act only as historians, setting down these genealogies as they stood in those public and allowed records. Therefore they were to take them as they found them. Nor was it needful they should correct the mistakes, if there were any. For these accounts sufficiently answer the end for which they are recited. They unquestionably prove the grand point in view, that Jesus was of the family from which the promised Seed was to come. And they had more weight with the Jews for this purpose than if alterations had been made by inspiration itself.[53]

To be sure, Wesley's words here reflect some degree of uncertainty in his dealing with these passages. Nonetheless, this perspective of Scripture's saving purpose, which Wesley understood had come from the inspiration of the Spirit, provided him with the conceptual foundation by which to interpret such problematic texts and issues.

Although Wesley did not articulate a systematic understanding of inspiration, his scattered comments and statements suggest that the three emphases included here were central to his understanding of inspiration. These three emphases concerning inspiration—in the writing process, in the reading process, and for the purpose of salvific response—provide some potentially useful points of congruence with literary approaches to Scripture—points of congruence to which we will return shortly.

TWO GENERAL ISSUES IN THE USE OF LITERARY-CRITICAL APPROACHES TO SCRIPTURE

Many questions that have surrounded the emergence of literary-criti-

---

cisco: HarperSanFrancisco, 1996), 133: "Christian faith has never—either at the start or now—been based on historical reconstructions of Jesus, even though Christian faith has always involved some historical claims concerning Jesus. Rather, Christian faith (then and now) is based on religious claims concerning the present power of Jesus."

51. Martin, "John Wesley's Exegetical Orientation," 112; and Shelton, "John Wesley's Approach to Scripture," 39.

52. Maddox, *Responsible Grace,* 15, 19, usefully orients his articulation of Wesley's thought around the concept of "responsible grace."

53. Wesley, *Explanatory Notes upon the New Testament,* 15.

cal studies of the Bible are related, at least in part, to a difference in what one identifies as the focus of one's study. Historical-critical methods have concentrated largely on "the world behind the text";[54] literary-critical methods, however, while not ignoring historical concerns, focus on "the world within the text" and/or "the world in front of the text."[55] With this significant shift in the study of biblical texts, one must reappraise methodological approaches to this field of study, not only considering established practices but also considering one's theological tradition. Since one's critical study of Scripture and one's faith affirmations relating to Scripture are overlapping categories, an appraisal of methodological issues becomes still more crucial. Thus, for present purposes, two crucial foci will be delineated for approaching the Bible and, more specifically, New Testament narratives from a literary-critical perspective.[56] These two foci—the literary text and the audience or reader of that text[57]—represent two of the three basic elements of the communicative act that are particularly relevant to literary criticism and have some congruence with Wesley's thought.[58]

As the designation "literary criticism" implies, the biblical text itself is the focus of critical reflection and analysis as a *literary* text.[59] Historical

---

54. "Text" refers to the complete work or biblical book, not merely the isolated passage.

55. For a useful but concise treatment of these issues for a general audience, see David L. Barr, *New Testament Story: An Introduction,* 2nd ed. (Belmont, Calif.: Wadsworth, 1995), 1-18. See also Meir Sternberg, *The Poetics of Biblical Narrative: Ideological Literature and the Drama of Reading,* Indiana Studies in Biblical Literature (Bloomington, Ind.: Indiana University Press, 1985), 1-23, who distinguishes between "source-oriented inquiry" (i.e., historical-critical approaches) and "discourse-oriented approaches."

56. Many different approaches to biblical studies may be described as "literary" approaches. The purpose here is not to present one type of literary approach as *the* model of choice, but merely to deal with the significant issues in the general field of literary studies of the Bible. For an assessment of the general field of literary studies of the Bible, see Mark Allan Powell, Cecile G. Gray, and Melissa C. Curtis, *The Bible and Modern Literary Criticism: A Critical Assessment and Annotated Bibliography* (Westport, Conn.: Greenwood, 1992).

57. Whether one should identify the recipient as a reader or an audience is an important critical issue but need not be sharply distinguished here. The original recipients were most likely "hearers" and not readers (i.e., an "audience"). However, "reader" will be used here to denote the activity of the one who seeks to understand a text.

58. The third element of any communicative act is, of course, the sender/author. See John A. Darr, *On Character Building: The Reader and the Rhetoric of Characterization in Luke-Acts,* Literary Currents in Biblical Interpretation (Louisville, Ky.: Westminster/John Knox, 1992), 16, who suggests: "What distinguishes literary theories from one another is how they define and address fundamental issues like the status of the text, the roles of author, audience, and critic in the production of meaning, the nature of reading and interpretation, and whether (or to what extent) cultural context controls the way we process a piece of literature." See Aristotle, *Rhetoric* 1.3.1; and Longinus, *On the Sublime* 8.1, 4.

59. The description "literary text" is, of course, redundant, since the written *text* has

criticism has tended to fragment the text and thereby violate the integrity of the whole literary composition.[60] Often, historical-critical approaches have attempted to extract theology from texts such as the Gospels and Acts and have not adequately considered these as *narrative* texts.[61] To approach the biblical text from a literary perspective, however, is to perceive the text both as a creation of some author and as a means of communication between that author and some reader. Thus, literary criticism recognizes that all texts function rhetorically, and that even the historical narrative text is composed with the purpose of effecting its audience or readers.[62] One identifies the different Gospels as narrative texts with different rhetorical aims. Literary criticism, then, examines not merely *what* the biblical text seems to convey (or its content, i.e., the *story*), but *how* the composed text conveys that story (i.e., its *discourse*) and *how* the whole text, with its various textual elements, may be interpreted or experienced in light of such rhetorical possibilities.[63]

Literary-critical approaches to biblical studies recognize that the narrative text is the product of the creative work of the author. The narrative text does not merely describe or tell what happened. Rather, one may identify the role of literary imagination in a number of important literary elements, including the plot, point(s) of view, selection, arrangement, and composition.[64] What the biblical narrative presents, then, is an "imaginary" world; the narrative is composed creatively and presented so that its readers may be able to imagine that world as though they are a part of it:

---

survived as a *literary* document. However, the description reminds us that approaching the biblical text as *literature* is not a peculiar idea.

60. Cf. Tolbert, *Sowing the Gospel,* 23-27.

61. See Beverly Roberts Gaventa, "Toward a Theology of Acts: Reading and Rereading," *Interpretation* 42 (1988): 146-57.

62. See, e.g., Richard P. Thompson, "Christian Community and Characterization in the Book of Acts: A Literary Study of the Lukan Concept of the Church" (Ph.D. diss., Southern Methodist University, 1996), 24-94; Sternberg, *Poetics of Biblical Narrative,* 15; and Robert C. Tannehill, *Luke,* Abingdon New Testament Commentaries (Nashville: Abingdon, 1996), 31.

63. See Seymour B. Chatman, *Story and Discourse: Narrative Structure in Fiction and Film* (Ithaca, N.Y.: Cornell University Press, 1978), an influential work in narrative-critical approaches to New Testament texts. One should note, however, that the story/discourse distinction is an artificial one, since one only has access to story through discourse. The distinction is helpful in identifying different rhetorical means by which the story is presented.

64. Cf. Gaventa, "Toward a Theology of Acts," 152: "As we read and reread 'the narrative itself,' we ask of what the narrative consists. What world does it create for the reader? What are its crises, its catharses, its developments? What connects various events and persons? What does the narrative repeat and what does it omit? . . . What kinds of characters occupy this story?"

to "see" the characters, to "hear" the dialogue, to become so involved that even their emotions may be stirred. In no sense should one perceive the identified role of creativity or imagination as undermining the historical integrity of these biblical narrative texts. Ancient and modern critics alike have noted that all writing includes, to varying degrees, the imaginative or creative contributions of the author.[65] Nonetheless, the reader is invited into *that* narrative world and not another, and has access to it only through the creative presentation of the narrative text. These imaginative elements, taken *together* to make up the whole narrative text, potentially guide the reader toward response.

Behind the argument that the biblical narrative text presents an imaginative world that would potentially create responses in its readers is the assumption that there were readers or an audience, at least ideally, who would have the necessary concepts, knowledge, and perceptive abilities to interpret the various elements of the text. Literary critics identify such persons as the "implied audience" or "implied readers."[66] In contrast, historical criticism has attempted to identify the historical audience or community to which a specific biblical writer wrote. Since a narrative text does not directly address the world of its readers but creates an imaginative world in which they may participate, it is doubtful that one can paint an adequate picture of the original addressees of any narrative text.[67] However, the text does imply much of what the readers would need to know if they were to make sense of that narrative. Although the precise definition of "implied reader" varies,[68] critics recognize that implicit expectations of the readers are embedded in the text, often including knowl-

---

65. Cf., e.g., Dionysius of Halicarnassus, *On Literary Composition;* Wayne C. Booth, *The Rhetoric of Fiction,* 2nd ed. (Chicago: University of Chicago Press, 1983), 68: "It should be unnecessary here to show that no author can attain to this kind of objectivity" [neutrality toward all things]; and Wolfgang Iser, *The Act of Reading: A Theory of Aesthetic Response* (Baltimore: Johns Hopkins University Press, 1978), 35. On the perceived tension between literary creativity and historical accuracy in ancient historiography, see Thompson, "Christian Community and Characterization in the Book of Acts," 58-94.

66. The idea of "implied reader" correlates with the idea of "implied author." However, only the implied reader will be considered here. Nor will this essay attempt to deal with other distinctions that relate to the implied reader such as "narratee," "ideal reader," or "critic." On these matters, see, e.g., Robert M. Fowler, *Let the Reader Understand: Reader-Response Criticism and the Gospel of Mark* (Minneapolis: Fortress, 1991), 25-40.

67. Cf. Tannehill, *Luke,* 24. See the conspicuous absence of any discussion concerning audience in Luke T. Johnson, *The Acts of the Apostles,* Sacra Pagina 5 (Collegeville, Minn.: Liturgical, 1992).

68. See, e.g., Booth, *Rhetoric of Fiction,* 138: "The author creates . . . an image of himself and another image of his [implied] reader; he makes his reader, as he makes his second self, and the most successful reading is one in which the created selves, author and reader,

edge of Scripture,[69] geography, cultural ideals, religious customs, and so forth.[70] Thus, narrative criticism attempts to enable readers to experience these imaginative texts in ways that are consistent with the textually embedded expectations of the implied reader.[71]

What should be readily apparent at this point is that an inseparable link exists between the literary text as one element of the communicative act and the reader of that text. One of the significant contributions of literary criticism and, more specifically, reader-response criticism has been the reinstatement of the reader to the study of biblical texts. This offers an important corrective to the role or place that has often been assigned to the reader merely as a "repressed reader" in traditional Gospel scholarship.[72] One reason for the repression of the reader may be found in the historical development of literacy, in which: (1) the written text became divorced from the speech act; (2) the evolving uniformity of printed language potentially led to the perception that language was something like a container that held meaning within it; and (3) the meaning or content of the text was identified as that which could be extracted from that literary container.[73] In this historical process, readers became unimportant to the objectified, static text. The "return of the reader"[74] has reintroduced the reading of the text

---

can find complete agreement"; and Iser, *Act of Reading*, 34: "He embodies all those predispositions necessary for a literary work to exercise its effect—predispositions laid down, not by an empirical outside reality, but by the text itself. Consequently, the implied reader as a concept has his roots firmly planted in the structure of the text; he is a construct and in no way to be identified with any real reader."

69. "Scripture" refers to those texts that would have been accepted and used by the earliest Christian groups. There is no need to distinguish here between the Septuagint and the Hebrew Scriptures.

70. See Mark Allan Powell, "Expected and Unexpected Readings of Matthew," *Asbury Theological Journal* 48 (Fall 1993): 31-51, who distinguishes between four types of assumed knowledge for Matthew's implied reader. See also Joseph B. Tyson, *Images of Judaism in Luke-Acts* (Columbia, S.C.: University of South Carolina Press, 1992), 19-41, who discusses the matter of the implied reader in Luke-Acts.

71. Cf. Darr, *On Character Building*, 21; Iser, *Act of Reading*, 152; Thompson, "Christian Community and Characterization in the Book of Acts," 146-47; and Tolbert, *Sowing the Gospel*, 54. Contrary to the complaints of some, literary-critical approaches to biblical studies *do* take seriously the historical elements of the text!

72. See Stephen D. Moore, *Literary Criticism and the Gospels: The Theoretical Challenge* (New Haven, Conn.: Yale University Press, 1989), 106.

73. Fowler, *Let the Reader Understand*, 43-44, draws on the work of noted orality/literacy scholar Walter J. Ong, especially *Rhetoric, Romance, and Technology: Studies in the Interaction of Expression and Culture* (Ithaca, N.Y.: Cornell University Press, 1971), and *Orality and Literacy: The Technologizing of the Word* (New York: Methuen, 1982).

74. See this emphasis within modern literary criticism in the title of Elizabeth Freund, *The Return of the Reader: Reader-Response Criticism* (New York: Methuen, 1987). For a collection of essays on reader-response criticism from a variety of perspectives, see Susan R.

as a temporal experience in which meaning emerges in the convergence of text and reader.[75] Some surviving texts on the subject of ancient literary thought reflected an understanding of this experience as that which created an effect and response—often a response of action.[76] Thus, a reader does not have a passive or nonexistent role in literary-critical approaches to the Bible; rather, this methodological family focuses both on the literary aspects of the biblical text and on the interaction of biblical text and reader.

The return of the reader has corresponded to the growing recognition in literary studies that all texts, including the biblical texts, require a reader for the text to come alive. Once the author hands over the text, it is dependent on its readers for its very life and significance. Both ancient and modern understandings of narrative texts identify the audience or reader as a key component in the realization of the text's potential purposes.[77] One aspect of the reader's contribution to the reading process is in the anticipation and retrospection that accompany that process. A reader progressing through a narrative looks forward and backward, both making judgments concerning what has been read and then revising them based on what is encountered subsequently in the text.[78] Another aspect of the reader's contribution in the reading process is the filling in of both the gaps and the blanks that arise in the reading of the text, since *all* the information necessary for the realization of a text is never provided.[79] These gaps and other ambiguities function as stimuli to the imagination of the reader in grappling with what the text does *not* state, yet the same text also constrains the reader to fill in what is lacking in a way that is consistent with what *is* stated.[80] Both aspects of the reader's contribution to the reading process are required, if indeed one seeks to fulfill the role of the implied reader.[81] This imaginative activity occurs in the reading event when

Suleiman and Inge Crosman, eds., *The Reader in the Text: Essays on Audience and Interpretation* (Princeton, N.J.: Princeton University Press, 1980).

75. Cf. Fowler, *Let the Reader Understand,* 41-58.

76. See, e.g., Aristotle, *Poetics* 6; Aristotle, *Rhetoric* 2.5.14; and Longinus, *On the Sublime* 7.3.

77. See, e.g., Aristotle, *Poetics* 6; Aristotle, *Rhetoric* 2.1.1-9; and Longinus, *On the Sublime* 1.4.

78. Wolfgang Iser, *The Implied Reader: Patterns of Communication in Prose Fiction from Bunyan to Beckett* (Baltimore: Johns Hopkins University Press, 1974), 275, 288. Cf. Iser, *Act of Reading,* 112.

79. For our purposes, let it suffice to say the following: that which is left unanswered is found both within the elements of the text and between the text and the reader.

80. Iser, *Act of Reading,* 163-231; Fowler, *Let the Reader Understand,* 45-46; and Sternberg, *Poetics of Biblical Narrative,* 235-37.

81. That is, since the implied reader/audience also needed to make similar judgments and contributions to the reading process, the real reader who sought to read "in a manner

the literary text and the reader converge. According to Wolfgang Iser, that convergence "brings the literary work into existence."[82] This understanding of the reading event corresponds to the ancient understanding of rhetoric and literature as having social, affective purposes.[83]

Although this convergence of the biblical text and the reader in the reading process brings the dead letters of that text to life, neither the text nor its author can control the process of interpretation. While the text does guide the reader's imagination by its various literary elements (such as textual codes, direct statements by the narrator, repetitious themes, allusions, etc.), both those members of the 1st-century audience and those among the 21st-century readers may come to a variety of conclusions about the text's meaning and the appropriate accompanying response. Literary-critical approaches to the Bible recognize what one finds both in meetings of professional biblical scholars and most Bible study settings of laypersons in local churches: different readers often produce different readings, since they will inevitably emphasize different elements of the biblical text or will fill in the gaps and blanks differently as they attempt to make sense of the whole.[84] Many are reticent to call these different readings anything but *mis*readings, for the perception is that one is merely making the text say what one wants.[85] Robert Tannehill has suggested, however, that the occurrence of different readings correlates with the possibility of different readings or interpretations by an implied audience of Luke's Gospel. These different readings may occur, according to Tannehill, because of the different perspectives that probably existed in such a group, which he identifies as being of diverse social composition.[86] Such useful insights into the potential readings of these biblical texts suggest that one need not limit a reading as the implied reader to one interpretation, effect, or response, provided that one's reading makes sense of the

---

expected of . . . the reader presupposed by the narrative" (Powell, "Expected and Unexpected Readings of Matthew," 32) would also need to read the text in this creative manner. Cf. Iser, *Act of Reading,* 34-35.

82. Iser, *Implied Reader,* 275.

83. See Thompson, "Christian Community and Characterization in the Book of Acts," 24-57.

84. Cf. Tolbert, *Sowing the Gospel,* 7, 26; Iser, *Implied Reader,* 281; and Iser, *Act of Reading,* 34-38.

85. The frequently voiced concern that acknowledging the potential for different readings may give a reader the license to make the text say whatever is wanted really proves the point most resisted, since such a reading of this acknowledgment shows how multiple readings can and do occur in any mode of communication, including a textual mode.

86. See Robert C. Tannehill, "'Cornelius' and 'Tabitha' Encounter Luke's Jesus," *Interpretation* 48 (1994): 347-56; and Tannehill, *Luke,* 24-27.

whole text.[87] Rather, literary-critical methods have opened the possibility for multiple interpretations of a biblical text. This opening accounts for the imaginative contributions of the reader—interpretations that are products of the convergence of the literary text and different readers.[88]

A literary approach to Scripture, therefore, considers both the features of the literary text and its readers as contributors to the reading process. The narrative text provides guidance for the reader through a variety of literary elements, thereby enabling the reader who seeks to fulfill the role of the implied reader to imagine the described narrative world. Nonetheless, this encounter with the biblical text leaves much to the reader's imagination that is provoked at that moment. Thus, the text does not and cannot control interpretation; with reading comes *both* freedom *and* responsibility for those interpretive responses.[89]

"INSPIRED IMAGINATION" AS AN INTERSECTION BETWEEN WESLEY AND LITERARY-CRITICAL APPROACHES TO SCRIPTURE

The previous two parts of this paper have focused on selected emphases in Wesley's concept of inspiration and on general issues in the use of literary-critical approaches to biblical studies. While the contention here is *not* that Wesley's concept of inspiration provided the conceptual framework for his thought and writings, one might argue that this concept provides a plausible starting point in exploring potential areas of compatibility and intersection between Wesley's understanding of Scripture and the emerging contributions of literary-critical methodology.

To be Wesleyan is to identify with John Wesley's ideals and emphases, which also opened windows and doors through which the freshness of new approaches may be appropriated. What one means by being identified as Wesleyan, however, need not be limited to what Wesley did or to exactly what he stated about the Bible. Some have suggested that canonical criti-

---

87. Contra Jack Dean Kingsbury, *Matthew as Story,* 2nd ed. (Philadelphia: Fortress, 1988), 38; and Powell, "Expected and Unexpected Readings of Matthew," 32, both of whom seem to suggest that the Gospel of Matthew guides toward only one possible effect.

88. Readers also bring presuppositions with them about how to analyze the text. These presuppositions come, according to Stanley Fish, from the "interpretive community" in which the reading occurs. See Stanley E. Fish, *Is There a Text in This Class? The Authority of Interpretive Communities* (Cambridge: Harvard University Press, 1980); Fish, *Doing What Comes Naturally: Change, Rhetoric, and the Practice of Theory in Literary and Legal Studies* (Durham, N.C.: Duke University Press, 1989); and Fowler, *Let the Reader Understand,* 35-36.

89. See Robert C. Tannehill, "Freedom and Responsibility in Scripture Interpretation, with Application to Luke," in *Literary Studies in Luke-Acts,* ed. Richard P. Thompson and Thomas E. Phillips (Macon, Ga.: Mercer University Press, 1998), 265-78.

cism best reflects Wesley's dominant concern to understand a passage within "the whole of Scripture."[90] Though this method is appropriate among Wesleyan readings of the Bible, other methods or approaches need not be ignored because Wesley did not advocate or appropriate them. In other words, the Wesleyan tradition need not attempt to become something like a modern mimic of an 18th-century Wesley.[91] George Lyons says: "Both the opponents and the partisans of complicated people like [Wesley] tend to deal with them by flattening them out, reducing them to one-dimensional figures. It is in fact easier to deal with a one-dimensional [Wesley], easier to put him in his place and keep him there, under control."[92] To identify ourselves as part of the Wesleyan tradition does not require that, if Wesley said or did it, we must believe it, and that settles it.[93] Nor must we conclude that Wesley has nothing to say to us in this new millennium. Both extremes—making Wesley out to be a "sacred cow" or a "white elephant"—are problematic.[94] However, the variety that one finds in Wesley's thought about the Scriptures does open other promising possibilities of congruence with recent methodological developments in biblical studies, such as one finds in literary criticism.

Basic correlations between Wesley's concept of inspiration and literary-critical approaches to Scripture are apparent in what has been examined above. To be sure, Wesley was not a literary critic, and neither his hermeneutic nor his use of Scripture reflects many of the concerns of a literary approach.[95] No attempts should be undertaken to dress Wesley in

---

90. See, e.g., Spina, "Wesleyan Faith Seeking Biblical Understanding," 26-49; and Wall, "Toward a Wesleyan Hermeneutic of Scripture," 50-67.

91. While a critique of canonical criticism is not the purpose of this essay, it is most difficult to reconcile the assumptions of that approach to current studies in the New Testament that focus on the integrity of the *single* text and examine matters of theology *primarily* in that single context. In addition, one should consider that Wesley also accepted the apocryphal writings as canonical (Jones, *John Wesley's Conception and Use of Scripture,* 140-43). See also Lyons, "Hermeneutical Bases for Theology," 69, who states concerns about canonical criticism.

92. George Lyons, "Biblical Theology and Wesleyan Theology," *Wesleyan Theological Journal* 30/2 (Fall 1995): 24-25, who adapts what was said of the apostle Paul by Victor Paul Furnish, "On Putting Paul in His Place," *Journal of Biblical Literature* 113 (1994): 4.

93. Cf. Lyons, "Biblical Theology and Wesleyan Theology," 25.

94. The "sacred cow" and "white elephant" analogies with reference to the apostle Paul's ethical teachings are found in Victor Paul Furnish, *The Moral Teaching of Paul,* rev. ed. (Nashville: Abingdon, 1980), 11-28.

95. See Jones, *John Wesley's Conception and Use of Scripture,* who divides his work into two parts, thereby assessing not only what Wesley *stated* about Scripture but also how Wesley *used* Scripture. Jones concludes that Wesley was not particularly successful in following some of his own suggestions and thoughts about Scripture.

the garb of modern literary theory and methods. Nevertheless, one may identify three basic areas of correlation, all of which are found in the reading process emphasized by literary critics.

One commonality lies in the nature of the biblical text. Both Wesley and literary critics recognize the rhetorical purposes of such texts. These writings do not merely convey information; these texts potentially guide the reader to a response. A second commonality lies in the role of the reader. Wesley and literary critics alike recognize both that the biblical text has no affective value unless a reader is involved, and that the reader's contributions to this reading process cannot be ignored. A third commonality lies in the recognition that the biblical texts do not *contain* meaning but that they *become* meaningful as the reader actively "engages" those texts.[96] These stated correlations do not exhaust other possible links between Wesley's concept of inspiration and literary-critical approaches to the Bible. Nonetheless, these correlations provide a general guide in considering more closely the potential contributions of such biblical approaches in a Wesleyan context.

Let us begin by considering the biblical texts themselves. Wesley might well have asked, "What is it that 'speaks' to the reader of the Bible?" The response to this question often focuses on the historical accuracy of the Scriptures. More than a small percentage of persons within the Wesleyan-Holiness tradition pinpoint the evidence for divine inspiration in the historical reliability of the Bible. To be sure, Wesley's statements about the Bible as free from error have been transported across the centuries and thereby misunderstood.[97] However, Wesley's greater concern was for the purpose of these writings, and this concern provided the focus as he expressed his thoughts on matters like inspiration. There is nothing inherently anti-Wesleyan in the acknowledgment of the rhetorical nature of the biblical texts. What we may recognize, with Wesley, is that historical fact alone has no inherent power to convince the reader of *anything*. The story level of the writing as historically accurate information does not convince the reader of its validity, nor does it provide evidence of divine inspiration in the compositional process.

Three points substantiate this claim. First, one may assume that there were probably those who witnessed the events in Jesus' life who could have and perhaps did write accurate accounts about him, yet these texts were not preserved (for whatever reasons) as products of divine inspira-

---

96. This expression is borrowed from Russell Pregeant, *Engaging the New Testament: An Interdisciplinary Introduction* (Minneapolis: Fortress, 1995).

97. See note 22 above.

tion.[98] Second, the mixed response of those confronted by Jesus and others as presented in the Gospels and Acts suggests that even firsthand access to historical facts did not have the power to create a positive response from all members of the audience. Third, the inclusion of four different Gospels in the New Testament suggests that these texts "were treasured for something other than their ability to render a historically accurate Jesus."[99] The likely conclusion, therefore, is that the biblical texts do not "speak" to the reader *simply* because of historically accurate presentations of events and persons.[100]

What, then, may one from the Wesleyan tradition identify in the biblical text as that which enables it to "speak" to its readers? What does one find that expresses the message of God that was divinely inspired? What may be offered as the most likely answer to this question is that the *discourse* level, not the *story* level, reflects the affective and rhetorical elements of the biblical text. That is to say, *how* the text presents something is crucial in *how* it may potentially affect its readers. This aspect of the text reflects the creative or imaginative contributions of the author.[101] At the same time, it is precisely here in the *creative or imaginative composition* of the biblical text where one may well find indications of the role of divine inspiration, as understood by Wesley. The Gospel writers, for instance, did more than gather collections of haphazard, colorless stories. Rather, these authors recognized God at work in the events and life of Jesus, and then imaginatively presented a selection of events in narrative form that would potentially guide an implied audience to make similar conclusions and to respond to what they had experienced. If the divine inspiration of the biblical writers involves the revelation of God through the text, then that element of inspiration will be found in the *imaginative* elements of that text. This convergence of divine inspiration and human imagination in the writing of what would eventually become part of the Christian Bible may be designated "inspired imagination." If inspired imagination is a plausible

---

98. For example, if there really was a "Q" document, why did it not survive? Why was "Q" not preserved, if it was a collection of the sayings of Jesus?

99. Johnson, *Real Jesus,* 147.

100. This statement reflects an understanding of historical narratives that is consistent with ancient historiographical concerns. See Thompson, "Christian Community and Characterization in the Book of Acts," 58-94.

101. See Booth, *Rhetoric of Fiction,* 436: "The author's single most important creative act is to invent what Aristotle calls the 'synthesis of incidents,' the 'plot' in the sense of the plotted narrative line. . . . It is always to some degree a doctoring of the raw chronology of events with a quite different chronology of telling. And it is always . . . ordered toward some powerful effect inherent in our picture of *these events happening to these characters, as perceived in the transforming vision of this storyteller.*"

concept that is consistent with the Wesleyan heritage, then literary-critical approaches provide particularly useful methodological means by which to read and appropriate the biblical texts.

A limitation of inspired imagination to the writing process and the written text, however, would not only present a partial understanding of Wesley's concept of inspiration but also ignore the role of the reader that both Wesley and literary critics recognize. While the biblical text, as a product of inspired imagination, guides and calls the reader into a particular narrative world, the reading process is not controlled by that text.[102] The contribution of the reader does, in fact, figure significantly in what one experiences and discerns through that process. This contribution is created as the imagination *of the reader* is provoked by the imaginative elements *of the writing.* Nonetheless, no text can dictate to the reader how to fill in *all* textual indeterminacies that arise from a particular reading, nor can that text prescribe a response for that reader. The real reader, even though taking on the role of the implied reader with its accompanying expectations for making sense of the biblical text, still must and does make judgments that imaginatively provide coherence to what the text does not state.

It is precisely here—in this imaginative activity that occurs in the reading process—where one may well find what Wesley stressed as the inspiration of the reader of Scripture. Such an element of inspiration in the reading process would contribute to the imaginative activity of the reader in attempting to create coherence of a biblical text.[103] To locate an aspect of inspiration here does not negate other contributions of the reader.[104] For instance, one should note here that the *possibility* for inspiration to work with the reader's imagination in reading the biblical text is also dependent upon the reader—a dependence that Wesley himself acknowledged.[105] The potential of multiple readings still exists. Nonetheless, a Wesleyan understanding of inspiration *in the reading process* would be consistent with the recognition of literary critics that the biblical text alone does not control that process—that something occurs within the reader as the text is encountered. The identification of inspired imagination *within the reader,* therefore, enables those in the Wesleyan tradition to perceive this conver-

---

102. Contra Lyons, "Biblical Theology and Wesleyan Theology," 11, who seems to hold a view that emphasizes textual determinacy and minimizes textual indeterminacy.

103. See William S. Kurz, *Reading Luke-Acts: Dynamics of Biblical Narrative* (Louisville, Ky.: Westminster/John Knox, 1993), 31, who speaks of the *reader,* not the author, as creating the narrative in the reading process.

104. Cf. Michael Lodahl, *The Story of God: Wesleyan Theology and Biblical Narrative* (Kansas City: Beacon Hill Press of Kansas City, 1994), 40-48.

105. See notes 32 and 41 above.

gence of biblical text and reader as something more than merely reading the Bible "as literature."[106] If we recognize the Bible as a collection of texts that reveal the salvific will of God, as Wesley stressed, then the inspired imagination of the *reader* will potentially be stimulated to read and respond appropriately.[107] Since this imaginative activity occurs in the interaction between the biblical text and the reader, we find neither the reader's manipulation of the text nor the textual control of its reader. Rather, the work of the reader's inspired imagination will seek coherence in a biblical text that is *itself* a product of inspired imagination on a different level.

The recognition of the role of inspired imagination in both the writing and reading processes coincides with Wesley's dual emphasis on the divine inspiration of Scripture. Wesley's insistence that readers "need the same Spirit to *understand* the Scripture which enabled the holy men of old to *write* it"[108] would not find substantially divergent emphases in the idea presented here as inspired imagination. This idea does not insist that one aspect of inspired imagination controls or dominates the reading process.[109] But, with Wesley, we may affirm that, if these texts reveal God's purposes of salvation for humanity, the Spirit who inspired the writing may also inspire those who read to experience and perceive those purposes, and potentially to respond in ways appropriate to those readings. Literary approaches to Scripture may assist us in such readings—readings that are done within the communities of believers in the Wesleyan-Holiness tradition.

In this new millennium, it is not surprising that questions are raised about our identity and distinctiveness as members of what we call the Wesleyan-Holiness tradition of Christianity. Often, we seek to highlight our distinctive doctrines, our distinctive hermeneutic, and/or our distinctive rituals and practices. Sometimes, we even seek to find a distinctively Wesleyan reading of Scripture. But could it be that, in our attempts to define what

---

106. See Spina, "Wesleyan Faith Seeking Biblical Understanding," 37-38, whose argument seems to downplay and misinterpret much of what literary criticism emphasizes when he states that "it is highly doubtful that appreciating the Bible's literary dimension takes serious enough the fact that in theological terms the Bible is more than a literary classic and must be read first and foremost as the church's Scripture." One should note, however, that the Greek word translated "Scripture" does literally mean "writing" or "literature," so one must use caution in making such a distinction between Scripture and literature.

107. Cf. Lyons, "Biblical Theology and Wesleyan Theology," 12, 17.

108. Wesley, "A Letter to the Right Reverend the Lord Bishop of Gloucester," in *Works* (Bicentennial ed.), 11:509.

109. Cf. Staples, "John Wesley's Doctrine of the Holy Spirit," 100: "John Wesley had a clear understanding of the bi-unity of Word and Spirit and that he held the two in proper balance, neither merging Spirit into Word so that the former is imprisoned in the latter, nor separating them to the extent that there are two separate sources of revelation. Word does not work automatically, and Spirit does not work autonomously."

makes us distinctive, we negate what truly *is* distinctive about us as Wesleyans? By attempting to limit our reading of Scripture to Wesley's methods or to a specific approach to Scripture, are we following the *letter* of Wesley but not his *spirit*? This essay has attempted to show that the intersection of Wesley's concept of inspiration and literary-critical approaches to Scripture—this idea of inspired imagination—may well cause us to reassess such ventures.[110] It may be that what is distinctive to the Wesleyan context and its understanding of Scripture—inspired imagination—may also include the richness of multiple readings of biblical texts that will provoke creative dialogue within the community of faith. Readings from this context will acknowledge the inspiring role of the Spirit of God and will result in a variety of possible responses to the salvific will of God. Thus, neither the questioning students nor we need to fear what literary-critical approaches to Scripture may do to our Wesleyan views concerning Scripture. Rather, such approaches may more adequately expose us as readers to what God, through those texts, seeks to do *in us*.

---

110. See Cobb, *Grace and Responsibility,* 159: "In short, a Wesleyan theology for today will draw from Wesley positively but only that which makes sense in terms of current understandings of the Bible and our own living experience. It will discriminate among elements of our own experience those that derive from more accurate understanding of the Bible and new knowledge gained from many sources, on the one hand, and those that express our confusion, our loss of zeal, our new idolatries, and our general sinfulness, on the other. In making these discriminations, it will be informed by the Bible as mediated by Wesley and as understood today on the basis of continuing Biblical scholarship."

Donald Thorsen, a senior professor of Christian theology, looks carefully in this chapter at the life and teaching of John Wesley. His purpose is to clarify Wesley's understanding of the inspiration, purpose, and authority of Scripture. John Wesley was clear in his commitment to the authority of Scripture for Christian faith and practice. When it came to the demanding task of biblical interpretation, however, he exhibited a concern for "catholicity." He felt the theological freedom to seek truth pragmatically through understanding spiritual experiences. He also was willing to profit from the wisdom available from several related and usually interactive sources. In particular, he was open to integrating his understanding of the text of Scripture with insights gained from tradition, reason, and experience, resulting in what now is often called the "Wesleyan quadrilateral." Scriptural authority is to remain basic and above question, but probing the Bible's meaning and applications is hardly to be viewed as an isolated and simple process.

Professor Thorsen notes that in John Wesley's writings one discovers a "dynamic" and "holistic" approach to biblical interpretation that is not legalistic or proof-texting, but focuses on enabling the reader to encounter God and experience salvation. This "inductive" approach necessarily leads to certain principles of biblical interpretation and theological method. Thorsen reviews these principles in this chapter, making clear Wesley's openness to more than the plain, literal meaning of biblical texts. Such clarification is very important for Wesleyans ministering today in contexts where "inerrancy" approaches to the Bible are relatively closed to the wisdom available in a more open, holistic, and inductive approach to biblical interpretation.

4

INTERPRETATION IN INTERACTIVE BALANCE: THE AUTHORITY OF SCRIPTURE FOR JOHN WESLEY[1]

Donald A. D. Thorsen

◆

Perhaps John Wesley's most enduring contribution to theological method stems from his concern for catholicity in including experience along with Scripture, tradition, and reason as genuine sources of religious authority. While maintaining the primacy of Scripture, Wesley functioned with a dynamic interplay of sources in interpreting, illuminating, enriching, and communicating biblical truths. He felt the theological freedom to seek truth pragmatically through understanding our experiences. But he did so without succumbing to the implications of a thoroughly pragmatic approach that reduces truth to what is relative to its practical value in our experiences of life.

Nevertheless, Wesley viewed his theological endeavors tentatively; that is, he remained open to new insights that might be uncovered by integrating and then interacting with Scripture, tradition, reason, and experience. He explicitly stated this openness in the preface to his "Sermons on Several Occasions"—his primary theological reference work.

> But some may say I have mistaken the way myself, although I take upon me to teach it to others. It is probable many will think this; and it is very possible that I have. But I trust, wheresoever I have mistaken, my mind is open to conviction. I sincerely desire to be better informed. I say to God and man, "What I know not, teach thou me."[2]

The humility demonstrated in this prefatory remark to his sermons reflects more than the quality of Wesley's inner character. It reflects his theological character as well—in particular, his methodological approach to biblical truth and other truths present in the world. Wesley recognized that one must humbly approach the experimental task of reflecting on theology.

---

1. Appeared originally as chapter 4 in Donald A. D. Thorsen, *The Wesleyan Quadrilateral: Scripture, Tradition, Reason and Experience as a Model of Evangelical Theology* (Grand Rapids: Zondervan, 1990; reprint, Indianapolis: Light and Life Communications, 1997). Used by permission of Light and Life Communications.

2. Preface, sec. 8, "Sermons on Several Occasions," in *Works* (Bicentennial ed.), 1:107.

In other words, we must remain open to the wealth of insight that God may reveal to us through a variety of sources about ourselves, our world, and our relationship with him. Each focus of religious authority makes a unique contribution to uncovering truth and formulating doctrinal ideas. To understand and appreciate the contributions Wesley expected from the various sources of religious authority, we need to investigate each of them individually. In so doing, we learn more of the theological gestalt that resulted from his integration of Scripture, tradition, reason, and experience.

We must begin by looking at Scripture. We could consider the other components in any order without obscuring their respective roles for his methodology, since Wesley never wrote anything specifically about the relationship between tradition, reason, and experience. In fact, there are good reasons for placing any of them after Scripture.[3] Yet our intuition suggests how Wesley might have wanted them ordered in a scholarly discussion. We do well to consider the formula most often invoked when referring to the popular conception of the Wesleyan quadrilateral: Scripture, tradition, reason, and experience.

The priority of scriptural authority goes without question. Yet the secondary placement of tradition behind Scripture possesses an intuitive order of importance in Wesley's theology. Especially as found in the classical orthodoxy of Christian antiquity, tradition provided genuine substance to our beliefs. Wesley hesitated to say that either reason or experience adds substance to our beliefs, but tradition served to fill in doctrinal lacunas not specifically addressed in Scripture. The canonization of the New Testament and the doctrinal summaries of the ecumenical councils offer the best examples of substantive contributions to the teaching of Scripture. Thus, tradition deserves second place among the four sources of religious authority.

It becomes less clear whether reason or experience should come

---

3. Wesley most often made explicit references to the authority of reason when speaking in conjunction with scriptural authority. And whenever he mentioned more than two sources of religious authority, he usually placed reason second in order after Scripture. So, especially in a larger discussion of theological method, it would seem logical to take up reason after considering Scripture.

Nevertheless, Wesley's understanding of experience could come immediately after Scripture because it is his most distinctive contribution to Christian thinking. Besides, the study of experience draws attention to the experimental dimension of religious truths so crucial to the life of believers and to the defense of Wesley's theology. Then again, Wesley always assumed the orthodoxy of his theology and the continuity of the Methodist movement with the truest, most primitive form of Christianity (which he believed to develop in spiritual succession through the Church of England). He did not try to create a new theology but only integrate reason and experience in ways that better reflected classical, orthodox beliefs. In sum, all three sources of religious authority could profitably be discussed in any order following Scripture.

next. The *Book of Discipline* for the United Methodist Church lists experience before reason, but it claims that "theological reflection may find its point of departure in tradition, 'experience,' or rational analysis."[4] From our perspective, either reason or experience could appropriately follow. But from our study of Wesley and the popular model of the quadrilateral, reason seems to be the source of religious authority to which Wesley appealed most often in the formulation and defense of his theology. Either because of his own regard for the importance of reason or because he knew his theology needed to be well-conceived from the standpoint of reason, Wesley regarded reason as inextricably bound up with the truths of Scripture and thus deserving of special recognition. This does not diminish the importance of experience. The point is, no theological method is complete without a genuinely catholic consideration of all historic authority claimants in reflecting on and formulating theology.

THE PRIMACY OF SCRIPTURE

Clearly, Scripture was to Wesley a source of religious authority unlike and superior to any other. His theology germinated from God's self-revelation as found in the Bible. All theology and experiences "are to be tried by a farther rule to be brought to the only true test—the Law and the Testimony."[5] In a letter to James Hervey, Wesley wrote, "I allow no other rule, whether of faith or practice, than the Holy Scriptures."[6] Out of concern for the ongoing faith of the Methodists, he wrote: "What I nightly wish is that you all keep close to the Bible. Be not wise above what is written. Enjoin nothing that the Bible does not clearly enjoin. Forbid nothing that it does not clearly forbid."[7] Although Wesley was willing to learn from other people and even other religious traditions, they needed to demonstrate their contentions "by plain proof of Scripture."[8] Not only did Scripture, as the "oracles of God," serve as the "foundation of true religion,"[9] but it also functioned as a kind of epistemological safeguard for the boundaries of true, experimental religion.

Wesley agreed with the greater Reformation and Anglican emphasis

---

4. *The Book of Discipline of the United Methodist Church 1984* (Nashville: United Methodist Publishing House, 1984), 81.

5. *Journal* (Curnock ed.), 2:226, 22 June 1739.

6. "To James Hervey," 20 March 1739, in *Letters* (Telford ed.), 1:285.

7. "To Johan Dickins," 26 December 1789, in *Letters* (Telford ed.), 8:192.

8. Preface, sec. 9, "Sermons on Several Occasions," in *Works* (Bicentennial ed.), 1:107.

9. "The Case of Reason Impartially Considered" (1781, sermon 70), I.6, in *Works* (Bicentennial ed.), 2:591.

on the primacy of scriptural authority. More specifically, he considered the Anglican Church "nearer the scriptural plan than any other" church either in England or Europe, which is largely the reason why he never wanted to separate from the Church of England. Scripture served as the only sufficient source commonly available to people for investigating the nature of God and of life. Because Scripture applies both to theology and the whole of life, Wesley considered tradition, reason, and experience viable resources in helping to understand and communicate the truths of Scripture.

Along with his theological respect for Scripture, Wesley gave it a special role in his personal life. Modern attempts to find antecedents of 19th-century liberal Protestantism in Wesley fail to do justice to his intimate trust and confidence in Scripture to serve as God's chosen means of self-revelation to individuals and to humanity in general. Wesley did not merely read Scripture; he listened to God personally speaking to him in its pages. Scripture represented the *living* words of God: "The foundation of true religion stands upon the oracles of God. It is built upon the prophets and apostles, Jesus Christ himself being the chief corner-stone. Now of what excellent use is reason if we would either understand ourselves, or explain to others, those living oracles!"[10] He believed that we can place ourselves in such a relationship to Scripture that God will speak to us through it. Thus he became highly excited when speaking of Scripture: "O give me that book! At any price, give me the book of God!"[11] It was existentially important to Wesley that he have the Bible and hold it as the primary rule of his life. Reading and then existentially listening to Scripture functioned in the same way as listening to God. God not only inspired the writing of Scripture but also continues to illuminate those who read it. The mere study of Scripture, of course, does not produce the necessary insight or inspiration for becoming a Christian. To enter into a saving relationship with Jesus Christ, one must be aided by the inner working of the Holy Spirit.

Commenting on the inspiration of Scripture in the *Notes upon the New Testament,* Wesley speaks of the ongoing need for inspiration or illumination from the Holy Spirit, who serves as a guide for those who approach the reading of Scripture in the context of prayer.

All Scripture is inspired of God—The Spirit of God not only once inspired those who wrote it, but continually inspires, supernaturally assists, those that read it with earnest prayer. Hence it is so profitable for doctrine, for instruction of the ignorant, for the reproof

---

10. Ibid., 2:591-92.

11. Preface, sec. 5, "Sermons on Several Occasions," in *Works* (Bicentennial ed.), 1:105.

or conviction of them that are in error or sin, for the correction or amendment of whatever is amiss, and for instructing or training up the children of God in all righteousness.[12]

Some theologians might refer to this theological understanding as the double-inspiration theory, when divine inspiration occurs in both the author and the reader of Scripture. Wesley did not formally elaborate such a doctrine, but he firmly believed in the continual inspiration or illumination of the Holy Spirit available to those who seek divine assistance in listening to God.

Although we need the continued presence of the Holy Spirit to guide us, Scripture remains a reliable source of God's self-revelation. Scripture does not supplant the Holy Spirit, but God has chosen to make it a sufficient resource for matters of religious faith and practice. Thus Wesley considered Scripture serving as much to *rule* our lives as God's Spirit serves to *guide* our lives.

> For though the Spirit is our principal leader, yet He is not our rule at all; the Scriptures are the rule whereby He leads us into all truth. Therefore, only talk good English, call the Spirit our "guide," which signifies an intelligent being, and the Scriptures our "rule," which signifies something used by an intelligent being, and all is plain and clear.[13]

Scripture and the Holy Spirit are not in conflict. Instead, they serve as perfect complements in communicating what Wesley liked to describe as heart-religion, religion in which knowledge and vital piety perfectly join in the life of a believer.

THE INSPIRATION OF SCRIPTURE

Belief in Scripture flows from belief in God, and not vice versa. Wesley did not assume the inspiration of Scripture without first committing himself, at least provisionally, to belief in God. Yet the growth of theistic beliefs came through reading Scripture and discovering its trustworthiness as a source of divine revelation about God and salvation through Jesus Christ. An almost dialectical interplay occurs between the reading of Scripture, the substantiation of experience, and the reasonably conceived insight that results from having committed oneself to Scripture as the self-revelation of God. The dialectical process comprises an active comprehension of things known whereby a person gains objective knowledge about God and salvation that may appear hidden to those unwilling to commit themselves to God.

---

12. 2 Tim. 3:16, *Notes upon the New Testament*, 794.
13. "To Thomas Whitehead (?)," 10 February 1748, in *Letters* (Telford ed.), 2:117.

Wesley committed himself at least by the year 1730—eight years before his well-known Aldersgate experience—to making the Bible the primary source of authority for his life.[14] Yet he sometimes doubted the truth of Scripture, for example, concerning the *instantaneous* nature of conversion by faith. He had not experienced the assurance of a personal conversion and knew of few who had. Although he desired such an assurance, he seriously questioned whether he could ever experience it. Peter Böhler and others encouraged him by introducing him to people who had experienced instantaneous conversions.[15] These witnesses, coupled with similar kinds of conversions described in Scripture, led Wesley to a point of belief when he, too, experienced a sense of personal assurance of salvation. It also led him to greater depths of commitment and willingness to participate in other truths mentioned in Scripture, for example, the possibility of living a holy life through the sanctifying grace of God.

Earlier Wesley had appealed to Böhler as to whether he should continue to preach despite his feeling "fully convinced of unbelief, of the want of that faith whereby alone we are saved."[16] Böhler replied, "Preach faith *till* you have it; and then, *because* you have it, you *will* preach faith."[17] This somewhat paradoxical comment by Böhler reveals the participatory nature of how we come to both believe *and* know. Without personally committing ourselves to something or someone as true, we will not fully understand the depth of truth present, nor will we experience the assurance of its truthfulness.

Similar participation motifs from the Catholic mystics were known to Wesley through what he had read, but it was his discovery of such truths in Scripture *and* his heartwarming experience of personal assurance that ultimately led him to the added assurance of the inspiration of Scripture. He believed that "all Scripture is given by the inspiration of God"—an affirmation found both in Scripture and in Anglican formularies.[18] This affirmation represented a faith commitment that Wesley used to distinguish himself and the Methodist movement from "Jews, Turks, and Infidels."[19] He

---

14. See "A Plain Account of Christian Perfection," sec. 10, in *Works* (Jackson ed.), 11:373.

15. See *Journal* (Curnock ed.), 1:454, 22 April 1738.

16. *Journal* (Curnock ed.), 1:442, 4 March 1738.

17. Ibid. Italics are Wesley's.

18. Compare Wesley's comments on 2 Tim. 3:16 in the *Notes upon the New Testament*, 794, with Anglican formularies concerning "The Scriptures" in Articles VI-VII of the Thirty-nine Articles in Philip Schaff, *The Creeds of Christendom* (New York: Harper and Brothers, 1919), 1:592-649, 3:486-516; and Edward J. Bicknell, *A Theological Introduction to the Thirty-nine Articles of the Church of England* (London: Longman, 1919), 128-46.

19. "The Character of a Methodist," sec. 1, in *Works* (Jackson ed.), 8:360.

also believed "the written word of God to be the only and sufficient rule both of Christian faith and practice; and herein we are fundamentally distinguished from those of the Romish Church."[20]

As we have seen, the confirmation of Wesley's belief in Scripture came at least in part from his personal experience of its truth for salvation and from the ongoing witness of the Holy Spirit. He fully expected God's Holy Spirit to witness to the inspiration of Scripture so that one would experience a personal sense of assurance of its truthworthiness. But beyond divine confirmation that we experience, Wesley appealed to several other arguments that he thought would further *induce* people to believe in the inspiration of Scripture. In "A Clear and Concise Demonstration of the Divine Inspiration of the Holy Scriptures," Wesley used empirical and rational arguments. First, he argued that the empirical facts that surround Scripture compel us to believe in its inspiration.

> There are four grand and powerful arguments which strongly induce us to believe that the Bible must be from God; viz., miracles, prophecies, the goodness of the doctrine, and the moral character of the penmen. All the miracles flow from divine power; all the prophecies, from divine understanding; the goodness of the doctrine, from divine goodness; and the moral character of the penmen, from divine holiness.[21]

The four arguments—divine power, understanding, goodness, and holiness, which Wesley called "the four grand pillars" for God—presuppose an already existing conception of God, and Wesley recognized this logical limitation. Nevertheless, the arguments served to substantiate a fundamental belief in God and characteristics about him that make belief in the inspiration of Scripture plausible as well as possible. Only after we encounter the living God in faith can we grasp the essential truths of Christianity. In a sense, these arguments provide a way in which a believing mind can form a rational understanding of inspiration.

A second rational argument used by Wesley comprised a logical problem on the necessary source of inspiration. Here he offered three propositions for possible motivations in writing Scripture and how it makes logical sense to believe that God inspired the Word.

> I beg leave to propose a short, clear, and strong argument to prove the divine inspiration of the holy Scriptures. The Bible must be the invention either of good men or angels, bad men or devils, or of God.

---

20. Ibid.

21. "A Clear and Concise Demonstration of the Divine Inspiration of the Holy Scriptures," in *Works* (Jackson ed.), 11:484.

1. It could not be the invention of good men or angels; for they neither would nor could make a book, and tell lies all the time they were writing it, saying, "Thus saith the Lord," when it was their own invention.

2. It could not be the invention of bad men or devils; for they would not make a book which commands all duty, forbids all sin, and condemns their souls to hell to all eternity.

3. Therefore, I draw this conclusion, that the Bible must be given by divine inspiration.[22]

This argument resembles popular arguments still used by such contemporary authors as C. S. Lewis. In *Mere Christianity,* Lewis argues that we have three options in our view of Jesus Christ. We must either consider him a liar, a lunatic, or the Lord of the universe.[23]

Of course, the options provided both by Lewis and Wesley are too simple for us to consider all possible approaches to the topic. In this instance, Wesley's intention to speak *ad populum* becomes quite evident because his reasoned approach to the inspiration of Scripture only made sense to those who already believed. In the final analysis, Wesley required the affective dimension of the testimony of the Holy Spirit to assure one of the inspiration of Scripture. Yet we may view the foregoing arguments as ways to *think* about inspiration rather than ways to provide *rational proofs* of inspiration.

Wesley never argued for a rationalistic conception of religion, but he continually argued for a conception of religion that is reasonable. As such, the objective of Wesley's discussion was not to discover rational, objective proofs for inspiration that we must then believe by faith. Inspiration was first known in experience through a personal encounter with God. The aim of Wesley's theological reflections was to understand the nature of this inspiration in depth. This reflection contributes to a Christian's sense of assurance about divine inspiration—an assurance experienced in both the head and the heart.

Colin Williams intimates that Wesley argued theoretically for the inspiration of Scripture from the standpoint of a static and mechanical biblical literalism. For example, Williams contends that Wesley's "interpretation of 'Thus said the Lord' . . . [is] a mechanical view which fails to do justice to the dynamic of the divine-human encounter."[24] But he moderates his interpretation by noting that the view of inspiration Wesley held in

---

22. Ibid.
23. C. S. Lewis, *Mere Christianity* (New York: Macmillan, 1943), 55-56.
24. Colin Williams, *John Wesley's Theology Today* (New York: Abingdon, 1960), 27.

practice reflected how "biblical interpretation was brought into relation with tradition, reason, and experience in such a way that he [Wesley] was relieved of the dangers of a static and mechanical literalism."[25] However, this modified interpretation gives Wesley very little credit for the sophistication of his theology and his understanding of language. On the one hand, Wesley said: "The language of his messengers, also, is exact in the highest degree: for the words which were given them accurately answered the impression made upon their minds; and hence Luther says, 'Divinity is nothing but a grammar of the language of the Holy Ghost.'"[26] On the other hand, Wesley did not work with a naive understanding of language in referring to the nature and work of God. In his sermon "The Witness of the Spirit," he used the same kind of *impression* terminology that we read above in his speaking of assurance. Yet he recognized the limitations of all language in describing God and his self-revelation.

> It is hard to find words in the language of men to explain "the deep things of God." Indeed, there are none that will adequately express what the children of God experience. But perhaps one might say (desiring any who are taught of God to correct, to soften, or strengthen the expression), The testimony of the Spirit is an inward impression on the soul, whereby the Spirit of God directly witnesses to my spirit, that I am a child of God.[27]

Wesley showed great confidence in God's continuous spiritual presence and work in the lives of believers both past and present. But he did not have a naive or simplistic approach to what that confidence involves. He considered religious experiences to provide objective knowledge of God, not merely subjective, but though it gives us objective impressions of the divine, our knowledge—because of our humanness—remains *in part*. This recalls the words of Paul in 1 Corinthians 13: "We know in part and we prophesy in part . . . Now we see but a poor reflection [of the way things are]."[28]

Although Wesley lived before the day of historical-critical questions about Scripture, he nevertheless had some sophistication concerning the limits of language and reason. We should not, even in theory, relegate his understanding to that of a static and mechanical literalism. He believed in the inspiration of Scripture because it proved sufficient for salvation and for growing in the Christian life. Scripture became functionally authorita-

---

25. Ibid.
26. Preface, sec. 12, *Notes upon the New Testament*, 9.
27. "The Witness of the Spirit, I" (1746, sermon 10), I.7, in *Works* (Bicentennial ed.), 1:274. Cf. "The Imperfection of Human Knowledge" (1784, sermon 69), in *Works* (Bicentennial ed.), 2:567-86.
28. 1 Cor. 13:9, 12.

tive for Wesley *before* he formulated his doctrine of Scripture. In fact, from his perspective, all conceptual formulations retain a hypothetical or tentative quality that mitigates against merely static or mechanical views of the inspiration and authority of Scripture.

To the extent that he affirmed Scripture as the primary authority of the Christian religion, Wesley agreed with the classical Protestant view of biblical authority. In his sermon "On Faith, Heb. 11:6," he explicitly aligned himself with the Protestant position on Scripture.

> The faith of Protestants, in general, embraces only those truths as necessary to salvation, which are clearly revealed in the oracles of God. . . . They believe neither more nor less than what is manifestly contained in, and provable by, the Holy Scriptures. . . . The written word is the whole and sole rule of their faith, as well as practice.[29]

Although Wesley fully aligned himself with Protestant Christianity, he was not content to use the principle of Scripture alone in a way that excluded other sources of religious authority. In keeping with his Anglican heritage, he was not afraid to introduce extrabiblical authorities into his method of approaching theology and Scripture. The whole theological task was too complex and interrelated to other sources of religious authority to ignore how they contributed to illuminating, vitalizing, and organizing the gospel message.

THE PURPOSE AND AUTHORITY OF SCRIPTURE

We discover in John Wesley that the primary purpose of Scripture is to communicate the full gospel message of salvation—salvation that produces both justification and sanctification in believers. Scripture contains a trustworthy record of how God provided a way of salvation, especially as revealed through the person and work of Jesus Christ. Scripture thus presents the "way of salvation."

Wesley articulated this way in such sermons as "Scriptural Christianity," "The Scripture Way of Salvation," and "On Working Out Our Own Salvation." If we want to be saved but do not know how, Scripture shows us "the steps which . . . direct us to take, in the working out of our own salvation."[30] Thus Scripture was always believed by Wesley to remain existentially essential to finding the way of salvation.

---

29. "On Faith, Heb. 11:6" (1788, sermon 106), I.8, in *Works* (Bicentennial ed.), 3:496. Cf. related discussions of Wesley's theological proximity with classical Protestantism in R. Larry Shelton, "John Wesley's Approach to Scripture in Historical Perspective," *Wesleyan Theological Journal* 16/1 (Spring 1981): 37-38; and Williams, *John Wesley's Theology Today*, 26, 37.

30. "On Working Out Our Own Salvation" (1785, sermon 85), II.4, in *Works* (Bicentennial ed.), 3:205.

Articulating the order of salvation *(ordo salutis)* found in Scripture facilitates the Word's intended purpose. Wesley recognized this practical application of theology and so attempted several times to delineate each stage in the way of salvation. Some scholars suggest that Wesley's order is one of his most systematic theological enterprises.[31] Indeed, Wesley generally regarded the order of salvation as the core of his theology. Harald Lindström presents a comprehensive study of Wesley's various attempts to articulate this order. Of these attempts, Lindström considers the 1765 sermon titled "The Scripture Way of Salvation" to provide the predominant factors Wesley placed in the *ordo salutis:* "(1) The operation of prevenient grace; (2) Repentance previous to justification; (3) Justification or forgiveness; (4) The New Birth; (5) Repentance after justification and the gradually proceeding work of sanctification; and (6) Entire sanctification."[32]

Larry Shelton notes that Scripture functions sacramentally for Wesley.[33] By sacramental use, Shelton explains: "When the means of Scripture is focused on the need for salvation, its purpose is fulfilled. . . . God works infallibly through the means of Scripture to bring salvation."[34] To Wesley, Scripture provided that means whereby God performs an action of grace corresponding to the finished and ongoing work of Christ in our lives for salvation. He described the "means of grace" as "outward signs, words, or actions, ordained of God, and appointed for this end, to be the ordinary channels whereby He might convey to men, preventing, justifying, or sanctifying grace."[35] He applied this sacramental principle to Scripture by saying, "All who desire the grace of God are to wait for it in 'searching the Scriptures.'"[36] Although Wesley did not formally describe the prayerful study of and meditation on Scripture as a sacrament, he certainly conceived of it as a channel of grace.

To the extent that Wesley claimed to be a man of one book, he affirmed the Reformation call to the authoritative principle of *sola Scrip-*

---

31. Cf. Harald Lindström, *Wesley and Sanctification: A Study in the Doctrine of Salvation* (Wilmore, Ky.: Francis Asbury Publishing, 1980; reprint, Grand Rapids: Zondervan, 1983), 105-12; Williams, *John Wesley's Theology Today,* 19-46; Randy L. Maddox, "Responsible Grace: The Systematic Nature of Wesley's Theology Reconsidered," *Wesleyan Theological Journal* 19/2 (Fall 1984): 26; Mitsuru Samuel Fujimoto, "John Wesley's Doctrine of Good Works" (Diss., Drew University, 1986), 1, 3; and Kenneth Collins, *Wesley on Salvation: A Study in the Standard Sermons* (Grand Rapids: Zondervan/Francis Asbury, 1989).

32. Lindström, *Wesley and Sanctification,* 113; cf. 105-19.

33. See Shelton, "John Wesley's Approach to Scripture," 23-50.

34. Ibid., 39.

35. "The Means of Grace" (1746, sermon 16), II.1, in *Works* (Bicentennial ed.), 1:381.

36. "The Means of Grace" (1746, sermon 16), III.7, in *Works* (Bicentennial ed.), 1:386.

tura.[37] But his affirmation of Scripture as primary appeared in the context of an overwhelming desire for salvation and not in the traditional mold, at least, of Continental Reformation thinking. Because the authority of Scripture ensued from its efficaciousness in bringing a person to the experience of personal salvation, it did not rest on proving the inspiration or dependability of it. Later in his ministry Wesley affirmed that Scripture contained no falsehood.[38] But earlier, he perceived the authority of Scripture resting more on its function in facilitating salvation than on its factual, historical, or theological dependability.[39]

No doubt Wesley affirmed the authority of Scripture with greater zeal after his famed heartwarming experience at Aldersgate. At that time Scripture asserted for him its supremacy as never before.[40] But he had to learn it experimentally from the context of his experience—even if at first he was only tacitly or subconsciously aware of the learning process. As mentioned earlier, Wesley had wondered pre-Aldersgate whether a person could be saved instantaneously. He knew that Scripture contained accounts of people who were thus converted, but he could not bring himself to believe it. After conferring with Peter Böhler and further reflecting on the words of Scripture, Wesley could only exclaim: "Here ended my disputing. I could now only cry out, 'Lord, help thou my unbelief!'"[41] Only later did Wesley develop a more complete understanding of Scripture that included an account of its authoritativeness.

What Wesley experienced as true, he expected to find confirmed under the experimental scrutiny of inductive investigation, which included the study of Scripture as well as the whole of life experiences. His articulation of the "four grand and powerful arguments"—miracles, prophecies,

---

37. Shelton states that "the *sola Scriptura* watchword in Luther is virtually the equivalent of Wesley's *homo unius libri* emphasis" ("The Trajectory of Wesleyan Theology," *Wesleyan Theological Journal* 21/1-2 [Spring-Fall 1986]: 160). Cf. Shelton, "John Wesley's Approach to Scripture," 33, 37.

38. In objection to Soame Jenyns's book titled *Internal Evidence of the Christian Religion,* in which Jenyns denies that all Scripture is given by the inspiration of God, Wesley said: "Nay, if there be any mistakes in the Bible there may as well be a thousand. If there be one falsehood in that book it did not come from the God of truth" (*Journal* [Curnock ed.], 6:117, 24 August 1776). Cf. *Wesley's Standard Sermons,* ed. E. H. Sugden, 2 vols. (London: Epworth, 1921), 1:249-50: "All Scripture is infallibly true."

39. John Alfred Faulkner argues that the Methodist movement "was soteriological, [and] not in the first place theological in the strict sense. It came round to God and Christ and Spirit by way of salvation" (*Modernism and the Christian Faith* [New York: Methodist Book Concern, 1921], 220).

40. See John S. Simon, *John Wesley and the Religious Societies* (London: Epworth, 1921), 283-84.

41. *Journal* (Curnock ed.), 1:455, 22 April 1738.

the goodness of the doctrine, and the moral character of the penmen—came many years after his conversion and after the revival movement had crested. By this time Wesley had the leisure to reflect theologically on the nature and authority of Scripture. Similar to his treatise "The Doctrine of Original Sin," he took an inductive approach, requiring empirical facts, logical argumentation, and a "clear and concise demonstration . . . which [would] strongly induce us to believe that the Bible must be from God."[42] Religious belief remained fundamental to establishing the authority of Scripture, but Wesley expected people to be persuaded of its authoritativeness by an accumulation of arguments.

On this subject, Albert Outler notes, "The great Protestant watchwords of *sola fide* and *sola Scriptura* were in fact fundamentals in Wesley's formulation of a doctrine of biblical authority. But early and late in his career, Wesley interpreted *solus* to mean 'primarily' rather than 'solely' or 'exclusively.'"[43] In support of this claim, Outler quotes from the "Minutes of Several Conversations," where Wesley said, in response to those who say they read only the Bible: "This is rank enthusiasm. If you need no book but the Bible, you are got above St. Paul. He wanted others too. 'Bring the books,' says he, 'but especially the parchments,' those wrote on parchment. 'But I have no taste for reading.' Contract a taste for it by use, or return to your trade."[44]

Wesley's affirmation of the authority of Scripture did not preclude his lifelong interest in and use of many other books, particularly those of theological relevance.[45] The 50-volume *Christian Library* that Wesley edited clearly attests to his concern to provide everyone with a diversity of intellectual and devotional resources for Christian belief—resources having a degree of authoritativeness, even if of a derived and supplemental nature.

But nothing could ever take the place of Scripture as the primary religious source of authority in Wesley's writings. He never wanted to become anything other than a biblical theologian. In the words of Thomas Langford:

---

42. "A Clear and Concise Demonstration of the Divine Inspiration of the Holy Scriptures," in *Works* (Jackson ed.), 11:484.

43. Albert C. Outler, ed., *John Wesley* (New York: Oxford University Press, 1980), 28 n101.

44. "Minutes of Several Conversations," Q.32, in *Works* (Jackson ed.), 8:315.

45. James R. Joy shows the breadth of Wesley's vast literary interests in "Wesley: Man of a Thousand Books and a Book," *Religion in Life* 8 (Winter 1939): 71-84. Ovna K. Boshears, Jr., expands on this theme in "John Wesley, The Bookman: A Study of His Reading Interests in the Eighteenth Century" (Ph.D. diss., University of Michigan, 1972).

> Wesley intended to be a biblical theologian. Scripture was the fundamental source of his theological expression; every doctrine must be measured against the standard presented in Scripture. . . . Hence the two principal resources Wesley left his followers for their theological guidance were his sermons and his *Notes upon the New Testament.*[46]

Wesley's use of Scripture flowed naturally from his mouth and pen. He did not merely preach Scripture; it became a part of him. His words, thought patterns, and concerns lived out in action all reflected the way Scripture became internal. Outler states that Wesley knew Scripture "so nearly by heart that even his natural speech is biblical."[47] In his *Notes upon the Old Testament,* Wesley said, "Tis not enough to have Bibles, but we must use them, yea, use them daily. Our souls must have constant meals of that manna, which if well digested, will afford them true nourishment and strength."[48]

PRINCIPLES OF INTERPRETATION

Wesley did not use Scripture glibly, nor did he use it in a legalistic or proof-texting way. His use of Scripture emanated from a holistic understanding of and trust in its sufficiency to "make you wise" for salvation and for living a holy life.[49] He may not have always exhibited the most gifted exegetical skills, but he was able to capture a gestalt or holistic understanding of Christian truths that exceeded his scholarship. He seemed especially capable of conceptually grasping and communicating the vital, dynamic character of Christian faith as it impinged on every aspect of a believer's life. At the same time, he sought to integrate its conceptual content into the warp and woof of his theology and ministry.

We must not expect to find in Wesley a highly developed and sophisticated understanding of the interpretation of Scripture. Although Christians have systematically reflected on hermeneutics since patristic times, and although early biblical criticism began in the century before Wesley, he preceded most of the historical-critical questions of the 19th century and onward. In Wesley's Anglican context there was no pressing need to develop an apologetic for one's doctrine of Scripture or biblical

---

46. Thomas Langford, *Practical Divinity: Theology in the Wesleyan Tradition* (Nashville: Abingdon, 1983), 25.

47. Albert C. Outler, "Introduction" in *Works* (Bicentennial ed.), 1:69.

48. Commentary on Deut. 17:19, *Notes upon the Old Testament,* 1:638n.

49. See Wesley's quotations from 2 Tim. 3:15*b* in "The Means of Grace" (1746, sermon 16), III.8, in *Works* (Bicentennial ed.), 1:388. Cf. "On Family Religion" (1783, sermon 94), III.16, in *Works* (Bicentennial ed.), 3:344.

hermeneutics. We cannot determine how Wesley might have responded to the many historical-critical issues that still challenge us today.[50] For instance, Wesley did not deal with questions of authenticity, authorship, and so on. Yet he did not slide past difficult passages in Scripture as though no problems existed.[51] He recognized that all people struggle to understand the mysteries of revealed as well as natural religion because "of our ignorance and inability to fathom his [God's] counsels."[52]

Interestingly, Wesley considered the possibility that religious knowledge, passed down from Noah and his children and his children's children, may have been affected by the addition of numberless fables.

> We may likewise reasonably suppose, that some traces of knowledge, both with regard to the invisible and the eternal world, were delivered down from Noah and his children, both to their immediate and remote descendants. And however these were obscured or disguised by the addition of numberless fables, yet something of truth was still mingled with them, and these streaks of light prevented utter darkness.[53]

Although Wesley did not speculate on how much such fables affected Scripture, he conceded that people can obscure and disguise even religious truths that have been handed down from ancestors.

As to the sometimes mysterious aspects of Scripture, Wesley said, "Even among us who are favoured far above these—to whom are entrusted the oracles of God, whose word is a lantern to our feet, and a light in all our paths—there are still many circumstances in his dispensations which are above our comprehension."[54] Possessing Scripture did not in itself safeguard complete understanding of God's truth, though it always re-

---

50. Some interpreters would disagree with this assessment of Wesley's view of Scripture. For example, Wilber T. Dayton squarely places Wesley in the tradition of biblical inerrancy ("Theology and Biblical Inerrancy," *Wesleyan Theological Journal* 3/1 [1968]: 35). The question, however, remains moot since Wesley did not address the historical-critical issues that arose largely in the following century.

51. Although Wesley sought to uncover "the plain, literal meaning of any text," he recognized that sometimes Scripture is obscure or "implies an absurdity." See "Of the Church" (1785, sermon 74), sec. 12, in *Works* (Bicentennial ed.), 3:50; cf. "To Samuel Furly," 10 May 1755, in *Letters* (Telford ed.), 3:129, and "Upon our Lord's Sermon on the Mount, I" (1748, sermon 21), sec. 6, in *Works* (Bicentennial ed.), 1:473.

52. "The Imperfection of Human Knowledge" (1784, sermon 69), III.2, in *Works* (Bicentennial ed.), 2:583.

53. "Walking by Sight and Walking by Faith" (1788, sermon 119), sec. 9, in *Works* (Jackson ed.), 7:258.

54. "The Imperfection of Human Knowledge" (1784, sermon 69), III. 2, in *Works* (Bicentennial ed.), 2:583.

mained sufficient for leading people to salvation and providing guidelines for holy living.

Thomas Langford holds that Wesley, in his *Notes upon the New Testament*, followed the lead of prominent scholars of his times, such as Hugo Grotius and especially Johannes Albrech Bengel, whose writings largely served as the basis for Wesley's commentary.[55] Langford writes: "His [Wesley's] intention was not so much to make any interpretation final, as to make the biblical source central. He reflected this openness in all his works as he attempted to join genuine piety with sound learning."[56] Scholars such as Mildred Bangs Wynkoop have described love as the theological hermeneutic behind Wesley's biblical interpretation.[57] Larry Shelton concedes that love motivates Wesley's examination of Scripture but suggests that "his methodology is primarily inductive, historical-literal, and soteriologically motivated."[58]

The Inductive Character. The inductive character of Wesley's theological method extends to his interpretation of Scripture, and Shelton provides helpful research into how Wesley approached hermeneutical questions. First, Shelton observes that in the preface to the *Notes upon the Old Testament*, Wesley developed the inductive characteristics of his approach to the study of Scripture.[59] At the end of his preface, Wesley summarized six devotional steps to the study of Scripture.

> If you desire to read the Scriptures in such a manner as may most effectually answer this end (to understand the things of God), would it not be advisable (1) to set apart a little time, if you can, every morning and evening for this purpose? (2) At each time, if you have leisure, to read a chapter out of the Old, and one out of the New Testament; if you cannot do this, to take a single chapter, or a part of one? (3) to read this with a single eye to know the whole will

---

55. Wesley admired and credited his reliance on the exegesis of Bengel's commentary, titled *Gnomon Novi Testamenti* (1742), in the preface to the *Notes upon the New Testament*, 7.

56. Langford, *Practical Divinity*, 25.

57. Mildred Bangs Wynkoop, "A Hermeneutical Approach to John Wesley," *Wesleyan Theological Journal* 6/1 (1971): 21. Cf. Wynkoop's chapter on "A Hermeneutical Approach to Wesley" in her book *Theology of Love* (Kansas City: Beacon Hill Press of Kansas City, 1972), 76-101.

58. Larry Shelton offers a helpful summary of Wesley's biblical hermeneutics in the article "John Wesley's Approach to Scripture in Historical Perspective," esp. 41. Cf. Preface, *Notes upon the Old Testament*, 1:i-ix, and Preface, sec. 5, in *Works* (Bicentennial ed.), 1:105-6.

59. Shelton, "John Wesley's Approach to Scripture," 41.

of God, and a fixed resolution to do it? In order to know His will, you should (4) have a constant eye to the analogy of faith, the connexion and harmony there is between those grand, fundamental doctrines, original sin, justification by faith, the new birth, inward and outward holiness. (5) Serious and earnest prayer should be constantly used before we consult the oracles of God, seeing "Scripture can only be understood through the same Spirit whereby it was given. . . ." (6) It might also be of use, if while we read we were frequently to pause and examine ourselves by what we read.[60]

These suggestions were given as preparation for more serious study of Scripture. But even on a devotional level, Wesley was concerned that Christians inductively study Scripture for themselves.

Second, Shelton observes that Wesley emphasized the primacy of the literal sense of Scripture. He states that Wesley did not advocate *literalism* per se, but the method followed by Luther and the other Reformers whereby the allegorical sense of Scripture was corrected by "the plain grammar and syntax [that] give the meaning of any statement without recourse to any esoteric spiritualizations."[61] As a corollary to historical and exegetical techniques, Shelton points out that Wesley used what he described as *the analogy of faith,* by which "he means the general themes of the Bible as they are correctly interpreted."[62] Similarly, Outler describes Wesley's use of the analogy of faith as "one's sense of the whole" by which an interpreter of Scripture is able to grasp a gestalt understanding of the truths of Scripture that supersedes a slavish dependency on the literal words.[63]

On close examination we find that Wesley always began by emphasizing the literal sense of the text. Yet he did not approach it simplistically or without the careful use of reason and, where possible, the confirmation or clarification of experience. He always revealed an openness to reconsider his interpretation of Scripture when given insights from reason and experience.

---

60. Preface, *Notes upon the Old Testament,* 1.

61. Shelton, "John Wesley's Approach to Scripture," 42. Cf. discussion of "literal interpretation" in Elliott E. Johnson, *Expository Hermeneutics: An Introduction* (Grand Rapids: Zondervan, 1990), esp. 9-11, 31-38, 87-96.

62. Ibid. As an example, Wesley might appeal to the historic doctrines of original sin, justification by faith, the new birth, and inward and outward holiness in order to interpret difficult passages of Scripture.

63. Albert Outler describes Wesley as having "twin principles of hermeneutics. The first is that Scripture is Scripture's own best interpreter; thus, 'the analogy of faith' (i.e., one's sense of the whole), should govern one's exegesis of each part. . . . The second is that one begins, always, with a literal translation and holds to it unless it should lead into a palpable absurdity; in which case, analogy and even allegory become allowable options" (*Works* [Bicentennial ed.], 1:473 n22).

Finally, Shelton notes the soteriological focus that is apparent throughout Wesley's writings—a focus motivated by what Wynkoop describes as Wesley's hermeneutic of love. Shelton maintains that although he was motivated by love, "Wesley's basic approach to interpretation and to the authority of Scripture is solidly in the historical-literal, Patristic and Reformation interpretative tradition."[64] Deeming faith and salvation to "include the substance of all the Bible, the marrow, as it were, of the whole Scripture,"[65] Wesley organized the whole of his theological investigations around the central focus of salvation, which was the raison d'être for the Methodist movement.

In describing Wesley's approach to Scripture as inductive, we do not find him systematically or formally using such an approach in all his writings. In fact, it could be argued that a deductive approach predominates in his approach to biblical hermeneutics. For example, Edward Sugden calls attention to the fact that Wesley "first worked out his theology by strict logical deduction from the Scriptures; and then he corrected his conclusions by the test of actual experience. His class-meetings were a laboratory in which he verified or modified his hypotheses."[66] One may interpret Wesley as merely deducing theological ideas from Scripture, under whose authority he had thoroughly and unquestioningly placed himself. But not even Sugden would want to say this, for even he realized that Wesley functioned as though he used a scientific method of hypothetical investigation, especially when verifying the correctness of his theological conclusions. Admittedly, Wesley believed that Scripture is entirely trustworthy, but also that it established its authority through the crucible of rational and experimental testing.

True to the Aristotelian tradition of logic that he admired and appropriated, Wesley's ideal was a deductive science. A deductive science proceeds logically from *general* biblical truths to *particular* truths of life experiences, showing that the particulars follow from the general by necessity. But Wesley saw that even though premises are logically prior to conclusions; in reality we don't necessarily come to know things in that order. Our knowledge starts from sense experience (including both physical and spiritual senses)—that is, from particulars—and finds there the general. Thus we reason inductively, a process that has as its goal a deductive science and which includes both induction *and* deduction as methodological components.

---

64. Shelton, "John Wesley's Approach to Scripture," 42.

65. "The Scripture Way of Salvation" (1765, sermon 43), sec. 2, in *Works* (Bicentennial ed.), 2:156.

66. *Standard Sermons* (Sugden ed.), 1:196 n2.

This was Wesley's way of working toward the ideal of a demonstrative theological science. For example, if he seemed biblically deductive in sermons or other theological writings, this was the result of inductive investigations that confirmed his general ideas *or* of the belief that such ideas would stand up to the test of inductive investigation and confirmation.

The Process of Interpretation: Discerning the Context. In interpreting Scripture, Wesley began by studying the texts themselves. Although he did not concern himself with higher critical questions that became the rage in the next century, Wesley saw the need to interpret Scripture beyond its plain, literal meaning. Biblical hermeneutics entailed investigation of the context. Wesley warned that "any passage is easily perverted, by being recited singly, without any of the preceding or following verses. By this means it may often seem to have one sense, when it will be plain, by observing what goes before and what follows after, that it really has the direct contrary."[67]

Scripture passages must stand under the scrutiny of other Scripture passages to clarify the meaning of the whole. As Wesley said, "The best way, therefore, to understand it [Scripture], is carefully to compare Scripture with Scripture, and thereby learn the true meaning of it."[68] In "An Address to the Clergy," Wesley added, "No less necessary is a knowledge of the Scriptures, which teach us how to teach others; yea, a knowledge of all the Scriptures; seeing Scripture interprets Scriptures one part fixing the sense of another."[69]

The use of Scripture to interpret Scripture is an important, explicit principle of Wesley's hermeneutics, though we may wish that he had been more consistent in applying it. No doubt he allowed his experience of and concern for salvation and concomitant holy living to shape his interpretation and exposition of Scripture. But the weakness stemmed not so much from poor methodology as from the lack of rigorously applying his stated rules of biblical interpretation.

The Process of Interpretation: Experience. In addition to the analogy of faith, Wesley relied on experience to help interpret Scripture. He used experience to confirm truths found in Scripture. He claimed he would not even believe the literal interpretation of Scripture unless it was confirmed

---

67. "On Corrupting the Word of God" (1727, sermon 137), in *Works* (Jackson ed.), 7:470.
68. "Popery Calmly Considered," I.6, in *Works* (Jackson ed.), 10:142.
69. "An Address to the Clergy," I.2, in *Works* (Jackson ed.), 10:482.

by experience. We may illustrate this through a conversation between Wesley and Peter Böhler:

> When I met Peter Böhler again, he consented to put the dispute upon the issue which I desired, namely, Scripture and experience. I first consulted the Scripture. But when I set aside the glosses of men, and simply considered the words of God, comparing them together, endeavouring to illustrate the obscure by the plainer passages, I found they all made against me, and was forced to retreat to my last hold, "that experience would never agree with the *literal interpretation* of those Scriptures." Nor could I therefore allow it to be true, till I found some living witnesses to it.[70]

Consequently Wesley insisted that debatable interpretations of Scripture and subsequent formulations of doctrine be "confirmed by your experience and *mine*."[71]

Since he expected experience to confirm Scripture, Wesley also allowed for the possibility of experience to clarify the meaning of Scripture when it is unclear or, more properly, clarify our interpretation of it. William Arnett notes that this "correctional value" of experience indeed operated in Wesley's interpretation of Scripture.[72] An excellent example may be found in Wesley's biblical understanding of entire sanctification. Some Wesley scholars suggest that his doctrine of entire sanctification sprang primarily from observation of Christians experiencing God's sanctifying grace in their lives.[73] Of course, observation of these experiences confirmed what Wesley already found to be true in Scripture.

A related example involves Wesley's response to the question of whether sin remains in a person subsequent to his or her entire sanctification. At least hypothetically, Wesley allowed for the possibility of experience correcting what might appear to be the plain and obvious meaning of Scripture:

> Q. But what does it signify, whether any have attained it or not, seeing so many Scriptures witness for it?

---

70. *Journal* (Curnock ed.), 1:471-72, sec. 12, 24 May 1738.

71. "The Witness of the Spirit, II" (1767, sermon 11), III.6, in *Works* (Bicentennial ed.), 1:290.

72. Cf. Sugden's interpretation of Wesley as one who "first worked out his theology by strict logical deduction from the Scriptures; and then he corrected his conclusions by the test of actual experience. His class-meetings were a laboratory in which he verified or modified his hypotheses." See *Standard Sermons* (Sugden ed.), 1:196 n2.

73. Cf. Lindström's interpretation of Wesley's doctrine of entire sanctification, of which Lindström says: "It was from this appeal to experience, moreover, that Wesley's doctrine of perfection sprang; the latter is regarded as a corollary of the former" (*Wesley and Sanctification*, 4).

A. If I were convinced that one in England had attained what has been so clearly and strongly preached by such a number of Preachers, in so many places, and for so long a time, I should be clearly convinced that we had all mistaken the meaning of those Scriptures; and therefore, for the time to come, I too must teach that "sin will remain till death."[74]

Of course, Wesley did not expect experience ever to contradict Scripture. Nevertheless, he expected that evidence gleaned from life experiences would crucially enhance proper interpretation and subsequent exposition and application of the Word.

The Process of Interpretation: Reason. Along with experience, reason played a vital role in Wesley's interpretation of Scripture. For Wesley, reason facilitates the entire thinking process, without which one could not hope or even begin to interpret Scripture. Reason constitutes a "precious gift of God. . . . [It is] 'the candle of the Lord,' which he hath fixed in our souls for excellent purposes."[75] The sinfulness of humanity may have effaced the moral image of God in individuals, but it did not utterly efface their natural image.[76] Reason, or understanding, functions as a part of that natural image and is a God-given capacity on which we may rely in the important process of scriptural interpretation.

Further, through reason God "enables us in some measure to comprehend his method of dealing with the children of men."[77] Reason guides us in understanding and responding to the important Christian ideas about repentance, faith, justification, the new birth, and holiness. Emphasizing the trustworthiness of reason, Wesley said: "In all these respects, and in all the duties of common life, God has given us our reason for a guide. And it is only by acting up to the dictates of it, by using all the understanding which God hath given us, that we can have a conscience void of offence towards God and towards man."[78] As such, Christians should not "despise or lightly esteem reason, knowledge, or human learning."[79] Rather, Chris-

---

74. "A Plain Account of Christian Perfection," sec. 19, in *Works* (Jackson ed.), 11:406.

75. "The Case of Reason Impartially Considered" (1781, sermon 70), II.10, in *Works* (Bicentennial ed.), 2:599. Outler notes that Wesley's use of the quote from Prov. 20:27 reflects a slogan of the Cambridge Platonists (*Works,* Bicentennial ed., 2:599 n58).

76. "The New Birth" (1760, sermon 45), I.1, in *Works* (Bicentennial ed.) 2:188; cf. "The End of Christ's Coming" (1781, sermon 62), I.1-7, in *Works* (Bicentennial ed.), 2:473-76.

77. "The Case of Reason Impartially Considered" (1781, sermon 70), I.6, in *Works* (Bicentennial ed.), 2:592.

78. Ibid.

79. "A Plain Account of Christian Perfection," sec. 25, in *Works* (Jackson ed.), 11:429.

tians may profitably employ reason in their biblical and theological investigations.

Wesley even considered the leadership of the Holy Spirit consistent with our rational capabilities.[80] To be sure, reason has its limits; it is not greater than Scripture as a source of religious authority. But reason remains essential in the entire hermeneutical process of exegesis, exposition, and application of Scripture.

SUMMARY OF THE PRINCIPLES

All these sources of authority complement one another in the methodological approach John Wesley used in his biblical and theological investigations. While not articulating a systematic approach, Wesley followed basic guidelines in his interpretation of Scripture, and these guidelines are discernible. Arnett distills six general rules of biblical interpretation characteristic of Wesley. While we have already seen the substance of these rules in our discussion, Arnett provides convenient summary:

First, the literal sense is emphasized.

Second, Wesley insists on the importance of the context.

Third, comparing Scripture is important.

Fourth, Wesley stresses the importance of Christian experience in interpreting the Scriptures. . . . Christian experience has both confirmatory and correctional value.

Fifth, reason is to be used as the "handmaid of faith, the servant of revelation."

Finally, we observe the rule of "practicality." Wesley was in large measure an apostle to the plain, unlettered people. Therefore he sought to eliminate the elaborate, the elegant, and the oratorical.[81]

Outler offers a similar summary of Wesley's principles of interpretation in his introduction to the Bicentennial Edition of the *Works*. He lists five principles.

The first was that believers should accustom themselves to the biblical language and thus to the "general sense" of Scripture as a whole. . . . This leads to a second rule, adapted from the ancient Fathers and from the Reformers as well: that the Scriptures are to be

---

80. See "To Thomas Whitehead (?)," 10 February 1748, in *Letters* (Telford ed.), 2:117.

81. These six rules are a summary of Arnett's study of Wesley's approach to scriptural interpretation. See William M. Arnett, "John Wesley—Man of One Book" (Ph.D. diss., Drew University, 1954), 89-96. The quotation in rule five comes from William R. Cannon, *Theology of John Wesley* (New York: Abingdon, 1946), 159.

read as a whole, with the expectation that the clearer texts may be relied upon to illuminate the obscurer ones. . . . This holistic sense of biblical inspiration suggested his third hermeneutical principle: that one's exegesis is to be guided, always in the first instance, by the literal sense, unless that appears to lead to consequences that are either irrational or unworthy of God's moral character as "pure, unbounded love." . . . A fourth hermeneutical rule follows from his doctrine of grace and free will: that all moral commands in Scripture are also "covered promises," since God never commands the impossible and his grace is always efficacious in every faithful will. His last rule is actually a variation on the Anglican sense of the Old Vincentian canon that the historical experience of the church, though fallible, is the better judge overall of Scripture's meanings than later interpreters are likely to be, especially on their own. Thus, radical novelty is to be eschewed on principle.[82]

The important thing to note about Wesley's rules or principles of biblical interpretation is his openness to investigating more than the plain, literal meaning of any text. Wesley showed a willingness to explore alternative interpretations when the text or evidence of Scripture appears "contrary to some other texts," "obscure," or "implies an absurdity."[83] Gerald R. Cragg confirms that Wesley was not a slavish literalist because he "invoked reason, tradition and experience in order to clarify the meaning of obscure passages."[84] Other scholars agree. Sugden argues that "Wesley was a critic, both higher and lower, before those much misunderstood terms were invented."[85] In support, Sugden cites the preface to the *Notes upon the New Testament:* "Those various readings which have a vast majority of ancient copies and translations on their side, I have without scruple incorporated with the text; which I have divided all along according to the matter it contains."[86] Sugden further suggests that in the preface to the Book of Joshua, Wesley stated almost exactly the modern critical view. Wesley wrote:

> Indeed it is probable they [Joshua to Esther] were collections of the authentic records of the nation, which some of the prophets were

82. Albert Outler, "Introduction" in *Works* (Bicentennial ed.), 1:58-59.

83. Quotations taken from the letter "To Samuel Furly," 10 May 1755, in *Letters* (Telford ed.), 3:129, and "Of the Church" (1785, sermon 74), I.12, in *Works* (Bicentennial ed.), 3:51.

84. Gerald R. Cragg, *Reason and Authority in the Eighteenth Century* (Cambridge: Cambridge University Press, 1964), 160.

85. Edward H. Sugden, "Introduction" in *John Wesley's Fifty-three Sermons,* ed. Edward H. Sugden (Nashville: Abingdon, 1983), 7.

86. *Notes upon the New Testament,* sec. 7, quoted by Sugden, *John Wesley's Fifty-three Sermons,* 7-8.

divinely directed and assisted to put together. It seems the substance of the several histories was written under divine direction, when the events had just happened, and long after put into the form wherein they stand now, perhaps all by the same hand.[87]

Along the same line, George C. Cell argues that Wesley may not have adopted the contemporary critical position on Scripture in *theory,* but certainly adopted it in *practice.*[88] Colin Williams cites several examples of how Wesley accepted textual criticism, refusing to approach doctrinal studies simplistically.[89] Outler agrees that Wesley was no "prooftexter" even though he viewed the entire Scripture authoritatively as "a whole and integral revelation."[90]

Other scholars disagree on the sophistication of Wesley's hermeneutics.[91] Despite attempts by Wesley to incorporate critical scholarship in his writings, he did not approach biblical studies as a professional scholar. His principles of interpretation were neither innovative nor consistent. But since he never intended to blaze new trails in biblical scholarship, we should not be too critical. Even critics of Wesley's hermeneutics such as Wilbur Mullen recognize that, however one analyzes Wesley's methodology, "the end result of his exegesis was fantastically successful . . . whether or not it would stand the test of twentieth-century hermeneutical analysis."[92]

In conclusion, the catholicity of Wesley's openness to all historic claimants of religious authority demonstrates that the inductive character of his theological method extended beyond theology to include biblical hermeneutics. Of course, he did not explicitly articulate this inductive process either in his biblical studies or in his theology, nor was Wesley always as rigorous as we would like in following such methodology. Yet the inductive character of Wesley's work may be discerned in his biblical studies even though he may not have used the methodology in the manner of a professional scholar. By recognizing inductive characteristics in his biblical studies, we understand better the pervasiveness and consistency of Wesley's use of a similar methodology in his approach to theology as a whole.

---

87. Preface to the Book of Joshua, *Notes upon the Old Testament,* 1:701.
88. George C. Cell, *The Rediscovery of John Wesley* (New York: Henry Holt, 1935), 88.
89. Williams, *John Wesley's Theology Today,* 26.
90. Albert C. Outler, *Theology in the Wesleyan Spirit* (Nashville: Tidings, 1975), 9; cf. "Introduction" in *Works* (Bicentennial ed.), 1:57.
91. For example, see S. Parkes Madman, *The Three Religious Leaders of Oxford and Their Movements* (New York: Macmillan, 1916), 338, and Wilbur H. Mullen, "John Wesley's Method of Biblical Interpretation," *Religion in Life* 47 (Spring 1978): 99-108.
92. Mullen, "John Wesley's Method of Biblical Interpretation," 107.

FRONTIERS
FOR
INTERPRETATION

In many ways, Professor Wall continues in this chapter where he left off in his earlier chapter within this collection. Here he calls again for a return to an understanding of the formative role of the Bible in the life of the contemporary church—a role that is consistent with those Wesleyan emphases regarding the nature of Scripture that are noted throughout this collection. In other words, he urges that Wesleyan readings of Scripture embrace the soteriological and sacramental dimensions of the whole biblical canon.

Professor Wall offers important insights regarding the ways that Wesleyans will potentially read the Bible. While he affirms traditional approaches to the study of biblical texts that have been practiced in scholarly circles, he also recognizes that biblical studies within Wesleyan circles must cherish the essential role of the Bible as the *church's* Scriptures. In other words, those in the Wesleyan tradition who read the Bible will find in these sacred texts words that speak about and call for salvation, grace, and faithful living.

5

FACILITATING SCRIPTURE'S FUTURE ROLE AMONG WESLEYANS[1]

Robert W. Wall

◆

The title of this paper invites two different although related responses. The first is the more general concern that inquires about the future of biblical studies. This is an especially appropriate concern in light of the dismal state of this discipline, the result of the continuing detachment of church from academy, and the academy of Christian theology from biblical studies. The second is the more specific and self-critical query that asks about the role that biblical studies might perform within a particular faith tradition. This more "tribal" concern actually presumes that the study of Scripture serves a theological and ecclesial end. The issue taken up in this paper is how biblical scholars should best understand and then facilitate Scripture's role within Wesleyan communions of believers.

There are at least three reasons for the divorce of biblical from theological studies in the academy.[2] They are: (1) the privatization of religious commitment in the church; (2) the hegemonic interest of academic biblical studies to protect the scholar's autonomy from theological commitments; and (3) the unwillingness to accept the legitimacy of theological reflection as an exegetical discipline in the professional guild of biblical scholars. Further, I want to emphasize the corrupting nature of the modern academy itself, which is profoundly skeptical of the supernatural and deeply suspicious of constructions of transcendent truth, scholarly and especially popular in nature. In his brilliant discussion of the modern university, M. R. Schwehn accepts Max Weber's suggestion as true concerning the present state of the academic life. The suggestion is that the solitary scholar functions in a routine of rationalization, which is best maintained by resisting the intrusive and "messy" concerns for ultimate, more normative questions of human life and relationships.[3] The result is that most con-

---

1. Appeared originally in the *Wesleyan Theological Journal* 33/2 (Fall 1998). Used by permission.

2. See Francis Watson, *Text and Truth: Redefining Biblical Theology* (Grand Rapids: Eerdmans, 1997), 4.

3. Mark R. Schwehn, *Exiles from Eden: Religion and the Academic Vocation in America* (Oxford: Oxford University Press, 1993).

temporary scholars remain disenchanted with the world, while pursuing truth by formal analysis of impersonal objects (e.g., biblical texts qua texts) without ever making normative claims (e.g., theological reflection on the universal meaning of biblical texts). If such is the character of academic culture in which biblical texts are studied, then the church's formative interest in Scripture is necessarily subverted.

THE STATE AND FUTURE OF BIBLICAL STUDIES

The battle for the Bible within first-world guilds of biblical scholarship is waged largely over hermeneutical issues. The protocols and prerequisites of the biblical guild and its sponsoring academy help to fashion upwardly mobile professional careers with little time for the different demands of a sacred vocation whose methodological interests are more ecclesial. Biblical scholarship tends to be funded by interpretive strategies that fail to privilege the current faith community as the normative location of Scripture's meaning or deny the importance of spiritual maturity as an important characteristic of the strong interpreter. Such failure or denial actually promotes, however unintentionally, a species of biblical studies largely irrelevant to the formation of theological understanding and so of a vital piety.[4]

I contend that if biblical studies is to survive modernity's assault and accomplish what the church formed Scripture to do, the singular aim of theological education is *to help the church be the church.* For the sake of academic purity and resistant to this more parochial definition of theological education, some in the world of academic biblical scholarship even name the church its "Babylon" and bid its practitioners to "come out of her, lest you take part in her sins, lest you share in her plagues."[5] The criti-

---

4. See, for example, the pair of essays written by Martin Marty and Jacob Neusner, published in *Religious Studies News* (12:3 [Sept. 1997]: 20-21, 48), which champion the academic study of religion. Both were perceptive and helpful—and typical. Neither defined the academic study of religion in ecclesial terms, which Marty suggested is an "apologetical" interest and prone to violence. The chief value of theological and biblical studies, even within the seminary and church-related university, is to serve the secular interests of a pluralistic culture rather than those more sacred interests of a pluralizing monotheism. In contending for this definition of a "public" religion whose voice is turned to the town square, they seem to follow Paul Tillich, for whom religion is the soul of culture and culture the form of religion. By this understanding, if the church is a public institution, the purpose of biblical studies is to help fashion civil dialogue over topics of general interest.

5. See, for example, Philip R. Davies, *Whose Bible Is It Anyway?* JSOT Supplemental Series 204 (Sheffield: Sheffield Academic Press, 1995). See also the helpful response to Davies by Francis Watson, "Bible, Theology, and the University: A Response to Philip Davies," *Journal for the Study of the Old Testament* 71 (1996): 3-16. Finally, see also Ulrich Luz's presidential address to the annual meeting of the *Studiorum Novi Testamenti Societas* (1997, Birmingham, England), which poses the question "Kann die Bibel heute noch Grundlage für die Kirche sein?" to which Luz answers (with some qualification) "yes."

cal suspicion of the modern interpreter directed toward Scripture, coupled with reading strategies that aim at original meanings or that serve political ideology, whether liberal or conservative, simply fail to read Scripture according to its original intention (which is to nurture the theological understanding and guide the moral praxis of God's people). It should come as no surprise, then, that within much of the first-world church, where Scripture has lost its practical authority to speak the Word of God to the people of God, Christian education has become increasingly more interested in secular ideology than in Christian theology, in pastoral care and church growth more than in rigorous biblical and theological studies, in liturgical form more than in biblical exposition. The alarming result, at least in the mainstream church, is a clergy that is biblically illiterate, a serious problem which is only compounded by the lack of a pedagogy that enables them to use Scripture effectively to "teach, reprove, correct and train" their congregations toward partnership with our Lord for the courageous work of holy living in an unholy world.

What a text is permitted or not permitted to say by biblical criticism rarely informs anymore the preaching and teaching offices of the mainstream church. Rather, under the formidable suspicion and skepticism still exacted by Enlightenment epistemology upon the church's magisterium, the one is put at risk by the other. Sharply put, most interpretation that aims at an academic study of Scripture, even when executed by believers, simply does not supply either the raw material or the incentive necessary for robust Christian theological reflection. In spite of the loud and persistent complaint from rank-and-file believers that biblical scholarship fails to offer a meaningful or even intelligible interpretation of Scripture for today's faith community, the gap between the public church and academy ever widens.

Now I move on to a *constructive proposal.* No battlefront is more strategic to win than that waged over the very idea of Scripture. The interpreter's judgments about the Bible determine in a decisive way what approach to and what results are anticipated from biblical interpretation. If the scholar allows that *Scripture is the church's normative rule of faith (or "canon"), whose subject matter is God and whose performance aims at Christian formation,* then the approach to Scripture will not presume it to be merely an anthology of ancient literary art, a record of historical events, or a depository of universal wisdom. Rather, the strong interpreter will approach the biblical text at its current address, which is the entire Christian Scriptures (OT and NT), and do so in light of its current ecclesial role, which is to bear witness to God's word and work in history and so to form the theological understanding of those who in faith submit to Scripture as "the word of the Lord Almighty" for today. Let me unpack four implications of this strategic initiative.

Implication One. The intended meaning of a biblical text is not the property of its author but of the church to which Scripture belongs.[6] The hegemony of the critical approach to biblical interpretation within the modern guild of biblical scholars, which tends to hold Scripture captive to serve an academic rather than sacred end, has greatly hindered the Bible's formative influence among contemporary believers as their rule of faith. In my opinion, the only hope for Scripture is to rescue it from the guild of biblical scholars for service in the church's theological understanding. In this light, today's great citadels of theological education must recover the Bible's intended role as the church's Scripture and train their students to use Scripture as a sacrament of divine grace in the formation of believers who seek a more precise and self-critical understanding of God in order to obey God's will. This point was made in other words at the 1997 Oxford Institute for Methodist Studies. Jose Miguez Bonino was asked following his plenary address about the mission of the church. His response was simply put: "To convert the world to Christ." But after a slight pause and with a smile, Miguez added, "The problem is, of course, to *what* Christ." Isn't the first task of biblical interpretation to describe with critical precision the Christ to whom all of Scripture bears witness, the Christ upon whom we call for our salvation and after whom we then follow as his disciples?

Not only is Scripture's normative meaning ecclesial rather than authorial, its reference point is theological rather than historical. Scripture points its reader to God and not to the social or literary worlds of its authors and first readers/auditors. It is only a slight exaggeration to say that

---

6. In defending the importance of ecclesial over authorial intent, consider the case of the NT writing, *Acts of the Apostles*. While the narrator told his story for a variety of reasons, among the most important was to defend Paul and his universal mission against detractors within the Jewish church, especially in Palestine. The cumulative case for this is based on internal evidence and, although exaggerated by F. Bauer and his Tübingen colleagues during the last century, is still entirely persuasive. Yet, when Acts is finally picked up and circulated with a collection of Pauline letters toward the end of the second century, subsequently recognized by the church in this new role as an inspired writing, Paul had long since triumphed and the Jewish constituency, especially in Palestine, had by that time become either mainstream or marginal. Paul was a problem no longer. Indeed, the intended role of Acts within the emergent NT was to introduce the Pauline inspired letters, an ecclesial intention that would have been impossible for its narrator to have imagined a century or more earlier. My point is that the historian's presumption is bogus that the author's original intention for a biblical text should norm the meaning the church now makes of it, since a text's current canonical address is sometimes at odds with that which occasioned its writing.

the gaps in a more precise historical understanding about the world behind the biblical text, which are then filled by competent historical critics,
typically contribute little that is essential to Scripture's performance as the
Word of God.[7] What the interpreter must know about a text's intended audience, the circumstances that occasioned its writing and the writer's response to it, a text's sociohistorical frame of reference, are details typically
found in the biblical writing itself and are available to the careful exegete.
My point is this: *If the aim of biblical interpretation is theological understanding and not historical reconstruction or literary deconstruction, the
test of sound interpretation is whether it makes the biblical text come alive
with meaning that makes sense of and empowers a life for God today.*

In this sense, biblical interpretation clarifies the Word of God, which
then must be adapted to and embodied in real life. When an interpretation of
Scripture accords with the church's intentions for Scripture, it will reproduce
in the life of its canonical audience a publicly and distinctively Christian wisdom and witness (see 2 Tim. 3:15-17). Beginning even before biblical texts
were written and then continuing today, faithful interpreters seek to render
Scripture as God's word for their faith communities so that they might better
understand what it means to be and do what God's people ought.

Implication Two. The Bible's authority within the church is imperiled
whenever believers perceive that Scripture lacks relevance for their contemporary life or its meaning is incomprehensible. When such a situation
persists, believers will neglect the biblical word and their functional illiter-
acy inevitably will lead to a serious distortion of their Christian faith and a
corruption of their witness to Christ in the world. When Scripture does not
perform its intended role as the community's rule of faith, some other rule
(typically secular) will take its place to delineate the church's theological
and moral boundaries.

The act of sound interpretation, when provoked by this theological
crisis, intends to demonstrate the Bible's authority for a particular congregation of readers by first clarifying what the text actually says (text-centered
exegesis) and then by recovering from the text that particular meaning that
addresses the theological confusion or moral dilemma of the canonical audience in meaningful ways. Of course, the legitimacy of any biblical interpretation is not determined by its mere relevance for a single readership,

---

7. The historical task that aims at a more precise reconstruction of the circumstances
that occasioned the writing and first reading of a biblical text actually undermines its canonical intent of a universalized meaning. That is, by making a text's meaning more particular, the inherent depth of its ambiguity and ability to transmit or mediate the Word of God
to an ever-changing people of God are imperiled.

but by its agreement with what the people of God have always confessed to be true according to our rule of faith, who is the incarnate Word, Jesus Christ. In other words, *the limits of sound interpretation are not determined by an interpreter's critical orthodoxy but by an interpretation's theological orthodoxy, whether or not it agrees with the church's rule of faith.*

Further, the performance of Scripture within a profoundly diverse faith community, which regularly must address new and different questions that challenge its faith in God, requires a multivalent text whose capacity to disclose the Word of God stems from an "inherent depth of ambiguity," as James Sanders calls it. That the text of Scripture gathers to itself a community of meanings, each theologically orthodox and at some particular moment relevant for the Christian formation of one or another congregation of readers, is easily illustrated by the history of biblical interpretation. In their ongoing interpretation, biblical texts have the effect of becoming authoritative whenever they are picked up again and again by different interpreters who seek to make clear their new meaning to "comfort the afflicted" or "afflict the comfortable." In the hands of faithful interpreters, past and present, the multiple meanings of a biblical text are discovered, always with the theological aim of forming a people who worship and bear witness to the word of the one true God.[8]

Implication Three. The discipline of biblical studies depends on the sound decisions made by the talented interpreter. But the issue is more one of character and less one of technique, with less emphasis on the authority of the author and more on the authority of the current interpreter—and this authority is predicated on character as much as on clever and informed technique. We should ask, *what characterizes the talented interpreter whose exegetical and interpretive decisions find meaning in biblical texts that serve Scripture's theological aim?* The question of the interpreter's authority to interpret Scripture meaningfully rests on two credentials. First, is the interpreter's understanding of Scripture's subject matter, including competency in those various interpretive strategies that facilitate a text-centered approach to biblical studies and a thorough knowledge of the history of

---

8. This point in no way intends to encourage any species of epistemological relativism that seeks to undermine a text's determinate meaning. Rather, it only suggests that a text's determinate meaning is not posited by a single tradition or interpretation, whether intended by the author (if ever this can be reconstructed with precision and confidence) or by its current readers (even critically trained scholars). The text's "determinate meaning" is, in any case, a theoretical construct and better or more concretely reconceived in the history of a text as its "full" meaning that is approximated by a community of talented and faithful readers (contra Watson, "Bible, Theology and the University," 10-12).

biblical interpretation. Second, while this informed knowledge of Scripture's teaching and interpretation should be the expected result of a formal theological education, the interpreter must also be spiritually mature since biblical studies must serve first of all the church's vocation of Christian formation.[9] Simply said, if biblical interpretation is faith seeking Christian understanding, then it is a sacramental as well as intellectual activity; and its proper setting is the *sanctuary* as much as the *library*. To the extent that the faithful interpreter enjoys a deep and vital relationship with God, which is brought to maturity primarily through worship of God, that interpreter will be better able to recover those meanings from Scripture that contribute to the spiritual formation of its current audience.[10]

If the act of sound interpretation adapts Scripture to life, the talented interpreter also pays close attention to the current audience's social and religious locations. The particularity of Scripture's meaning derives from the particularity of its current audience, what faith tradition it belongs to, and what spiritual crisis threatens a more robust faith in God. That is, the status of believers in a particular setting requires discernment of their spiritual crisis so that Scripture may be used by the interpreter to "afflict the comfortable" (prophetic meaning) or "comfort the afflicted" (pastoral meaning). Further, the religious location of a particular audience also determines the theological accent sounded. For example, believers who seek theological understanding as members of a Wesleyan communion will naturally intensify the importance of a "responsible grace," to borrow Randy Maddox's term for the orienting concern of Wesleyan theology. Sound interpretation works from within a faith tradition to revitalize its particular contribution to the whole people of God.

Implication Four. This reformation of theological education will stand against the methodological relativism that currently plagues the academy. It will privilege *text-centered exegetical strategies* that seek to

---

9. Cf. Michael A. Fishbane, *The Garments of Torah: Essays in Biblical Hermeneutics* (Bloomington, Ind.: Indiana University Press, 1992), 16-18.

10. By this emphasis on a "talented/strong" interpreter who can make exegetical and theological decisions that map a distinctively Wesleyan theological trajectory within the church catholic, I am not proposing a species of sectarianism that disregards all other Christian interpretation or interpreters. The focus in this paper is more narrowly restricted to *Wesleyan* biblical scholars and proposes a *Wesleyan* reading strategy for Scripture. My more essential assumption, however, is that, within a more catholic community of interpretation, different interpretations will surely result from different theological loyalties and will finally form a complement of self-correcting and mutually informing conversations. I celebrate and depend on these differences and the robust conversation. They serve to generate a more collective and dynamic understanding of a text's "determinate meaning."

describe with critical precision the theological subject material of the biblical text in its final literary (i.e., canonical) form. Why? For practical and theological reasons. Not only is the canonical text the authorized medium of divine revelation for the church, but unlike some reconstructed authorial meaning, we actually have the text before us to study together—once biblical scholars have settled a range of text-critical and translation issues, which may well be easier said than done.

Further, the history of interpreting a biblical writing should be scrutinized in order to anticipate the range or limits of a text's normative or full meaning. Since a biblical writing is a hermeneutical writing, the careful student may learn more of the interpretive strategy employed by the biblical writer, which in turn is used to interpret their texts. The critical investigation into how writers used their Scripture illumines the texture of their writings. This more historical-critical species of intertextuality contributes to but is finally different from the literary interest in viewing the whole of Scripture as a discrete world of meaning, where different texts repeat similar phrases or ideas and are joined together by the interpreter to thicken the meaning of the whole.

In my view, the most profound loss in the academic study of Scripture is the neglect of the *discipline of biblical theology.* The reductionism of modern biblical studies, which separates Old from New, Hebrew from Christian, and then scrutinizes the meaning of only selected parts of the whole Christian Bible, often in ways that are adversarial to its other parts, has made it difficult if not impossible to think of a truly "biblical theology." Most modern critics have thus concluded that Scripture's various theologies cannot possibly be formed into a coherent whole, since there isn't a single biblical thematic or theological construct that can account for all of Scripture's various theologies.

Indeed, modern biblical studies have taken on the likeness of Humpty Dumpty, with scholars playing the king's men who have no interest in putting the pieces of poor Humpty Dumpty back together again. Against this backdrop, a reformation of biblical studies would embrace Scripture's simultaneity in principle and interpretive strategies for putting these pieces back together again, not by artificially harmonizing Scripture's different theological conceptions or by treating similar linguistic or thematic expressions as necessarily carrying the same theological freight, but rather by considering each theology as integral to and a complementary part of the whole biblical witness.[11] Indeed, the coherence and unity of the Bi-

---

11. For this more positive definition of Scripture's simultaneity, which also funds my understanding of Scripture's intertextuality, see Jon Levenson, *The Hebrew Bible, the Old*

ble's theological subject matter may well force us back to a precritical-disposition view that Scripture is a book finally authored by the one true and holy God and read best in terms of divine intent and therefore toward the end of our entire sanctification.[12]

PUTTING THE "WESLEYAN" BACK INTO BIBLICAL STUDIES

In many ways, the 1997 Oxford Institute for Methodist Studies was an exhilarating, even haunting experience for most of us in the biblical studies working group. The institute is among the few meetings remaining where biblical scholars gather together as confessing Christians to make theological sense of Scripture in service of their church. Here was a truly international community of well-trained men and women, some from Asia and Africa, and others from Latin America, Europe, the UK, and North America, all of whom felt a profound call to be scholars of and for a variety of Methodist communions of believers. Our common lament was and is that we lack the experience to do it well; and our awkward, even artificial attempts to move from critical exegesis to constructive theology during our two weeks together revealed both the importance and the absence of a critical methodology that would allow us to do so in the distinctive idiom of the Wesleyan theological tradition.

A part of the lament of this group, sometimes heard loudest of all, is that the educational institutions of Methodism in the first world have done a poor job, at least when compared with our Reformed Protestant or Roman Catholic counterparts, in producing a competent and theologically sensitive biblical scholarship for and of the church. A colleague even wondered aloud whether there was something deep within the Wesleyan tradition, when viewed as experiential religion, that actually works against biblical studies. For evidence, yet another colleague mentioned that the biblical studies working group had its inception late in the institute's history—at its 8th meeting in 1982—and even at the 10th gathering of Methodist scholars 15 years later all agreed that Scripture was rarely used by

---

Testament, and Historical Criticism: Jews and Christians in Biblical Studies (Louisville, Ky.: Westminster/John Knox, 1993).

12. This shift of focus from the authorial to the divine intent of Scripture envisages a theological commitment to Scripture's role as the church's canon rather than to some conception of its production. Depending on a reader's essential understanding of God, the result of this shift of meaning's locus from authorial to divine intent carries substantial hermeneutical implications. For instance, if a text's normative meaning is now located in the "mind of God" whose word is not timeless but dynamically open to the changing character of God's relationship (or partnership) with the covenant community, then the aim of biblical interpretation is not to seek after a timeless truth but rather a timely (or meaningful) meaning that unfolds over and within time itself.

any of the other 10 working groups when reflecting on the institute's theme, "Trinity, Community, and Power." A strange silence indeed. Biblical scholars have sometimes been made to feel like unwanted guests even at annual meetings of the Wesleyan Theological Society. Indeed, if the cadre of biblical scholars who interpret Scripture under the light of a Wesleyan theological conception is to have an influential voice in the life of the church, we must not only encourage those spiritual disciplines that will make us truly a people of one book but also give a more prominent place in our educational curricula and scholarly meetings to the role biblical studies performs in shaping our church's understanding of God's law and gospel.

What is our starting point? I believe we must begin by working together on reading strategies that can relate the theological subject matter of Scripture to the Wesleyan tradition in persuasive ways. Let me briefly sketch a working model of one such strategy as a conversation piece, before concluding with an exhortation that such a conversation be as interdisciplinary as possible. Indeed, the *only* way to negotiate the chasm between biblical studies and theology is for biblical scholars to begin talking with theologians about these issues of common interest and concern for the whole people of God.

James Sanders argues that the act of interpretation must fully realize these three major factors of the canonical process in pursuit of the meaning of biblical texts: the text itself, the spiritual crisis of the audience addressed, and the hermeneutics of comparative midrash by which the ancient interpreter "caused" the sacred tradition to interpret and respond to the crisis of a people's faith in God.[13] By dynamic analogy, the text picked up again and cited by a biblical writer mirrors and illumines the spiritual crisis to which that writer was responding. Sanders calls this "the tool of the triangle"[14]—the three points of which are the biblical text, social con-

---

13. Sanders defines "canonical process" differently than does Brevard Childs. Whereas Childs understands the hermeneutical value of the canonical process in terms of the literary shaping of the final form of the biblical witness, Sanders sees the process in terms of the interpretive strategy of the faith community by which texts were constantly adapted to ever-changing social worlds in order to maintain the community's religious identity and witness to God. Thus, Childs is primarily interested in the *literary* formation of discrete texts into a canonical text, whereas Sanders is primarily interested in the *social* formation of the community that read and shaped these canonical texts in order to maintain its faith in God. For my discussion and integration of each into another hermeneutical model, see "Reading the New Testament in Canonical Context," in *Hearing the New Testament: Strategies for Interpretation* (Grand Rapids: Eerdmans, 1995), 370-93.

14. James A. Sanders, *Canon and Community: A Guide to Canonical Criticism* (Philadelphia: Fortress, 1984), 77-78.

text, and the theological tradition by which the unrecorded hermeneutics of biblical writers are employed and may be discerned by their readers. The image of a triangle reminds the interpreter of the "necessary and essential interrelatedness" of these three factors whenever the sacred tradition is adapted to life. My present proposal will adapt this theoretical tool of the triangle by defining in broad strokes an interpretative strategy for Wesleyan interpreters of Scripture.

Central to this interpretative model is the biblical text itself, whenever it is called upon, recited, or alluded to as the Word of God for today. Certainly every critical strategy is a gift of God in due season, when employed to the end of clarifying the theological meaning of the text itself. Most important to this exegetical enterprise, however, are those literary and linguistic strategies that are text-centered and seek to relate a particular text to its wider compositional and still wider canonical contexts. I have already mentioned the value of intertextual analysis in this regard. Also important is a study of the history of a text's effect upon its readers. In our case, the performance of a particular text among Wesleyan and holiness readers is a feature of its textual analysis. For example, a Wesleyan reading of the Book of Acts should consider how Acts was used in 19th-century holiness preaching; the education of the biblical interpreter should also include how Scripture is arranged in our lectionaries and read in Christian worship today.

The nexus of Scripture's performance as the Word of God is supplied by the interplay of biblical text and social context; this is where the Spirit of God is at work, inspiring biblical texts to function in inspiring ways. In fact, the meaning of a particular text is produced from within a particular social location. In the words of Severino Croatto, "what is genuinely relevant is not the 'behind' of a text, but its 'ahead,' its 'forward'—what it suggests as a pertinent message for the life of the one who receives or seeks it out."[15] In this sense, biblical theology is a variety of contextual theology, since the point of a text's departure is a concrete experience of some kind in some space at some time. The biblical word springs from a historical event and seeks to interpret its meaning for a particular community of its readers. Not only is the biblical text itself a response to some ancient event or a narrative of events, but a text's rereading as Word of God also happens in a particular social context where its current interpreter seeks to make Scripture's message intelligible for its new readers and auditors in light of their current experiences.

---

15. J. Severino Croatto, *Biblical Hermeneutics: Toward a Theory of Reading as the Production of Meaning*, trans. Robert R. Barr (Maryknoll, N.Y.: Orbis Books, 1987), 50.

This observation suggests that careful reconstruction of the ancient social setting and discernment of the spiritual crisis of the authorial audience are important investigations; but the importance of this interplay between text and ancient historical context fully unfolds as the interpreter imaginatively, analogically relates the ancient and contemporary settings, the authorial and canonical audiences. In particular, the location of Wesleyan readers of Scripture should be extended to include their experience of God's transforming and sanctifying grace.

Finally, the "unrecorded hermeneutics which lie in and between all the lines of biblical texts"[16] reveals the strategic importance of the interpreter's own theological commitments whenever Scripture is adapted to the living context of faith. Scripture's witness to God is discerned and dissected as analogous to the interpreter's own rule of faith.[17] No interpretative strategy should be theologically neutral; "to practise theology is always to practise a particular theology."[18] The word of God to which Scripture bears witness is analogous to the rule of faith confessed and expressed differently by particular and various theological traditions. Thus, the self-critical Wesleyan interpreter seeks after meaning in biblical texts and stories that congrues around the distinguishing themes and deeper logic of a Wesleyan typology of God's Word, without denying that these same texts and stories might yield other meanings to other interpreters from other theological traditions.

An essential feature of the interpreter's social location is theological. That is, the particular ways we live our lives of faith are shaped and justified by the traditions of particular communions of faith. How an interpreter shapes the theological meaning of Scripture, or how Scripture is related to those of a particular social setting or spiritual crisis, is nurtured within a discrete theological trajectory, whether via formal instruction or informal experience. For example, Wesley's understanding of Scripture as a sacrament of divine grace influences a more functional view of its inspiration and authority. Again, a community's conception of God's salvation, its experience and

---

16. Sanders, *Canon and Community,* 78.

17. My model of canonical criticism differs somewhat at this point from James A. Sanders. Whereas Sanders understands the principle of "dynamic analogy" in terms of comparable social contexts, ancient and modern, within which the biblical text continues to address God's people as God's word, I have come to downplay the usefulness of such historical constructions for biblical theology. Rather, in my view, the canonical witness is approached and interpreted as analogous to the community's rule of faith. Yet, such rules are hardly static; rather, different faith traditions conceive and express the church's rule of faith differently. Hence, the interpreter approaches the biblical witness to make meaning of it in ways that are analogous to a particular communion's rule of faith.

18. Watson, *Text and Truth,* 13.

its idea, reproduces a certain conception of theological orthodoxy that inter-preters seek to maintain by the meanings they make of Scripture.

When I speak of a Wesleyan reading of Scripture, then, I do not mean that Wesleyans simply adopt as normative Wesley's particular read-ing of Scripture or return to a crude, uncritical version of proof-texting. Rather, the particularity of the unrecorded hermeneutic of the Wesleyan trajectory is acquired in more subtle ways, first of all by living and wor-shiping within a congregation of Methodists who seek to preserve and even privilege: a Wesleyan perspective of Scripture's authority; a Wesleyan typology of the *via salutis,* which posits accent on believing humanity's sanctifying responses to God's justifying grace; a Wesleyan variety of Christian spirituality that is more developmental and affectual; of social justice which privileges our ministry to the poor and powerless; a duty-bound resistance to an "almost Christianity" in support of a "practical di-vinity"; and so on.[19] In this sense, a Wesleyan setting for the reading of Scripture should seek after those particular meanings that occur as the natural and logical yield of participating in a community of believers whose teaching and life are guided by a rule of faith composed in a dis-tinctively Wesleyan heritage context.

This more positive species of a Wesleyan "tribalism," which is neither apologetic in interest nor triumphalist in tone, should also sponsor more self-critical and intentional readings of Scripture whose performance is a word on target for those of and for this particular faith tradition. If the role of exegesis is to deliver the raw material that facilitates theological reflec-tion and Christian formation, then biblical studies in a Wesleyan idiom should reflect on Scripture's meaning in ways that more narrowly inform and thus form a Wesleyan communion of believers. Whether to afflict *our* comfortable or to comfort *our* afflicted, the orienting concern of Wesleyan biblical studies should aim at nurturing an understanding of what Scripture teaches us about being Wesleyan and doing what Wesleyans ought. I ask, where is this currently happening? Unless we do this and do it well, serious biblical studies have no future within the ongoing Wesleyan tradition.

A CONCLUDING EXHORTATION

The hermeneutical project before biblical scholars of Wesleyan her-itage as I have sketched it is fully interdisciplinary. For this to happen, cur-

---

19. For my understanding of this point, see Robert W. Wall, "Toward a Wesleyan Her-meneutic of Scripture," *Wesleyan Theological Journal* 30/2 (1995), 50-67 (and reprinted in this volume), which draws upon several recent treatments of Wesley's theology, especially Randy L. Maddox, *Responsible Grace: John Wesley's Practical Theology* (Nashville: Abing-don/Kingswood, 1994).

rent disciplinary boundaries must be relativized. Every vital element of the proposed reading strategy requires the work of others: contextual theologians from every social location should be recruited to help biblical scholars exegete the currents of contemporary society; and systematic theologians should be gathered to help Wesleyan biblical scholars understand what particular arrangement of Christian beliefs lies at the epicenter of the Wesleyan theological tradition. Surely, if the aim of Wesleyan biblical scholarship is the formation of a holy people actively engaged in holy work, the more practical concerns of pedagogy and preaching must also have voices in this community of interpretation. Indeed, every single methodological interest of biblical scholarship, if employed to serve the end of Wesleyan theological understanding and faithful praxis, must be an active collaborator in this sacred deliberation. There is no longer theologian or biblical scholar, academic or devotional readings of Scripture, critical or postcritical interests in Scripture, Christian clergy or faithful scholars, for all are one in Christ Jesus.

Joel Green is a prolific writer, professor, and seminary administrator. This chapter is an adapted version of what was originally offered as a response to what Robert Wall offers in the immediately preceding chapter. Here he offers additional reflections on what is truly Wesleyan in any Wesleyan reading of Scripture. At the center of his contribution is the idea that such readings do not come out of a formulaic kind of approach to these texts, where Wesleyans use certain techniques and not others to come to some expected end. Rather, a Wesleyan reading of Scripture simply means that such reading is shaped and performed by persons who *themselves* have been shaped by Wesleyan communities of faith and practice.

What Professor Green offers is a helpful guide through what many often see as a confusing maze of methodological issues within biblical studies. While his significant work elsewhere and this essay affirm the vast contributions within the larger discipline of biblical studies, here he touches on key critical issues within that discipline as they relate to the task of reading and interpreting Scripture in the church today.

6

IS THERE A CONTEMPORARY WESLEYAN HERMENEUTIC?[1]

Joel B. Green

◆

At the close of his meticulous analysis of *John Wesley's Conception and Use of Scripture,* Scott Jones writes hopefully of the promise of a genuinely Wesleyan view of Scripture articulated for our times. The first mark of such an approach, Jones observes, would be its high view of the authority and inspiration of Scripture.[2] This is obvious even to the casual reader of Wesley, who may be stunned with how freely Wesley is willing to embrace the derisive labels directed at him and his movement: Bible-bigots, Bible-moths, and the like;[3] and how simplistic his appeals to Scripture can appear: "Bring me plain, scriptural proof for your assertion, or I cannot allow it."[4] The higher the view of Scripture, though, the more crucial the issue of interpretation—indeed, the more crucial the twin issues of validity and relevance in interpretation.[5] Communities where the authority of the Bible is affirmed are necessarily concerned with validity in interpretation. Against the backdrop of Wesley's articulation of the authority of Scripture, his hermeneutical motto—"plain truth for plain people"—has heightened significance.

Is it possible to speak of a Wesleyan hermeneutic, a way of reading Scripture peculiar to those who find their identity in the Wesleyan tradition? On the one hand, the question itself presents problems for those of

---

1. This is a revision of an essay that appeared originally under the title "Reading the Bible as Wesleyans," in *Wesleyan Theological Journal* 33/2 (Fall 1998): 116-29. Used by permission.

2. Scott J. Jones, *John Wesley's Conception and Use of Scripture* (Nashville: Abingdon/Kingswood, 1995), 222-23.

3. John Wesley, "On God's Vineyard," sec. 1.1.

4. John Wesley, *Advice to the People Called Methodists with Regard to Dress,* sec. 5.1. See further, e.g., Jones, *John Wesley's Conception and Use of Scripture;* Thomas C. Oden, *John Wesley's Scriptural Christianity: A Plain Exposition of His Teaching on Christian Doctrine* (Grand Rapids: Zondervan, 1994), 55-65; Mack B. Stokes, *The Bible in the Wesleyan Heritage* (Nashville: Abingdon, 1979).

5. This concern was helpfully signaled for the wider evangelical community by Robert K. Johnston, *Evangelicals at an Impasse: Biblical Authority in Practice* (Atlanta: John Knox, 1979).

us who have been nurtured on the "scientific method." Weaned on historical criticism, we may justifiably assume that the identity of the hermeneut
—whether Wesleyan or urban or Hispanic or whatever—is irrelevant to
the task of interpretation. On the one hand, then, we have been taught to
make as our aim dispassionate, disinterested readings of Scripture. "What
it meant"—the decisive question in the modern era of biblical studies—
must be segregated from, not contaminated by, our social location or
theological commitments.

On the other hand, in spite of officially sanctioned attempts to exclude
readerly bias, anecdotes indicating the practice of a Wesleyan hermeneutic
are easy to document. During the days of my doctoral work, for example,
the New Testament postgraduate seminar at the University of Aberdeen
spent some months reading Romans. Happily for me, the seminar was led
by Prof. I. Howard Marshall, a committed redaction critic *and* British Methodist, who, perhaps unknowingly, ensured that Calvinist readings of Paul on
matters related to the atonement or election were held at bay. This, of
course, was much to the consternation of the Calvinists among us, who
must have outnumbered Wesleyans by a margin of seven to one! Even those
who eschew contemporary forays into reader-response hermeneutics thus
find themselves drawn to some readings instead of others.

At the same time, we may agree that it is often easier to spot a Wesleyan reading of Scripture than to articulate a hermeneutic that is distinctively Wesleyan. We know it when we see it, perhaps, but how do we articulate this "it"? The current scene in biblical and theological studies
provides an opportunity for celebration and fresh thinking on questions of
this sort—questions about the practice of biblical studies within and for
faith communities. Indeed, contemporary proposals for a text-centered,
canon-oriented, interdisciplinary engagement with Scripture, which locate
meaning in Scripture's witness to God and the faithful life of God's people,
are suggestive of a hermeneutic that draws deeply from the well of Wesley's own perspective on and use of Scripture. Although underscoring the
importance of these hermeneutical considerations, in this essay I want also to urge that much of what characterizes a Wesleyan hermeneutic must
be that Wesleyans do it. To put this differently, a Wesleyan mode of interpretation cannot be reduced to a particular set of techniques; there is no
Wesleyan apparatus into which biblical texts can be dumped, the handle
cranked, and a Wesleyan result guaranteed on the other side. What is
needed, rather, is involvement in biblical interpretation by persons formed
in Wesleyan communities.

How, then, might we read the Bible as Wesleyans? Let me attempt to
move our thinking forward by sketching four theses.

TOWARD A CONTEMPORARY WESLEYAN READING OF SCRIPTURE

1. To read the Bible as Wesleyans is not to adopt a precritical stance with respect to the nature and interpretation of Scripture, but to find ways of being critical that cohere with the Bible's character as Scripture. Characterizations of biblical studies prior to the tectonic shifts in hermeneutical foundations of the 19th and early 20th centuries as "precritical" are now legion. Reacting against medieval modes of interpretation, Protestant Reformers emphasized the one meaning of Scripture; hermeneutical handbooks developed criteria for legitimate readings—especially philological, including the historical exigencies governing the meaning of words. At the turn of the 19th century, new emphases on the related notions of cultural context and cultural relativism led interpreters to stress the distance between text and reader, and to construe this distance primarily along historical lines. Biblical study began to devote its energies to the mediation of this distance, and this led to various forms of "higher criticism" characteristic of the historical-critical paradigm that has until recently gripped the academy.

Against the backdrop of these developments, perhaps we should not be surprised to hear students of Wesley say of him that, in his use of Scripture, he is "not critical."[6] Such indictments typically bemoan the fact that Wesley paid little notice to the sacred cows of the historical-critical paradigm, especially the original meaning of a biblical text according to the (reconstructed) historical context and/or the (reconstructed) intent of the author. One might suppose, then, that calls for a reappropriation of a Wesleyan hermeneutic might serve best the agenda of a naive primitivism interested in recovering "precritical" modes of interpretation, or of those hoping to be rescued from the perils of modern, higher criticism of the Bible. This is not the case.

Those who lament Wesley's precritical approach to Scripture, and who might imagine that recovering Wesley for biblical studies entails our embracing precritical assumptions and practices, are mistaken on at least three grounds. First, the term itself, "precritical," when applied to Wesley is a dismissive anachronism that has gained its force from the assumption

---

6. E.g., Wilbur H. Mullen writes, "In a brief summary reaction to his method I would conclude that Wesley is not critical" ("John Wesley's Method of Biblical Interpretation," *Religion in Life* 47 [1978]: 99-108 [106-7]). See also Duncan S. Ferguson, "John Wesley on Scripture: The Hermeneutics of Pietism," *Methodist History* 22 (1984): 234-45 (esp. 238, 244); George A. Turner, "John Wesley as an Interpreter of Scripture," in *Inspiration and Interpretation,* ed. John F. Walvoord (Grand Rapids: Eerdmans, 1957), 156-78 (esp. 165-66).

that the only legitimate reading of a biblical text is one oriented toward tradition-critical and historical concerns. Lurking in the shadows here is the fallacy of presentism, the erroneous assumption that our methods and state of knowledge always evolve into higher forms, so that the way things are done in the present is necessarily better than in the past. But dismissing Wesley's hermeneutic in this way begs important questions about the aims of biblical interpretation; in particular, if we begin from the presumption that at least one of the aims of Bible reading is for Scripture to have a formative role in those communities who turn to it as Scripture, then we might conclude that historical criticism has not been "critical" enough![7]

Moreover, labeling Wesley's hermeneutic in this way overlooks the degree to which Wesley himself participated in the Enlightenment project—according significance in his theological enterprise to reason, limiting the authoritative voice of Scripture in deference to scientific discovery, and even engaging in the empirical method of contemporary science. Although he held to the unity of Scripture and steered an alternative course to that of the Deists, his position was not that of a man caught unawares with his head buried in the sand.[8] To take seriously Wesley's engagement with Scripture, then, should not lead us to a simplistic acceptance or rejection of, nor to a defensive posture vis-à-vis science.

Of even greater consequence, however, is the simple absurdity of assuming that the only style of reading worthy of the designation "critical" is historical criticism. The critical tradition is much more inclusive than the hegemony of historical criticism might have allowed us to imagine. Some readings are mimetic in theoretical orientation, others pragmatic, others expressive, and still others objective. Each finds the locus of meaning in its own place—in "the universe," in "the work," in "the artist," or in "the audience"—and so each in its own way is critical insofar as each is concerned both theoretically and performatively with validity in interpretation.[9] The Bible is susceptible to critical exploration in each of these ways and, undoubtedly, each has a contribution to make to our understanding of these texts. This is not to say, however, that all are equally compatible

7. Cf. Kevin J. Vanhoozer, "Hyperactive Hermeneutics: Is the Bible Being Overinterpreted?" *Catalyst* 19/1 (1992), 3-4; James Callahan, "The Bible Says: Evangelical and Postliberal Biblicism," *Theology Today* 53 (1997): 449-63; and the earlier, more programmatic essay by Peter Stuhlmacher, *Historical Criticism and Theological Interpretation of Scripture: Toward a Hermeneutics of Consent* (Philadelphia: Fortress, 1977).

8. See Jones, *John Wesley's Conception and Use of Scripture,* 36-41.

9. See M. H. Abrams, *The Mirror and the Lamp: Romantic Theory and the Critical Tradition* (Oxford: Oxford University Press, 1953); cf. Hazard Adams, ed., *Critical Theory Since Plato,* rev. ed. (Fort Worth: Harcourt Brace Jovanovich, 1992).

with our engagement with the Bible as "the church's book." If our aim embraces the religious significance of these books, what modes of critical inquiry are best suited to our critical task? On this point, as we will explore momentarily, Wesley is a helpful pathfinder.

Wesley himself was capable of adjudicating competing views on biblical texts in his concern for validity in interpretation. That he did not locate validity in interpretation in the intent of the human authors of biblical books, nor in the world or traditions behind the text, does not render him uncritical or precritical. Neither will it necessarily render us uncritical or precritical, nor allow us to be uncritical nor precritical—those of us who wish to take on something of the Wesleyan mantle of scriptural exegesis. This, of course, raises the question, how did Wesley involve himself in a critical mode of interpretation? And this brings us to our second thesis.

2. A properly chastised concern with the "literal meaning" of Scripture allows the Bible to lay its claims on contemporary readers and provides space for diversity in our reading strategies. Like those of the Protestant Reformation before him, Wesley rejected the four senses of Scripture characteristic of much medieval exegesis in favor of "the plain, literal meaning." "You are in danger of enthusiasm every hour," he wrote, "if you depart ever so little from Scripture; yea, or from the plain, literal meaning of any text, taken in connection with the context."[10] Such an emphasis today faces a number of challenges, two of which demand immediate attention.[11]

First, innovations in hermeneutics in the 20th century have emphasized interpretation less as the achievement of understanding and more as the production of meaning. "Meaning," accordingly, is not so much to be stalked and captured as to be cultivated, actualized, and embodied. One of the corollaries of this shift, however, is that interpretation can no longer be viewed as an objective enterprise, and the whole hermeneutical process is viewed in some quarters as to varying degrees embodying latent ideological commitments. In such an environment, literal interpretation

---

10. John Wesley, *Farther Thoughts on Christian Perfection.* For this emphasis in Wesley, see, e.g., Oden, *John Wesley's Scriptural Christianity,* 57-58; and especially Jones, *John Wesley's Conception and Use of Scripture,* 114-23.

11. In addition, we should not overlook the fact that, in using the phrase "literal sense," Wesley was assuming the classical theory of language that distinguishes between metaphor and everyday language. This view can no longer be sustained (cf., e.g., George Lakoff and Mark Johnson, *Metaphors We Live By* [Chicago: University of Chicago, 1980]; George Lakoff, *Women, Fire, and Dangerous Things: What Categories Reveal About the Mind* [Chicago: University of Chicago Press, 1987]), though the significance for biblical studies of "the contemporary theory of metaphor" (Lakoff) has not been explored.

smacks of attempts at a power game aimed at masking one's own commitments while parading them as God's. Indeed, the horizons of the history of interpretation are marred by examples of recruiting "the literal sense of Scripture" toward heinous ends—to undergird apartheid in South Africa, classism in Great Britain, the treatment of Native Americans in the United States, and the almost global disparaging of women, to name only four. Even against such a backdrop, it is nonetheless arguable that a properly chastised literal interpretation of Scripture may be embraced. This would require, first, that we self-consciously own the reality that we Wesleyans are not approaching Scripture in a value-free mode, but do so precisely as Wesleyans. Second, we must allow that, even though we come with certain theological, even ideological commitments to Scripture, we do so in order "to penetrate so deeply into the text that even these assumptions are called into question, tested, and revised by the subject matter [of Scripture] itself."[12] To put it differently, attention to the literal sense of Scripture is for us held in tandem with a commitment to the Bible's right to speak over against the church.

The second significant obstacle facing a literal construal of Scripture's meaning has to do with the challenge of any endeavor today to understand Scripture in a way that does not accord privilege to its historical meaning. One of the legacies of the historical-critical paradigm is that a primary emphasis on literal meaning will seem naive to some, ahistorical or even docetic to others. In fact, the paradox we face as Christians reading Scripture is more complex than historical criticism has allowed. For Christians, Scripture has as its primary referent *not* "the world of events behind the text" (as in the old historicism), but the nature of God and life before God. Accordingly, a premium must be placed on text-oriented readings of biblical narrative. At the same time, Christian faith is essentially incarnational, so that we can never be content with the gnosticizing tendencies of new literary readings of biblical narrative.

Seen in this light, a literal reading of Scripture does not share with historical criticism a commitment to locating meaning behind the text. Nor can we follow Wesley and others of his generation in seeking to ascertain the sense implied by the authors of those biblical texts. Scripture is constituted by the text itself, so that concern with literal meaning relates above all to the meaning, as it were, intended by the text.[13] Accordingly, "validity

---

12. So Brevard S. Childs, "Toward Recovering Theological Exegesis," *Pro Ecclesia* 6 (1997): 16-26 (19).

13. Francis Watson has recently insisted that "the literal sense is the sense intended by the author in so far as this authorial intention is objectively embodied in the words of the text" (*Text and Truth: Redefining Biblical Theology* [Grand Rapids: Eerdmans, 1997], 115;

in interpretation" would be measured by how a given interpretation *(a)* accounts for the text in its final form; *(b)* accounts for the text as a whole and is consistent with the whole of the text, without masking unfortunate aspects of the text that continue to haunt the interpreter; *(c)* accounts for the cultural embeddedness of language, refusing the interpretive imperialism that assumes that all people everywhere and in all times have construed their life-worlds as we do; *(d)* is consistent with itself; and, for Wesleyan Christians; and *(e)* coheres with the Rule of Faith (see below).

What of history and historicism in hermeneutics? In focusing so fully on the text, even when accounting for the text as the product of a particular sociocultural context, have we not adopted a mode of textual engagement that is at best naive and at worst docetic? In reply, we may inquire, Which is more naive—the precritical presumption that everything in Scripture happened in just the way it is described, or the critical assumption that interpretation can be sliced away from events/facts by the precision instruments of the historical-critical paradigm? Which is more naive—the historicism of a John Wesley or the historicism of a scholarly enterprise like today's Jesus Seminar? In point of fact, as philosophers of history have been arguing for decades, historical criticism has left us grasping for false alternatives. Verification and narrative run inescapably together in genuine historiography, so that every single sentence carries with it both an interpretative and a documentary force.[14] Undoubtedly, it is here, in the struggle for a new historicism, that more work is needed, but this does not detract from the reality that a Wesleyan interpretation of Scripture can embrace neither the old historicism that continues to occupy many of our colleagues nor the new literary formalism that arose as its antidote.

Finally with regard to Wesley's interest in a literal sense, it is important to remember that, for Wesley, this sense of Scripture was grounded in the intention not only of human authors but, even more so, in the intent of Scripture's one author, God. Hence, the literal sense must coincide with the general tenor of Scripture[15]—an emphasis that introduces for us our fi-

---

cf. already Richard Freadman and Seumas Miller, *Re-Thinking Theory: A Critique of Contemporary Literary Theory and an Alternative Account* [Cambridge: Cambridge University, 1992]), but this is not "authorial intentionality" in the usual sense.

14. So Albert Cook, *History/Writing: The Theory and Practice of History in Antiquity and in Modern Times* (Cambridge: Cambridge University Press, 1988), 55.

15. Cf. Jones, *John Wesley's Conception and Use of Scripture*, 197; and see the parallel remarks in Childs: "The literal sense was never restricted to a verbal, philological exercise alone, but functioned for both Jews and Christians as a 'ruled reading' in which a balance was struck between a grammatical reading and the structure of communal practice or a 'rule of faith' *(regula fidei)*" ("Toward Recovering Theological Exegesis," 20).

nal two theses, the one concerned with "the analogy of faith" and the other with "the whole of Scripture."

3. In contrast to the historical-critical paradigm, which accords privilege to cognitive objectives, a Wesleyan reading of Scripture will be characterized by its soteriological aims. For Wesley, the plain sense of Scripture would have been construed in relation to the grand story of Scripture. In actuality, this story was for Wesley not one but two. There is, on the one hand, the overarching story running from creation to new creation, which places its stamp on every biblical text. As important as this might be, the more critical story for Wesley was the soteriological progress of the person coming to faith and moving on to perfection. Thus, for Wesley, the purpose of biblical interpretation is singular:

> I want to know one thing, the way to heaven—how to land safe on that happy shore. God himself has condescended to teach the way: for this very end he came from heaven. He hath written it down in a book. O give me that book! At any price give me the Book of God! I have it. Here is knowledge enough for me. Let me be *homo unius libri.* Here then I am, far from the busy ways of men *[sic].* I sit down alone: only God is here. In his presence I open, I read his Book; for this end, to find the way to heaven.[16]

It is as puzzling as it is disturbing that one so fully committed to the social nature of Christian faith, to conferencing—that is, to the ecclesiology for which Wesley is justly celebrated—could thus emphasize the practice of reading Scripture *in solitude,* and it is here that a contemporary Wesleyan hermeneutic might offer a corrective to Wesley's own rhetoric. The crucial issue before us at this point lies elsewhere, however, with regard to how the motif of the soteriological journey, so central to Wesley's biblical hermeneutic, might become operative in a contemporary hermeneutic.

First, it must simply be acknowledged that, in positing a soteriological aim for the reading of Scripture, Wesley could hardly have found himself more out of step with the mainstream of biblical study that would soon come to flourish. The various modes of tradition criticism that were

---

16. John Wesley, Preface to *Sermons on Several Occasions,* sec. 5. That the aim of Wesley's hermeneutic was soteriological is noted by everyone—e.g., Donald A. D. Thorsen, *The Wesleyan Quadrilateral: Scripture, Tradition, Reason and Experience as a Model of Evangelical Theology* (Grand Rapids: Zondervan, 1990; reprint, Indianapolis: Light and Life Communications, 1997), 135-39; Robert W. Wall, "Toward a Wesleyan Hermeneutic of Scripture," *Wesleyan Theological Journal* 30/2 (Fall 1995): 50-67 (63-65); Jones, *John Wesley's Conception and Use of Scripture,* 104-27.

subsequently developed and practiced were oriented toward countering the sort of "interested" exegesis Wesley claimed for himself. For many critical scholars of the 20th century, acknowledging the search for contemporary significance is already enough to poison the water. It is no surprise, then, that voices bemoaning the irrelevance of modern biblical criticism to the theological task, to ethical discourse, to homiletics, and the like have become so pervasive and increasingly vibrant. If, as Karl Barth would have it, systematic theology "does not ask what the apostles and prophets said but what we must say on the basis of the apostles and prophets,"[17] it is little wonder that systematic theologians have typically looked askance at modern biblical scholarship. We biblical scholars have generally provided little by way of access to "what the apostles and prophets said," since *(a)* biblical scholarship has taken on the guise of a profession open only to those specialists guided by accredited procedures, and *(b)* the modern paradigm of study has portrayed "the strange world of the Bible" as profoundly remote from our own world, so that the nature and relevance of the truth claims of Scripture are (almost?) impossible to negotiate. Consequently, were we to put the "Wesleyan" back in biblical studies, we would find ourselves swimming very much against the stream.

Second, happily, the rediscovery of the reader in philosophical hermeneutics provides us with a means for swimming against just such a stream. As Wolfgang Iser and Umberto Eco have helped us to appreciate, texts are not self-interpreting, semantically sealed, meaning-making machines.[18] For Eco, texts like those in Scripture are characterized by the invitation for readers "to make the work" together with the author, so that texts might achieve a vitality that cannot be reduced to the cognitive domain. Rather, they are rendered meaningful in personal and communal performance. Iser observes that narrative texts—incapable of delineating every detail, even in plot—are inevitably characterized by gaps that must be filled by readers; even if the text guides this "filling" process, different readers will actualize the text's clues in different ways. For both Eco and Iser, then, texts are capable of a range (though not an infinite number) of possible, valid meanings, depending on who is doing the reading, from what perspectives they read, what reading protocols they prefer, and how they otherwise participate in the production of significance.

---

17. Karl Barth, *Church Dogmatics,* vol. 1: *The Doctrine of the Word of God,* pt. 1 (Edinburgh: T. & T. Clark, 1975), 16.

18. See, e.g., Wolfgang Iser, *The Implied Reader: Patterns of Communication in Prose Fiction from Bunyan to Beckett* (Baltimore: Johns Hopkins University Press, 1974); Umberto Eco, *The Role of the Reader: Explorations in the Semiotics of Texts,* Advances in Semiotics (Bloomington, Ind.: Indiana University Press, 1979).

How are these theoretical musings relevant to a Wesleyan reading of Scripture? A large part of what makes a reading Wesleyan is that those doing the reading are nurtured in the Wesleyan tradition of according privilege to some theological categories over others—the pursuit of holiness, for example, and the primacy of grace. In a sense, the perspectives on reading from such persons as Iser and Eco *(a)* indicate the absurdity of reading as the "discovery of meaning," substituting in its place the notion of reading as text-guided production and performance, and *(b)* show how our reading of Scripture is and can legitimately be self-consciously Wesleyan with respect to the aims of our interpretive strategies and habits. As Mack Stokes intuitively discerned, our heritage as Wesleyans shapes our reading of Scripture as Wesleyans. We read with a constant eye to "the Scripture way of salvation,"[19] and we do so in ways oriented toward the ongoing formation of the people of God in holiness.

This does not mean that our readings as Wesleyans are complete, or that they constitute the only possible ways of construing texts, but it does indicate how, from diverse communities of reading, we may hear the same pattern of words in new keys. Neither does it sanction every reading as equally valid, but it does indicate in one significant way how diverse readings of the same text might lay claim to legitimacy.

4. Finally, in their engagement with Scripture, Wesleyans can no longer allow for the invidious divisions that have determined our theological map; divisions between biblical studies and systematic theology, biblical studies and ethics, biblical studies and homiletics, and so on— such walls as these must be razed. The most deplorable barricade from a Wesleyan vantage point, however, is that which separates study of the Old Testament from study of the New. Like Wesley's grasp of the soteriological aim of biblical interpretation, so his emphasis on "the whole of Scripture" is well documented and widely recognized.[20] On the one hand, this phrase refers to the "unity of Scripture" according to the analogy of faith, the nucleus of which is holy love. On the other, it refers to his notion of the unity of Scripture—one Bible, two Testaments. Although it would be anachronistic to view Wesley as an early proponent of canonical criti-

---

19. See Stokes, *The Bible in the Wesleyan Heritage,* chaps. 2—3; also, Oden, *John Wesley's Scriptural Christianity,* 60; cf. Kenneth J. Collins, *The Scripture Way of Salvation* (Nashville: Abingdon, 1997).

20. For discussion, see Ferguson, "John Wesley on Scripture," 239-40; Jones, *John Wesley's Conception and Use of Scripture,* 43-61, 219-21; Oden, *John Wesley's Scriptural Christianity,* 57-60.

cism,[21] it can still be observed that one who moves so easily from one Testament to the other, and who finds witness to God's purpose equally in Old and New Testament, would surely find much to criticize about a church that has in so many arenas proven itself to be Marcion's child and an academy that so easily takes for granted the segregation of biblical studies into testamental specializations.

An analogous criticism would undoubtedly arise from Wesley the pastoral theologian regarding the ease with which we compartmentalize theological education, as though study of Scripture ought naturally to be done in relative isolation from exploration of the church's social witness, for example. One might insist that theological education necessarily requires that students do the work of integration. One might argue further that our pastors-in-training must know something about the Bible before they are able to integrate it with the study and work of pastoral care or spiritual direction or theological ethics. But this argument betrays its own, foundational commitment to a particular epistemology and pedagogy that, arguably, Wesley would have found extraordinarily foreign. It begs the question whether faithful study of Scripture can be other than reflection on pastoral care, spiritual direction, theological ethics, and so on. The practice of interdisciplinarity is capable of conceptualization and practice in more organic ways than this.[22]

Though Wesley did not contend with such issues as these in his historical situation, it might still be said that he has provided a way forward in our struggle. This has to do with his commitment to "conferencing." Even if we cannot turn back the clock of academic specialization, we can find more organic and dynamic ways to engage in vital discussion across, perhaps even through the walls that divide us in our disciplinary commitments and practices.

CONCLUSION

For those with eyes to see, the contemporary landscape is cluttered with the rubble of the Enlightenment experiment that has pervaded the totality of our lives and life-worlds in ways acknowledged and unacknowledged. The assured results of modern scholarship are much less assured, and the time is ripe for hermeneutical reflection on fresh fronts. We are

---

21. Cf. the helpful discussion in Robert W. Wall, "Reading the New Testament in Canonical Context," in *Hearing the New Testament: Strategies for Interpretation,* ed. Joel B. Green (Grand Rapids: Eerdmans, 1995), 370-93.

22. See Julie Thompson Klein, *Interdisciplinarity: History, Theory, and Practice* (Detroit: Wayne State University, 1990).

discovering that the years separating us from Wesley have not in every case been favorable to our understanding of and engagement with Scripture. Returning to Wesley, as though the 21st century could be the 18th, or as though the 18th were not in need of the hermeneutical correctives that would come, may not be a worthy aspiration, but this does not require that we relegate Wesley's conception and use of Scripture to exhibits in a museum. We live in a time alive with new possibilities. In our attempts to realize the promise of our era, we would do well to learn from one who stood at an earlier wellhead, to appropriate his wisdom in this new time. Reflecting on biblical study in the Wesleyan spirit, we are urged to loosen our grips on the tradition of modern biblical scholarship, and to loosen its grip on us, in order that we might participate in forms of biblical study that take with utmost seriousness our location within the church, and more particularly within the Wesleyan tradition of the church.

Professor Barry L. Callen has written the intellectual biography of Clark H. Pinnock (*Clark H. Pinnock: Journey Toward Renewal*, 2000), presented in brief in this chapter as an enlightening case study. Beginning in the 1970s, Clark Pinnock has journeyed from being a fierce defender of a Reformed, fundamentalistic view of biblical inspiration to a carefully nuanced, although still revelationally rooted view of the Bible that is quite compatible with that common in the Wesleyan theological tradition. He has become less a doorkeeper of "assured biblical truth" and more a grateful believer celebrating the Spirit's work in making the biblical text transformingly relevant in the present. This shift highlights a significant divide in the thought world of evangelicalism today. One side focuses strongly on the "text horizon" of the faith; the other is very aware of the equally significant "reader horizon." Evangelicals too often have spent great energy defending the presumed "inerrancy" of the biblical text and much less on methods of thoughtful interpretation of the text.

Pinnock questions the concept of divine revelation being primarily religious "information" that we humans can capture and catalog. While clear that divine revelation does yield necessary content for faith, Pinnock is concerned about the tendency of interpreters of the Bible to bring their own systems of human thought to the text, often effectively muting the text itself. He has sought to remain thoroughly biblical by freeing himself (to the degree possible) from prejudged and restrictive human rationalisms. Biblical revelation is said to be progressive in character, a living Word centered finally in a person, Jesus. The Christian agenda should be less a preoccupation with a theory of biblical inerrancy and much more a concern for the spiritual power of God's Spirit who speaks through the ancient text and illumines the contemporary reader to understand in currently relevant ways.

7
THE STRUGGLE OF EVANGELICALISM: AN INSTRUCTIVE CASE STUDY

Barry L. Callen

◆

For most Christians, especially conservative Protestants, the Bible is an authoritative point of beginning for identifying the orthodox substance of the faith. There is, for instance, the Wesleyan quadrilateral that Randy Maddox explains helpfully as "a unilateral *rule* of Scripture within a trilateral *hermeneutic* of reason, tradition, and experience."[1] All interpreters use all of these elements in their biblical reference and understanding, but in differing degrees and ways.

An instructive case study is available for highlighting the pivotal issues of biblical authority and hermeneutics. Clark H. Pinnock's early teaching and writing career focused major attention in this significant area of biblical authority. Beginning in the 1970s and proceeding to date, he journeyed from being a fierce defender of a Reformed fundamentalistic view of biblical inspiration and authority to a carefully nuanced, although still a revelationally rooted view of the Bible quite compatible with the Wesleyan theological tradition. His major transition of perspective highlights well a key struggle of contemporary evangelicalism.

A TRANSITION FROM TECHNICAL FOUNDATIONALISM

Between his books *A Defense of Biblical Infallibility* in 1967 and *The Scripture Principle* in 1984, Clark Pinnock obviously had been on a journey in regard to his understanding of the precise nature of revealed truth. Both early and later on this journey he has cared deeply and spoken convictionally about the reality of biblical revelation as a central principle on which the Christian faith rests. He would, however, make significant adjustments to his own thought along the way, adjustments he found warranted and important, ones that some of his evangelical colleagues have judged questionable and even unacceptable. Always he would think of himself as a committed and loyal evangelical. Finally he would emerge as a self-styled peacemaker on the controversial issue of the nature of bibli-

---

1. Randy L. Maddox, *Responsible Grace: John Wesley's Practical Theology* (Nashville: Abingdon/Kingswood, 1994), 46.

cal authority and interpretation.[2] His journey on this subject sheds light on contemporary evangelicalism and the key role that Wesleyan ways of Bible reading have and might play.

Of particular concern to Pinnock has been "the skeptical attitude toward the unique authority and relevance of Holy Scripture."[3] Into this concern area he boldly stepped, first ready to defend the presumed technical, foundationalist, and revelational integrity of the Bible against all comers. Later he found himself reviewing critically some aspects of the nature of his own vigorous defense and the motivations for the intensity of it. The influential periodical *Christianity Today* helped make inerrancy the badge of evangelical authenticity, even as Francis Schaeffer insisted that it was the watershed of evangelical fidelity. This periodical once lauded Pinnock's stalwart fidelity, saying that his "bareknuckles challenge of current leading theological ideas will be cheered by people who possess but cannot adequately articulate a disdain for the irrational abstractions sweeping through the ecclesiastical intelligentsia."[4] Later this magazine would take a much more cautious approach to the value of Pinnock's contributions, seeming to judge the "revised" Pinnock in a way similar to the 1986 conclusion of Henry Holloman. In the *Journal of the Evangelical Theological Society* Holloman commended Pinnock for capably criticizing the "liberal theological revision" with its "flat denial of the Scripture principle in the classical sense," and yet insisted that "unfortunately Pinnock's proposed Scripture principle with its very lenient view of inerrancy does not offer evangelicals a Biblically sound and logically consistent position to stabilize Christian faith and to withstand the onslaughts of destructive Biblical criticism."[5]

Pinnock's journey toward renewal in the evangelical understanding of biblical authority had led him, to use his own terms, from a "philosophical biblicism" to a "simple biblicism." This postmodern shift had begun with an early preoccupation with verifiable revelational data that could speak

---

2. Trent Butler, in reviewing Clark Pinnock's book *The Scripture Principle* (San Francisco: Harper and Row, 1984) for the *Journal of Biblical Literature* (105/4 [Dec. 1986]: 700-701), highlights Pinnock's obvious awareness of excess on all sides of the debate about biblical inspiration and interpretation and Pinnock's expressed hope of supplying a model that might help transcend the impasse. For an extensive exploration of Pinnock's intellectual journey and thought in general, see Barry L. Callen, *Clark H. Pinnock: Journey Toward Renewal* (Nappanee, Ind.: Evangel, 2000).

3. Clark Pinnock, "Evangelicals and Inerrancy: The Current Debate," *Theology Today* 35 (April 1978): 65-66.

4. *Christianity Today* endorsement on the cover of Pinnock's book *Set Forth Your Case* (Nutley, N.J.: Craig Press, 1967).

5. Henry Holloman, review of Pinnock's book *The Scripture Principle* in the *Journal of the Evangelical Theological Society* 29/1 (March 1986): 96-97.

with certainty to the world. He championed the assumption of divinely given propositional truths that could save humankind from relativism. The journey later moved him to a focus that he always had in an incipient way, but one that became dominant for him and now lacked the heavy foundationalist overlay. By the resulting "simple biblicism" Pinnock means

> the delight evangelicals experience from meditating on Scripture and submitting to it. They feel immense gratitude for this means of grace that the Spirit has bestowed on the church to equip it. Scripture is a gift of the Spirit, and evangelicals want to be open to all that God says in this text. Scripture for them is the tangible sacrament of the Word of God nourishing them like milk and honey. Not a theory about the Bible, simple biblicism is the basic instinct that the Bible is supremely profitable and transforming, alive with God's breath. Without being free of every difficulty, the Bible nevertheless bears effective witness to Jesus Christ. . . . Although wanting a reasonable faith, simple biblicism is not overly anxious about erecting rational foundations in the modern sense. It reflects a postmodern lack of anxiety about such foundations and is content with soft rather than hard rational supports.[6]

To begin his career in the 1960s, Pinnock was primarily a vigilant doorkeeper of "assured biblical truth." Soon he journeyed to the place where most of his energy was being expended in ways other than withstanding "the onslaughts of destructive biblical criticism." He has begun "listening" to the Bible, learning all he could, not defensively, but openly and expectantly. Like the Wesleyan tradition, he has opened himself to both the historic and contemporary work of God's Spirit.

Regardless of his sturdy commitment to revealed truth, which Pinnock ties directly to biblical authority and still defines intentionally by use of the word "inerrancy," he has remained in creative motion on the subject. By the early 1970s he had become better able to reign in his enthusiastic crusading and make any needed confrontation increasingly constructive. Then came Pinnock's three years of teaching at Regent College in Vancouver, Canada (1974-77), where he experienced freedom to quest and be creative. In this context he was impacted significantly by Stephen Davis's book *Debate About the Bible: Inerrancy Versus Infallibility*[7] that openly challenges certain assumptions about biblical inerrancy then held

---

6. Clark Pinnock, "New Dimensions in Theological Method," in *New Dimensions in Evangelical Thought,* ed. David Dockery (Downers Grove, Ill.: InterVarsity Press, 1998), 200.

7. Stephen Davis, *Debate About the Bible* (Philadelphia: Westminster, 1977).

by Pinnock. So Pinnock began to review carefully and revise cautiously his inerrancy views.[8] Increasingly he was questioning openly certain traditional defenses and expressions of inerrancy treasured by many conservatives.[9] In his early period of fundamentalism he had leaned on 2 Timothy 3:16-17, the only place in Scripture where the term "inspired" *(theopneustos)* occurs. But now, as a "neoevangelical," he was looking beyond the inspiration issue to appreciate also Paul's emphasis on practical spirituality—what is inspired is "useful for teaching, for reproof, for correction, and for training in righteousness, so that everyone who belongs to God may be proficient, equipped for every good work."[10] That is, God's Spirit breathes through the text to transform believers into maturing and obedient disciples. The focus should be less on textual technicalities of the past (the original text no longer wholly available) and more on faithful and transformative relevance in the present.

It was immediately obvious that reforming a cherished element of fundamentalism like biblical inerrancy would be slow and painful at best. Pinnock quickly found himself being sharply criticized by some traditionalists, including Harold Lindsell who earlier had counted Pinnock a valuable ally in the "battle for the Bible." Pinnock was beginning what would become his common experience—walking a tightrope, explaining to the liberals why so few revisions were being made and to the fundamentalists why there were so many.[11] Recalling his two early mentors, F. F. Bruce and Francis Schaeffer, Pinnock would characterize his shifting in the 1970s as a move from Schaeffer's militant rationalism to Bruce's more bottom-up irenic scholarship.[12] His move bore similarity to another key figure in his eyes, C. S. Lewis. This Englishman represented for him a reasonable, com-

---

8. See his "Three Views of the Bible in Contemporary Theology," in *Biblical Authority,* ed. Jack Rogers (Waco, Tex.: Word, 1977), 45-73; and "Evangelicals and Inerrancy," 65-69.

9. Later Pinnock would see the degree to which the foundationalism of modernity had been reflected in his own early work. "It did so in a covert way," he reported, "since I was not tuned in to these subtleties. Because religion appeals to the need for security in life, it is easy to fall into foundationalism as a way of attaining it. It has a particularly seductive appeal for fundamentalists with their passion for certainty" (as in the unpublished paper of Pinnock delivered in 1997 to the evangelical-process dialogue convened at Claremont School of Theology).

10. Clark Pinnock's 1963 doctoral dissertation at the University of Manchester in England was titled "The Concept of the Spirit in the Epistles of Paul."

11. For example, Pinnock's eventual book *The Scripture Principle* (1984) was reviewed critically by James Barr (judged unacceptable from the left—Pinnock did not go far enough) and by Roger Nicole (judged unacceptable from the right—Pinnock went too far) in *Christianity Today* 29 (1 February 1985): 68-71.

12. Clark Pinnock in his interview with Barry Callen, November 21, 1998.

monsense approach to Christian belief that is enriched with wonderful visions and the ability to live with ambiguity.

What intervened to alter Clark Pinnock's view? His own explanation is that he realized that he had "inflated the biblical claims for inspiration in the interests of a rationalist paradigm. . . . I had been engaged in making the Bible say more than it wanted to in the interests of my system."[13] In fact, for him the rationalism of a scholastic theological system was slowly crumbling in light of an enhanced appreciation for the dynamic work of the Spirit in relation to the biblical authors/editors and his own thought and life (and potentially the thought and lives of all contemporary Bible readers). Such divine work came to have a substantive impact on Pinnock's view of biblical revelation and interpretation. He now affirms a progressiveness of revelation and thus the need for the interpreter to give heed to the letter, spirit, and direction of the principles of a text. Thus, with the Spirit's help, one "may need to go beyond Scripture in carrying out its intentions."[14] Pinnock had come to recognize that Jesus and the apostles, while holding a high view of biblical inspiration and authority, used the text in more practical and flexible ways than inerrantists typically have allowed. He now is open to a more inductive approach to the text that avoids the tendency to strained exegesis forced by a preheld theory. He had been helped by scholars like Edward Farley and James Barr to realize without embarrassment that God in fact has given the Scriptures in human forms and languages.

The Bible, so it increasingly has appeared to Pinnock, should be allowed to teach God's will and way out of its distinctive diversity rather than out of a forced uniformity. Robert Johnston reflects as follows on the reasons for Pinnock's broadening use of the term "inerrancy": "The perfect errorlessness of non-extant autographs was an abstraction that, for Pinnock, died the death of a thousand qualifications. More importantly, it failed to prove the dynamic authority of the present text."[15] After all, it is the Spirit who causes the reader to be receptive to a text's "surplus of

---

13. Clark Pinnock, in Ray C. W. Roennfeldt, *Clark H. Pinnock on Biblical Authority: An Evolving Position* (Berrien Springs, Mich.: Andrews University Press, 1993), xix. He attributes much of his new viewpoint to the writings of I. Howard Marshall, F. F. Bruce, James D. G. Dunn, and James Barr.

14. Clark Pinnock, "An Evangelical Theology of Human Liberation," *Sojourners* 5 (Feb. 1976): 30. This article was originally a 1975 address to a workshop sponsored by Evangelicals for Social Action.

15. Robert Johnston, "Clark H. Pinnock," in *Handbook of Evangelical Theologians,* ed. Walter Elwell (Grand Rapids: Baker, 1993), 434.

meaning" and, observes Pinnock, "whatever the reason, stress on the Spirit is noticeably lacking in the literature of inerrancy."[16]

The force that can liberate the message of Jesus for the needs of life today is the Bible read in the wisdom and power of the Spirit. Focusing inordinately on the presumed necessary accuracy of all textual detail, however marginal, can easily become dysfunctional. There was a growing realization that for many believers strict adherence to the inerrancy doctrine endangers rather than protects evangelical faith.[17] Accordingly, Pinnock commended the 1977 anti-inerrancy polemic of Stephen Davis for its "pastoral service" to those who are troubled with marginal difficulties in the Bible but who, nonetheless, are deeply committed to a biblically based evangelical faith. The theory of errorlessness sometimes leaves such persons stranded "if a single point however minute stands in any doubt."[18] The intent of divine revelation surely is human transformation. People are to be changed, not stranded by their rational engagement with the biblical text.

From his new academic post at McMaster Divinity College, Pinnock began in 1977 to reflect his maturing thought to ever-widening Christian publics and to an increasing range of possible implications. Regarding biblical inspiration and authority in the modern world, he now was identifying three general positions within evangelicalism. The first, his own personal heritage, centers in a militant advocacy of a virtually unqualified biblical inerrancy, an errorless Bible presumed to be the essential anchor of true Christianity. The second position actively opposes such strict inerrancy. Although a minority of evangelicals, there were prominent names here, including Pinnock's own revered teacher F. F. Bruce of the University of Manchester in England. These thinkers questioned the assumption of scientific precision and accuracy usually connoted by inerrancy, arguing that such an inerrancy mentality is a modernistic approach not appropriate to the biblical text and not evidenced in how the Bible treats its own material or in what it claims for itself. They saw inspiration as "a much less

---

16. Clark Pinnock, *The Scripture Principle* (San Francisco: Harper and Row, 1984), 154.

17. This judgment, of course, was hardly universal in the world of evangelical theologians. Roger Nicole, e.g., reacted in his *Christianity Today* review of Pinnock's 1984 book *The Scripture Principle* under the provocatively critical title "Clark Pinnock's Precarious Balance Between Openmindedness and Doctrinal Instability." Nicole's inference was that there is an establishment evangelical theology that should not be threatened by a methodology that is dynamic enough to be open to any significant theological alterations. Obviously, Pinnock had come to disagree.

18. Clark Pinnock, "Foreword" to Stephen Davis, *The Debate About the Bible* (Philadelphia: Westminster, 1977), 12.

formal and more practical affair," a divine action on behalf of the sufficiency of Scripture meant to "nourish and instruct the church for its faith and life, and not to [guarantee] an abstract perfection" in regard to the technicalities of its text or its incidental references to matters outside its central concern.[19]

The third position, which by 1978 had become Pinnock's own, involved a preference for the term "inerrancy," but only after modifying its definition so as to take into account certain biblical phenomena not compatible with any absolute view of an errorless text (like the presence of a Semitic cosmology, variants of parallel material appearing in the Synoptic Gospels, etc.). Pinnock's own book *Biblical Revelation* (1971) was representative, as soon would be his "softer" *Reason Enough* (1980) and then his major work *The Scripture Principle* (1984).[20] In the 1984 work he rethought biblical authority in light of its witness to itself, including both its divine and human character and its spiritual dynamic. His style of argument was less rationalistic than his earlier apologetic works and his stance a less strict and more nuanced form of "inerrancy." On the one hand, he was acknowledging the need to deal with the biblical text as it is, not with the abstraction of an ideal text (the "autographs") that God did not choose to give the church across the centuries. Reverently pursued critical scholarship has its place, he judged, as does a Spirit-led dynamic reading of the biblical text. On the other hand, such scholarship and hermeneutical focus do not lessen the fact that Scripture is genuinely authoritative in what it intends to teach. There is an objective content to biblical revelation that should caution both against skeptical and subjective biblical criticism and any Spirit focus that disassociates itself from the control of the revealed biblical text. The word "inerrancy" can be retained legitimately, Pinnock concluded, when defined as "a metaphor for the determination to trust God's Word completely."[21]

---

19. Pinnock, "Evangelicals and Inerrancy," 67.

20. A portion of the material in this 1984 book was first presented at Fuller Theological Seminary as the 1982 Payton Lectures. The title of Pinnock's lectures was "Holy Scripture: Divine Treasure in Earthen Vessels."

21. Pinnock, *Scripture Principle*, 225. The review of Pinnock's *Scripture Principle* by Randy Maddox affirms the book as "the most nuanced and critically aware exposition of biblical inerrancy available." Even so, Maddox was perplexed by Pinnock's argument for retaining the term "inerrancy" after defining it basically as the belief that Scripture never leads one astray in regard to what it intentionally teaches. Retaining it when it is thus defined appeared to be essentially a political move, "using the approved password to placate a constituency," a move that will not be accepted by others who use the term and retain its traditional meaning (*Wesleyan Theological Journal* 21/1-2 [Spring-Fall 1986], 206). For evidence that Maddox was correct, see Roger Nicole, *Christianity Today* 29 (1 February 1985): 68-71.

Pinnock now was championing a potentially awkward and certainly controversial middle position criticized by advocates of both the other positions. He assesses the resulting awkwardness this way: "The militant advocates suspect them [and me] of watering down the inerrancy conviction close to meaninglessness, and left wing Protestants like James Barr ridicule the effort to be critically honest and still retain biblical inerrancy in any form."[22] Regardless of criticisms from representatives of both alternatives and his increasing willingness to qualify carefully the exact meaning of his own inerrancy stance, Pinnock continued to maintain at least this: "The Bible, not modernity, is normative, and our thoughts are to be shaped by its teaching, not the reverse. Only by acknowledging this can we prevent revelation from being buried under the debris of human culture and opinion and from disappearing as a liberating Word from outside the human situation."[23]

By 1984 he was speaking in terms of "the Scriptural principle," by which he meant that the Bible is to be viewed as God's own written Word. God "has communicated authoritatively to us on those subjects about which Scripture teaches . . . and we believers willingly subject ourselves to this rule of faith." The Bible is "a contentful language deposit" that addresses us with God's authority, a deposit that should not be reduced to a mere expression of human experience and tradition."[24]

Delwin Brown rightly observes that Pinnock's *Scripture Principle* "is as much an internal self-criticism of conservatism as it is an external critique of liberalism."[25] For Pinnock, inerrancy had come to mean that the Bible can be trusted in what it teaches and intentionally affirms. A key passage like 2 Timothy 3:15-16 authorizes sturdy belief in the instructional significance of the Bible in matters relating to human salvation, but not necessarily in marginal matters unrelated to the need for, basis of, and practice of new life in Jesus Christ. All Scripture is to be regarded as authoritative, but the character of the authority is relative to the actual content and form of any given text. Those portions of the Bible that plainly intend to teach the will of God constitute the core of authoritative Scripture. The Christian should accept the Bible as teacher in a way consistent with the diversity that the Bible contains. For instance, the way the New Testament uses the Hebrew Scriptures ("Old" Testament) makes plain that a text

---

Nicole quotes Carl F. H. Henry (68): Pinnock "retains inerrancy as a concept, but seems to thin it out almost to the breaking point."

22. Pinnock, "Evangelicals and Inerrancy," 66-67.
23. Pinnock, *Scripture Principle,* 213.
24. Ibid., 62.
25. Delwin Brown, "Rethinking Authority from the Right," *Christian Scholar's Review* 19/1 (1989-90), 67.

can possess "a surplus of meaning potential that transcends the meaning it originally had." The original meaning is to be the anchor of interpretation, but under the guidance of the Holy Spirit "the significance of the text for us needs to be searched out. . . . The picture is that of a canon in which the truth unfolds gradually and dialectically."[26] The Bible remains the norm of belief and must rule in opposition to the liberal reformers who "are in rebellion against the content of the Bible and are determined to adapt it to the 'itching ears' of the present."[27]

Innovative and on journey Pinnock surely *was;* rebellious and anti-biblical he clearly *was not.* It had become crucial for him that one both affirm biblical authority in principle and define it with care. He was seeking to claim middle ground in a crucial and complex issue. He had moved in a direction highly compatible with a Wesleyan/Holiness way of Bible reading.

THE HERMENEUTICAL CHALLENGE

It has remained the firm assumption of Pinnock that true Christianity depends on a truth deposit once delivered to the saints, a deposit that must be maintained and accepted by faith. This is why he holds staunchly to the "text horizon" of the faith in the face of the obvious role always played by the "reader horizon." The problem he now sees, however, is that evangelicals, for whom the Word of God is of utmost importance, "have spent a great deal of energy defending the authority or inerrancy of the Bible and [have] given little attention to the equally important matter of its interpretation." They have, in fact, often evidenced a "naivete in hermeneutics" that threatens "to drag the meaning of the text into the range of what we want it to say." The text is not there to do human bidding, and it does not mean whatever readers want it to mean. But interpretation is no easy process, in part because "the Bible is not a flat text but a symphony of voices and emphases."[28] Pinnock thus places himself today in an "in-

---

26. Pinnock, *Scripture Principle,* 45, 186. He says further: "The Bible in the form it comes to us is the kind of teacher that draws us into the process of learning and helps us learn to think theologically and ethically ourselves in new situations" (194).

27. Ibid., 208, 211. Some conservatives, of course, now insist that Pinnock himself is a liberal reformer still trying to wear inerrancy clothes. Norman Geisler, for instance, judges: "Strangely, some neotheists such as Clark Pinnock claim to believe in the infallibility and inerrancy of the Bible. However, this is clearly inconsistent" (*Creating God in the Image of Man?* [Minneapolis: Bethany, 1997], 131).

28. Clark Pinnock, "Catholic, Protestant, and Anabaptist: Principles of Biblical Interpretation in Selected Communities," *Brethren in Christ History and Life* 9 (Dec. 1986): 268, 275.

errancy of purpose" category that allows room both to significantly nuance the specific textual meanings of inerrancy[29] and continue to sign the statement of the Evangelical Theological Society that affirms that "the Bible alone, and the Bible in its entirety, is the Word of God written, and is therefore inerrant in the autographs." He actually prefers the wording of the Lausanne Covenant that says the Bible is "inerrant in all it affirms" or that of the Chicago Statement of Biblical Inerrancy that says: "We deny that it is proper to evaluate Scripture according to standards of truth and error that are alien to its usage or purpose." In other words, the Bible may *contain* errors of incidental kinds, but it *teaches* none.[30]

Clearly, by the 1980s Pinnock had opened himself to modern biblical scholarship to a degree he had previously rejected. In 1968 he had warned Southern Baptists about new teachers then in their ranks who "had found it expedient to jettison the historic high view of Scripture and accept a scaled down version. . . . Scholarship is the gift of God. But scholars have erred time and time again, while Scripture has never erred!"[31] The next year he had joined the faculty of Trinity Evangelical Divinity School and affirmed its statement of belief, point one of which was: "We believe . . . the Scriptures, both Old and New Testaments, to be the inspired Word of God, without error in the original writings, the complete revelation of His will for the salvation of men, and the Divine and final authority for all Christian faith and

---

29. Note, for instance, Pinnock's "Climbing Out of a Swamp: The Evangelical Struggle to Understand the Creation Texts," *Interpretation* 43 (April 1989): 143-55. He is concerned that evangelicals be true to their own premise of "letting Scripture speak definitively above the noise of human opinions" (153). He also is concerned, however, that near the surface of evangelical interpretation is a "docetic" tendency, "an unconscious wish not to have God's Word enter into the creaturely realm" (153). He concludes: "Evangelicals are understandably nervous about existential hermeneutics, but that is no reason to overreact and make the Bible a victim" (154). Modern scientific perspectives and calls for "factual" information may be quite other than the biblical intent in the Genesis texts (and elsewhere). To honor biblical authority is to affirm claims to assured truth only within the context of the intent of biblical teaching (which relates to salvation and not science, for instance).

30. Note this from Donald Bloesch (*Holy Scripture: Revelation, Inspiration and Interpretation* [Downers Grove, Ill.: InterVarsity, 1994], 116): "I affirm that the message of Scripture is infallible and that the Spirit infallibly interprets this message to people of faith. But the perfect accuracy of the letter or text of Scripture is not an integral part of Christian faith. Because the term *inerrancy* is so often associated with the latter position, I agree with Clark Pinnock that it is not the preferable word to use in theological discussion today, even though it should not be abandoned, for it preserves the nuance of truthfulness that is necessary for a high view of Holy Scripture." Bloesch refers to this statement of Pinnock (*Scripture Principle*, 225): I wish to retain the word *inerrancy* because it "has come to symbolize in our day that full confidence that Christians have always had in the Scriptures."

31. Clark Pinnock, "A New Reformation" (booklet, Tigerville, S.C.: Jewel Books, 1968), 7, 10.

life." But by the 1980s he had qualified the precise meaning of appropriately affirming an inerrant Bible, insisting that "qualify" and "scale down" differ in meaning. For him the Bible's authority and reliability had not thereby been diminished.

Pinnock, both early and late in his personal journey, has believed the Bible to be inerrant in all that it intentionally affirms. What changed in his view is the identification of exactly what the Bible actually affirms. Doing such careful identifying is a central and ongoing challenge for contemporary Christians. The task of interpretation would be much easier, of course, if the actual words of the Bible were identical with divine revelation. But it may be said that human words are to divine revelation what form is to content. Therefore, there is danger in any rote application of Augustine's classic statement: "What the Bible says, God says." When such a statement is applied mechanically to the biblical text, there is the tendency "to dehistoricize the vehicle of revelation and to make each text an immutable and inherent proposition." In fact, tradition, experience, and reason (key elements of the Wesleyan quadrilateral) all are needed to assist the community of faith in understanding and applying the Word of God. *Sola Scriptura* may have been a distinguishing slogan of the Protestant Reformation, but it was never literally practiced. Probing the sacred text is always done within some reading tradition that relies at least in part on a given pattern of logic and experience. Even so, it remains the case for Pinnock that the Bible—with all its humanness—extends beyond being merely a crucial cultural heritage for believers to being the normative rule of faith that should define belief and practice.

This revised inerrancy position came to be judged by Pinnock as both justified by the facts, textual and contextual, historical and hermeneutical, and able to provide a viable position to mediate the authority struggle in the evangelical community.[32] In 1965 he had seen the Southern Baptist Convention, into which he then was entering as a new professor, in danger of serious infiltration by a Bible-evading and doctrine-eroding liberalism. This he fought. By 1987, however, Pinnock saw the primary danger to the SBC having shifted from the external assault of liberalism to a dangerous division within the convention itself, nearly a holy war among the parties

---

32. Carl F. H. Henry was a stalwart evangelical defender of the distinctiveness and even propositional nature of divine revelation, the one thing, he argued, on which evangelicals can confidently construct a substantial, coherent, and trustworthy theological system. Clark Pinnock, however, countered that it is impossible to set forth an infallible Scripture as the foundational axiom of Christian theology. Argues Pinnock: "The problem in a nutshell: If reason is given its head, will it reliably lead to orthodox conclusions? Progressives certainly do not believe that it will" (*Tracking the Maze* [New York: Harper and Row, 1990], 46-47).

of its nonliberals (ranging from moderates to fundamentalists). A primary dividing line was between competing theories of biblical inspiration. The truly frightening prospect, as judged by Pinnock, was that in a time of unprecedented worldwide mission potential "the possible fragmentation of believers could have disastrous consequences for world evangelization," even causing Baptists to "snatch defeat from the jaws of victory."[33] He announced to a large gathering of Baptist scholars that there was the option of peace without compromise, saying that "the key issue is to maintain the right amount of form and freedom." He supported this perspective with his own experience: "I did not see my colleague at L'Abri, the strict inerrantist Francis Schaeffer, spending his time seeking to drive out my doctoral mentor, the moderate F. F. Bruce, from the evangelical coalition just because of a difference of opinion over a theological theory and not the gospel."[34]

Pinnock spoke in 1987 to a large body of mostly Southern Baptist scholars gathered for the Conference on Biblical Inerrancy at Ridgecrest, North Carolina. In the midst of presentations by persons ranging from strict inerrantists to significant revisionists, Pinnock's inclination was to be a peacemaker. He supported the 1978 Chicago Statement of the International Council on Biblical Inerrancy, which declared in its famous Article 13 that textual phenomena like chronological order, loose quotations, and disagreeing numbers should not be considered "errors." He argued that Bible believers over the centuries have come to no consensus on the precise meaning of inerrancy, that the Chicago Statement made room for nearly every well-intentioned Baptist, and that "old-fashioned love and understanding" was the real need of the hour. On the one hand, there should be correction of any "unbalanced over-belief which overlooks the human and historical dimension of the Bible"; but, he warned on the other hand, "let us never fail to express our unsurpassed confidence in the divine treasure which the Bible surely is." What is the bottom line? It should be mission, said Pinnock, not fruitless and debilitating internal combat over technicalities largely of human devising. What he saw happening was that the liberals already had lost the day, while conservatives, properly but not very gracefully, were now "trying to get the wrinkles out of their sounder view of inspiration."[35] Pinnock's own approach was to adopt "a simpler, more spontaneous biblicism" that trusts the Bible without reserva-

---

33. Clark Pinnock, *The Proceedings of the Conference on Biblical Inerrancy, 1987* (Nashville: Broadman, 1987), 73.

34. Ibid., 74.

35. Clark Pinnock, "Afterword," in *The Unfettered Word: Southern Baptists Confront the Authority-Inerrancy Question,* ed. Robison B. James (Waco, Tex.: Word, 1987), 186-87.

tion, but at the same time does not "burden the Bible reader with too much human theory lest he or she miss what God is saying in the text."[36]

This more simple and spontaneous biblicism approach was similar to that of fellow Baptist theologian Bernard Ramm who, according to Pinnock, toward the end of his career "was able to experience freedom from the methodological fixation."[37] Ramm had wearied of evangelicals fighting over inerrancy and "longed for them to be able to rejoice in its [the Bible's] solid testimony to Jesus Christ in the power of the Holy Spirit." Pinnock himself had come to the place to which Ramm also had arrived. For him, the Bible seldom addresses its authority and says nothing about its inerrancy. The rationalistic (Western) model of biblical authority that Pinnock had learned early from B. B. Warfield and others had exaggerated these concepts to fit a system that had been adopted in advance. Pinnock and many other evangelicals are now learning "not to force the Bible onto a Procrustean bed of extra-scriptural assumptions about authority and perfection."[38] Wesleyan scholar Timothy Smith was right:

> Those of us who come from Wesleyan, Lutheran or Calvinist backgrounds draw upon the writings of the Reformers themselves to affirm our conviction that the *meanings,* not the *words,* of biblical passages are authoritative, and that understanding these meanings requires close and critical study of the texts, rather than incantation of supposedly inerrant words.[39]

Gary Dorrien offers good perspective. In midcareer Pinnock had realized that evangelicalism was needlessly struggling and dividing over an assertion of total biblical inerrancy, an assertion that cannot be sustained by the biblical text itself. So "he redrew the line at infallible-teaching inerrancy and invested the same passion he had earlier shown for strict inerrancy in defending this fallback position against theological relativism."[40] Pinnock now knew that Karl Barth had good reason for rejecting the con-

---

36. Pinnock, *Proceedings of the Conference on Biblical Inerrancy,* 75. For an excellent overview of the apparent strengths and weaknesses of this "later" position of Pinnock, see Roennfeldt, *Clark H. Pinnock on Biblical Authority,* 321-41.

37. Clark Pinnock, "Bernard Ramm: Postfundamentalist Coming to Terms with Modernity," in *Perspectives on Theology in the Contemporary World: Essays in Honor of Bernard Ramm,* ed. Stanley Grenz (Macon, Ga.: Mercer University Press, 1990), 26.

38. Clark Pinnock, "New Dimensions in Theological Method," in *New Dimensions in Evangelical Thought,* ed. David Dockery (Downers Grove, Ill: InterVarsity Press, 1998), 204.

39. Timothy L. Smith in *The Christian Century* 94 (2 March 1977): 198. At the time of this writing, Dr. Smith, a Wesleyan, was a member of the Department of History of Johns Hopkins University.

40. Gary Dorrien, *The Remaking of Evangelical Theology* (Louisville, Ky.: Westminster/John Knox, 1998), 140.

cept of revelation as primarily "information" (which turns revelation into an object that is available for human control); but he also remained troubled about how this "neo-orthodox rejection had led so much of modern theology to retreat from the belief that revelation yields necessary content, leaving theologians "free to pursue enticing doctrines of their own making and preference."[41] There must be forged a middle ground where revelation is real and meaningful without being prejudged and restricted to a human system of thought that is brought to the biblical text more than found in it.

Pinnock had found a relative freedom from an epistemology that is mechanical and rationally restrictive. Biblical texts are not free of the issues of cultural relativism. Biblical revelation is progressive in character, requiring attention to where a text lies in the living organism of Scripture. What something meant originally and what it means authoritatively now may differ, at least at the language and cultural levels. Even so, the "Scripture principle" holds. For Pinnock, the needed nuancing of the inerrancy concept had not violated the heart of what evangelicals had taught all along. Scripture can be trusted to be truthful in all that it intentionally affirms, especially on matters pertaining to salvation. Rather than the "hard rationalist" approach to biblical authority and interpretation, Pinnock had come to appreciate the story and mystery of Scripture, the key role of the Spirit's ministry in original inspiration and current illumination,[42] and the need to listen as well as reason. He now often speaks of "growing as hearers of the Word of God."

The core conviction of Pinnock had become one of certainty of truth arising more from the work of the Spirit through the biblical text than from a tight rationalism rooted in the supposed human theory of biblical errorlessness of the text per se. He nonetheless sees a retaining of the "inerrancy" word as the path of wisdom given circumstances in the evangelical community (more a political than a theological stance). He also sees the need to carefully nuance the implications of this word given the circumstances of the biblical text itself. He recalls that Paul in 1 Corinthians 2:4 speaks about a certainty that does not result from the wisdom of human words. It is born of the Spirit's witness to human hearts. Finally, then, for adequate biblical interpretation, attention must be given to the key place of authentic piety or Spirit reality in Christian life. Such is a historic Wesleyan-Holiness position.

---

41. Pinnock, *Scripture Principle,* 26.

42. For discussion of the coordinate roles of inspiration and illumination as taught by John Wesley, see Barry L. Callen, *God As Loving Grace* (Nappanee, Ind.: Evangel, 1996), 316-23.

THE PIVOTAL PLACE OF PIETY

Clark Pinnock's whole agenda in his early years appears to have been centered in his deep concern to enable conversions to Jesus Christ. As changes came in some of his views, he did not retreat from his central evangelistic concern or rebel and generally reject evangelical Christianity once he had examined it critically. Many others did bolt from their evangelical upbringings and become some of today's liberal theologians. Why not Pinnock? He has suggested that it might have been his temperament, maybe his ability to make changes without throwing out the baby with the bathwater. Perhaps it was "the depth of my conversion which would not be denied, or the fact that I was raised in liberal Christianity and knew how little it has to offer. . . . Not having been a fundamentalist culturally was a definite advantage."[43] Whatever the reasons, he was on a journey of renewal that later he would characterize as finding his way "from the scholastic to the pietistic approach" to Christian believing and living. In fact, he would see postmodern developments in the late 20th century, with their emphasis on the particular and experiential, as favoring an "evangelical pietism."[44]

Previously Pinnock had expressed suspicion about any evangelical focus on "charismatic" renewal that was not thoroughly checked by biblical definitions and restrictions. He tended to denigrate subjective religious experiences as indistinguishable from a case of indigestion unless there was an inerrant Bible to separate the true from the false.[45] There was worry that Baptists, mixing noncreedalism with revivalism, tend to locate truth in the saving encounter with Christ—maybe a key reason why many were "ravaged by liberal and later neo-orthodox theology" and thus became vulnerable to theological compromise. This tendency, he judged, "is even more true of the world-wide Pentecostal movement whose emphasis on religious subjectivity is even more complete."[46] During the 1970s, howev-

---

43. Pinnock in Roennfeldt, *Clark H. Pinnock on Biblical Authority,* xvii.

44. Clark Pinnock, "Evangelical Theologians Facing the Future: Ancient and Future Paradigms," *Wesleyan Theological Journal* 33/2 (Fall 1998): 11. Note the similar thesis of Pinnock's colleague Stanley Grenz (*Theology for the Community of God* [Nashville: Broadman, 1994], x): "I discovered anew the importance of the pietist heritage in which I had been spiritually nurtured. Since 1988, I have been seeking to integrate the rationalistic and pietistic dimensions of the Christian faith. . . . Thus, while theology may be an intellectual search for truth, this search must always be attached to the foundational, identity-producing encounter with God in Christ. And it must issue forth in Christian living."

45. Pinnock, *Set Forth Your Case,* 73.

46. Clark Pinnock, "Baptists and Biblical Authority," *The Journal of the Evangelical Theological Society* 17 (1974): 203.

er, Pinnock came to soften his negative critique of Pentecostalism, but without granting to spiritual experience a position of equal partnership with biblical authority in defining Christian truth. Soon he would freely endorse a more overtly "charismatic" spirituality like John Wesley, who did not separate spiritual experience from the defining roles of the Bible and church tradition, but granted enough significance to religious experience to be accused of being an enthusiast. Concludes Robert Rakestraw about Pinnock: "For a Southern Baptist leader in the conservative South in the 1960s this was a remarkable occurrence, indicating in him a thirst for God and His truth wherever that may lead and regardless of whose theological system it may violate."[47] Pinnock later would report a divine healing in one of his own eyes, commenting: "I know from personal experience that one such incident can be worth a bookshelf of academic apologetics for Christianity (including my own books)."[48]

Now Pinnock published pace-setting articles in *Christianity Today* with the provocative titles "A Truce Proposal for the Tongues Controversy" (Oct. 8, 1971), "The New Pentecostalism: Reflections by a Well-Wisher" (Sept. 14, 1973), and "Opening the Church to the Charismatic Dimension" (June 12, 1981). He argued that Bible-believing evangelicals would have to find a way to get over their rigid rationalism and inordinate fear of emotional excess in order to avoid a quenching of the Spirit. He had no personal case to make for any divisive spiritual elitism or for anyone insisting that a divine gift like "speaking in tongues" is for every believer as a necessary sign of the reception of the Spirit. It was just that he appreciated charismatics as "those evangelicals with a little more spiritual voltage." He was one with them, at least in their newly claiming the "heart dimension" of the faith—what to him was like returning to the best of the older and less scholastically bound evangelicalism (such as is often found in the Wesleyan-Holiness tradition).

Pinnock now has written convincingly and movingly about the coordinate roles of mind and heart (for instance, *Flame of Love,* 1996) so much so that Pentecostal scholar Terry Cross offered this generous judgment in 1998:

> Because of its method and message, *Flame of Love* [Pinnock, 1996] is a vital theological treatise for Pentecostals and charismatics. It is the most needful and yet most provocative book I have read in a

---

47. Robert Rakestraw, "Clark Pinnock," in *Baptist Theologians,* ed. Timothy George and David Dockery (Nashville: Broadman, 1990), 662.

48. Clark Pinnock, "A Revolutionary Promise," review of *Power Evangelism* by John Wimber and Kevin Springer, *Christianity Today* 30 (8 August 1986): 19.

decade. It is needful for the church at large since the doctrine of the Spirit is visibly absent and the urge to consider the work of the Spirit in our lives is also missing; it is needful for the renewal movement since we are lacking good systematic theological reflection on the whole.[49] Regarding biblical inspiration and authority, Pinnock has retained a sturdy grip on the significance of real divine revelation dependably made available in the biblical text for serious seekers. Nonetheless, he has been on a spiritual journey and, as Millard Erickson has observed, "It is apparent that his aim is not to propound a Barthian view of revelation but to revitalize the evangelical doctrine of illumination of Scripture by the Holy Spirit."[50] Clearly, Pinnock has come to value *function* as much or even more than *form* in the area of biblical authority and meaning, looking with disfavor at any excessive intellectualism and abstraction that detracts from concrete Christian discipleship and mission. The important question for him has come to be: How can Scripture be a lamp to our feet and a light to our path, the vital function of Scripture that "has little to do with the perfect errorlessness of non-existent autographs and a great deal to do with the continuing authority of a (slightly) imperfect document"?[51] The Christian agenda should be less a preoccupation with a theory of precise inerrancy and much more with a healthy concern for a spiritual power enabled by the Spirit of God who both speaks through ancient Scripture and illumines the contemporary reader for real life and mission.

What about Robert Price's judgment that Pinnock's own theology is profoundly experience-centered, even experience-generated, making him more of a "liberal" than he himself recognizes—a fear at the heart of any proposed change among evangelicals? Without question Pinnock has been on a spiritual journey that he refuses to separate from his theological work. Also without question has been his persistent intent to retain a good balance between revealed and experienced truth. On the one hand, he openly and repeatedly rejects the theism of most "process" theologians, in part because he judges their concept of God inadequate in the face of the "evangelical experience" and the religious needs of fallen humans.[52] On the other hand, he also rejects the suggestion of Price that, like Schleiermacher, he (Pinnock) has been extrapolating theology from the conscious-

---

49. Terry L. Cross, "A Critical Review of Clark Pinnock's *Flame of Love: A Theology of the Holy Spirit,"* *Journal of Pentecostal Theology* 13 (1998): 4.

50. Millard Erickson, *The Evangelical Left: Encountering Postconservative Evangelical Theology* (Grand Rapids: Baker, 1997), 79.

51. Pinnock, "Evangelicals and Inerrancy," 68.

52. See, e.g., Clark Pinnock, "Between Classical and Process Theism," in *Process Theology*, ed. Ronald Nash (Grand Rapids: Baker, 1987), 313-25.

ness of piety. Responds Pinnock: "Just because a person sees more importance in experience than he used to does not make him/her a liberal!"[53]
Regarding Schleiermacher's use of religious experience as a critical criterion for assessing the teachings of Christian faith, Pinnock argues:

> The use of an outside criterion by which to understand the ke-
> rygma appears to allow the Gospel itself to come under alien con-
> trol. Instead of Scripture being the norm, theology is governed by the
> 19th or 20th century cultural ego instead. . . . We are often attracted
> by the novel theology which comes up with a brilliant fusion be-
> tween the Bible and something contemporary. But this is not what
> God is after. He desires us to be faithful stewards of his Word, who
> do not seek glory in this age, and do not value what man thinks
> above what God has said, but open ourselves to his Spirit, walk by
> faith and not by sight, and proclaim the Gospel with fearlessness and
> undiminished power.[54]

Such perspective offers a constructive solution to the ongoing theological
struggle in evangelicalism. It reflects wisdom long resident in the Wesleyan-Holiness tradition. The Wesleyan scholar Paul Bassett, for instance,
highlighted the classic Protestant insistence on *sola Scriptura* (Scripture
alone), but immediately added the necessary *testimonium Spiritus sancti*
(testimony of the Holy Spirit) if the biblical text is to come alive as an informing means of grace in each new present.[55]

---

53. Clark Pinnock, Letter to Diane De Smidt, Bethel Theological Seminary, 11 November 1988. Also see Pinnock's *Tracking the Maze,* 99 ff., for more on his view of the theological method of Schleiermacher.

54. Clark Pinnock, *Three Keys to Spiritual Renewal* (Minneapolis: Bethany, 1985), 95,
100.

55. Paul Bassett, "The Holiness Movement and the Protestant Principle," *Wesleyan
Theological Journal* 18/1 (Spring 1983): 22.

Clark Pinnock is a retired professor and Christian theologian who has pioneered what often is called an "open theism" approach to understanding the God revealed in the Bible. Assuming as basic for Christians the rule of Scripture within an interpretive context that involves tradition, reason, and experience, Professor Pinnock goes on in this chapter to explore how this approach to the Bible is able to serve up "a sumptuous feast." He insists that, once an interpreter establishes the apparent past meaning of a biblical text, the job is not done. The pressing question is: How does Scripture avoid becoming antiquarian, a dead letter from a distant past, and instead come alive as the Word of God in new and very different contexts? Pinnock insists that responsible interpreters must reflect on the Word of God in relation to contemporary experience and contexts, just as Jesus said (Luke 12:56). The fullest feast of Scripture is not locked in the past; therefore, we present Bible readers must learn to grow as more effective hearers of God's gracious and living Word.

After exploring four factors that provide the rationale for seeking future meanings of ancient biblical texts, Pinnock presents seven brief case studies of key issues in our present time that illustrate possible directions in which God may be leading in our interpretation of Scripture today. He is not suggesting that we understand the Bible in ways that go *beyond* biblical revelation, but in ways that *penetrate more profoundly* into the biblical revelation. The Spirit of God, after all, is always able to cause what has been written to be revealed in new light for the needs of a new time. The Bible remains the primary source of authority for Christians. Thus, the never-ending task is to discern what the Word of God is for this time and place. There is urgent need for caution and prayer in this process, of course. It also is urgent that believers not shy from this task or the very mission of the church will be undermined.

8
THE PAST AND FUTURE MEANINGS
OF BIBLICAL TEXTS[1]
Clark H. Pinnock

In an earlier article recently published in the *Wesleyan Theological Journal*[2] I referred to the need of reform in theological method and explained how to get beyond the rational/propositional method and adopt a larger concept symbolized by what is called the "Wesleyan quadrilateral" or (more precisely) the rule of Scripture within a trilateral hermeneutic of tradition, reason, and experience.[3] In this essay, I want to explore the fecundity of this excellent rule and in particular how it is that Scripture is able to serve up such a sumptuous feast.[4]

THE TEST OF CRUCIALITY

Millard Erickson has remarked: "I think that the issue of contemporizing the biblical message is possibly the single most important issue facing evangelical hermeneutics today."[5] Erickson is referring to what could be called the test of cruciality in theology. He recognizes that, in order to follow Jesus in our generation, we need to have an ear *for* the Word of God even as we listen *to* the Word of God. We need to be able to discern and speak a timely word in modern situations and circumstances. This is not so easy for evangelicals who often have a certain fear of new interpretations because of the trauma of their experience with liberal theology; but God is calling us nonetheless to grow as hearers of the Word of God.[6]

---

1. Appeared originally in the *Wesleyan Theological Journal* 34/2 (Fall 1999). Used by permission.

2. Clark Pinnock, "Evangelical Theologians Facing the Future: Ancient and Future Paradigms," *Wesleyan Theological Journal* 33/2 (Fall 1998): 7-28.

3. W. Stephen Gunter, Scott J. Jones, Ted A. Campbell, Rebekah L. Miles, and Randy L. Maddox, *Wesley and the Quadrilateral: Renewing the Conversation* (Nashville: Abingdon, 1997).

4. For an extended exploration of the thought of Clark H. Pinnock, see Barry L. Callen, *Clark H. Pinnock: Journey Toward Renewal* (Nappanee, Ind.: Evangel, 2000).

5. Millard Erickson, *Evangelical Interpretation: Perspectives on Hermeneutical Issues* (Grand Rapids: Baker, 1993), 56.

6. On this point, see Daniel L. Migliore, *Faith Seeking Understanding: An Introduction to Christian Theology* (Grand Rapids: Eerdmans, 1991), 211, 179. Evangelicals often have

Some readers of the Bible seem content to be antiquarian with regard to its meaning. Once they have established (as they suppose) the past meaning, they think the job is finished, although it is not. We have also to be concerned about the Word of God coming alive in new contexts. Scripture ought not to remain a dead letter, but should constitute a living challenge to people of every present time.

When I speak of future meanings of the biblical text, I refer to the ways in which the Bible addresses us today. Dietrich Bonhoeffer once asked: "Who is Jesus Christ for us today?" To be sure, one could say in reply that Jesus Christ is the same yesterday, today, and forever. Nevertheless, the proclamation of Jesus comes to people in ever new ways through the Spirit, and the present context always represents an opportunity for a fresh hearing of the gospel. Bible reading that is mature requires the readiness on our part to consider fresh interpretations and applications, even if they shake us up. Our Lord says: "Every scribe who has been trained for the kingdom of heaven is like the master of a household who brings out of his treasure what is new and what is old" (Matt. 13:52, NRSV).

Cruciality is an important test of theological faithfulness. It means that we ask not only whether a given interpretation is true to the original meaning but also whether it is pertinent to the present situation or an evasion of what really matters now. Is this reading (we ought to be asking) what God wills or is it not? We must distinguish between the original meaning of the words and the truth toward which they are pointing us. Martin Luther King, Jr., had a good sense of this when he wrote to fellow clergy from a Birmingham jail saying it was time for white churches to stop standing on the sidelines and take a stand against racism. In his discernment of the will of God, King named the truth toward which the Scriptures were pointing at that moment—and time has confirmed the rightness of his conviction. He was sensitive to Jesus' distinction: "You tithe mint, dill, and cummin, and have neglected the weightier matters of the law: justice and mercy and faith" (Matt. 23:23, NRSV).[7]

Having listened to the text and attempted to grasp what it is saying in its own context, we have to let it speak to us. The language of "applying" the

---

difficulty with the call to timeliness and cruciality in the task of biblical interpretation. Fear was palpable in the symposium titled "The Future of Evangelical Theology" by Roger E. Olson and others in *Christianity Today* (9 February 1998, 40-50) when Timothy George expressed the conviction that a theologian who questions tradition and projects a fresh interpretation is a self-seeker, not a servant of the church.

7. See Martin Luther King, Jr., *Why We Can't Wait* (New York: Harper and Row, 1964). On cruciality as a test of theological faithfulness, see Christopher Morse, *Not Every Spirit: A Dogmatics of Christian Disbelief* (Valley Forge, Pa.: Trinity Press International, 1994), 65-66.

text to a situation is too weak an expression to render what has to happen. More than a rational exegetical decision, we must be open to God challenging our very being and impacting our world through the text. Hermeneutics has the responsibility to reflect on the Word of God in relation to contemporary experience and contexts. Not to do so is to invite Jesus' criticism: "You know how to interpret the appearance of earth and sky, but why do you not know how to interpret the present time?" (Luke 12:56, NRSV).[8]

FUTURE MEANINGS

Witnesses to the gospel cannot be content with past meanings in an antiquarian way. In order to be timely in our testimony, we need to be able to access future meanings as well. That is, we need to cultivate an eye and an ear not only for the meanings of human authors in their various historical settings but also for the directions and trajectories that belong to the flow of God's historical redemptive project. While making use of literary and historical scholarship, we are not the prisoners of a textual past but are privileged for the opportunity and accountable for listening for the Word of the Lord and watching for the fulfillment of God's promises that are still outstanding.

The historical study of Scripture can help us hear God's Word, because God has become self-revealed in the particularities of history—in specific persons, places, and events. So naturally we want to know as much about them as we can. It is the same with Jesus Christ, the Word made flesh. Because we respect his humanity and historicity, we want to know as much as we can about his historical career. In the same way, we respect the human reality of the biblical witnesses and pay close attention to how they express themselves. At the same time, we want to avoid being like the scribes of Jesus' day who studied the text carefully but were blind to ways in which its message was being worked out in their own generation. They were scriptural positivists (as it were) in relation to the past meanings of texts. They were not sensitive to the fact that the reason we engage the narratives of Scripture

---

8. Theology at its best always has been contextual and correlational and has sought to be timely. In the Bible itself, the themes are interpreted in different contexts and cultures creating the rich diversity with which we are all familiar. Classic church theologians also sought to make sense of the faith in terms of culture. Augustine leaned on Plotinus and Thomas used Aristotle as material for a synthesis of Christian doctrine. But evangelicals are more often warned about the dangers of giving context a voice instead of the danger of not working contextually. Harvie Conn makes this point in "Contextual Theologies: The Problem of Agendas," *Westminster Theological Journal* 52 (Spring 1990): 51-63, and it is the theme of Stephen B. Evans, *Models of Contextual Theology* (Maryknoll, N.Y.: Orbis Books, 1992), chap. 1.

is not just to refresh our memories about what they said, but also because the history of salvation of which they speak is not finished and we anticipate greater actualizations of the promises of God.

Tom Wright offers a helpful analogy. Suppose we discovered a Shakespearean play (he suggests) whose fifth act has been lost. The four extant acts contain a wealth of characterizations and dynamics of plot and so the work cries out to be performed. But what should we do? Wright suggests that we should not try to write a fifth act in a detached, scholarly way but rather commit the text to experienced actors who, having immersed themselves in the four extant acts, would work out what the fifth act might reasonably be like had the Bard himself written it. It would be based, as it were, on the authority of the first four acts, and the drama would be brought to completion in an appropriate manner. Living as we do after Acts 28, it is our responsibility to fill in details of our faith and practice out of a patient watching and waiting on God.[9]

The event of Jesus Christ, which is the centerpiece of Scripture, cannot fully be understood apart from the future that it has put into motion. It is not a story to be read with nostalgia for Bible times. To read it properly, we have to go beyond the historical descriptions and consider the extension of the story into the present and future. We need to read the Bible both historically and with prayerful sensitivity to the directions in which it is moving us. Migliore comments: "We must ask of Scripture, not only what past it calls us to remember, but what promises it wants us to claim and what future it wants us to pray and work for."[10]

The full significance of the Christian message was not actualized in the life of the early church. The need for Christians, individually and corporately, to grow as hearers of the word of God remains, because interpretation is an unfinished task. Even if revelation were mainly a deposit of propositions essential to faith (which it is not), we would still be in the position of having more to learn about God and God's reign than we presently know. Our best knowledge, as Paul says, is like seeing things in a mirror dimly. At the same time, our knowledge, limited though it is, anticipates a fuller understanding toward which God is leading. Theology is therefore a venture in hope and always capable of enrichment and reform.[11]

9. N. T. Wright, *The New Testament and the People of God* (Minneapolis: Fortress, 1992), 140-43.

10. Migliore, *Faith Seeking Understanding,* 51.

11. Wolfhart Pannenberg, *Systematic Theology,* 3 vols. (Grand Rapids: Eerdmans, 1991), 1:16, 55-58.

The meaning of the Bible is not static and locked up in the past but is something living and active. There is untapped potentiality of meaning in these texts, a surplus that can be actualized by succeeding generations of disciples in their various situations. The Bible is more than a collection of facts requiring analysis; it has a potentiality of meaning that is waiting to break forth as it engages real-life situations by the Spirit.

THE UNDERLYING RATIONALE

The existence of this potentiality of meaning that is waiting in the biblical text to be realized is due to a number of factors. Let me enumerate the ones that come to my mind most forcibly. No doubt there are others.

Factor One. One factor leading to a potentiality of meaning in the biblical text is the nature of divine revelation itself as seen in the gracious self-disclosure of God in the history of Israel and in the life and ministry of Jesus. Revelation refers first of all, not to the Bible, but to God's activities in history where the purposes of God are disclosed for all to see. Revelation, while including rational and propositional dimensions, goes beyond these by being a form of interpersonal communication that cannot be totally pinned down conceptually. Such revelation, therefore, is always open to deeper penetration by Spirit-led interpreters.

This openness may be glimpsed in the way in which Old Testament texts are said to be fulfilled in the New Testament, often in surprising ways that go beyond the terms of the original propositions. This phenomenon shows God moving forward and expanding the scope of divine promises by a pattern of divine responses to new situations. These responses sometimes are unprecedented and give humankind more than was actually promised in the beginning. Was it not the scriptural literalists in Jesus' day who, because they only had room for past meanings, could not bring themselves to recognize who Jesus was? They refused to accept the central fact that God was (is) free and sovereign in the making of divine decisions about how God's kingdom project should be worked out. They had their own restrictive view of God's freedom that ruled out God's doing new things that had not been specifically spelled out in advance.[12]

---

12. On the liberty taken in the fulfillment of Old Testament promises, see Stephen Travis, *I Believe in the Second Coming of Christ* (Grand Rapids: Eerdmans, 1982), 135-43, and James DeYoung and Sarah Hurty, *Beyond the Obvious: Discover the Deeper Meaning of Scripture* (Gresham, Oreg.: Vision House, 1995). Also see Clark Pinnock, *Flame of Love* (Downers Grove, Ill.: InterVarsity Press, 1996), 223-27.

Factor Two. A second factor that fosters the retrieval of future meanings arises from the nature of Scripture as a grand metanarrative. Apart from the Bible, we would know little of the good news of God's revelation in history through Jesus Christ. Were Scripture to be ignored, the availability of God's revelation would be diminished drastically. Scripture gives us access to Jesus, the Word of God, and the light that shone on his face gets transmitted to us through the prism of the biblical witnesses. The central authority of the Bible resides in its witness to God's world-transforming revelational activity culminating in Christ, and it is the Bible's character as story that opens the text to future meanings.

Often people think of the Bible in a Koran-like way, as a book of rules to obey and doctrines to believe. This intellectualistic approach is a legacy of the Enlightenment and helps explain why many Christians cannot get very far with the idea of future meanings. But if story is the comprehensive category that best describes the Bible, and if it is the book that tells the story of God's care for the world, stretching from creation to new creation, then its basic authority lies in the narrative and upholding its authority involves a believer entering, inhabiting, and becoming part of the story. In that case, something more than intellectual assent is required because, like all great stories, the Bible draws us into its own world, engages us imaginatively, and calls us to grow up into Christ from within it.[13]

In terms of interpretation, the story character of the Bible gives it a flexibility with regard to future meanings that the Bible, viewed as a collection of abstract truths, would not. Consider the way in which the Koran binds people to ancient Arab culture and hinders the ability of Islam to contextualize itself in the modern world. The results have been cataclysmic for these nations. By way of contrast, the nature of the Bible as story makes it flexible when it comes to the adapting of its message to changing circumstances and to yielding future meanings. The Bible encourages us to believe, not so much in the Bible itself as in the living God rendered by the Bible's story. In a variety of ways, the Bible brings us into a relationship with God in Jesus Christ and thus with others and with the whole creation. The Bible witnesses to God's liberating activity in Jesus in whom God is identified and by which we are led into new life.

Nicholas Wolterstorff uses speech-act theory to illuminate how God

---

13. Alister McGrath calls our attention to the centrality of story in the Bible and the evangelical neglect of it. See his *A Passion for Truth: The Intellectual Coherence of Evangelicalism* (Downers Grove, Ill.: InterVarsity Press, 1996), 105-16. Along the same lines, see Richard Bauckham, "Scripture and Authority," *Transformation* 15 (April 1988): 5-11. Neglecting this results in a barren, rationalistic type of hermeneutics.

speaks to us through the Bible. Classic texts (he rightly says) not only *say* something but also *do* something. They do not just communicate content but through the Spirit propel readers into a confrontation with God. They transform readers by getting in touch with the depth of our very selves. Through Word and Spirit, the revelatory activity of God is kept open and the process of ever-fresh interpretation goes on.[14]

Factor Three. A third factor that keeps the meaning of the text open for the future is (paradoxically) its ambiguity and variety. Texts normally have several possible interpretations that require us to discern how to take them. For example, does Paul teach double predestination in Romans chapter 9 or not? John Piper says yes and John Ziesler says no. Both cannot be right, but the ambiguity takes us back to root metaphors, to systematic considerations, and to issues of discernment. It forces one to ask why we read texts the way we do and to become more self-conscious about issues of our social location and other matters. Often texts open up different paths that could be followed and the resulting communal reflection can be rich and beneficial.

Diversity can have the same kind of effect on us.[15] Different answers are given in the Bible to similar sorts of issues because the text itself has been contextualized in different ways. This leaves room for us to decide about future meanings and applications. Sometimes there are even trajectories developing within the Bible, as Richard N. Longenecker has shown. Using Galatians 3:28, he reveals how gospel principles are applied to specific situations and how texts can be viewed as signposts at the beginning of a trajectory, indicating paths to be followed by future disciples. God's project is an ongoing historical project; therefore, texts may not only set a standard but *also* indicate a direction in which we ought to be moving.[16]

Factor Four. A fourth factor that opens up future meanings is the illuminating work of the Holy Spirit. Interpretation is dynamic because the Spirit is integral to our theological method. Having inspired the text and guided the people of God to a canon, the Spirit continues to open up its

---

14. See Nicholas Wolterstorff, *Divine Discourse: Philosophical Reflections on the Claim That God Speaks* (Cambridge: Cambridge University Press, 1995).

15. Consider the diversity discussed by John Goldingay, *Theological Diversity and the Authority of the Old Testament* (Grand Rapids: Eerdmans, 1987), and by James D. G. Dunn, *Unity and Diversity in the New Testament* (London: SCM, 1977).

16. Richard N. Longenecker, *New Testament Social Ethics for Today* (Grand Rapids: Eerdmans, 1984), 14-15, 26-28.

meaning to us. Jesus gave the Spirit so that there might be a fuller understanding of his life and ministry by disciples in the future. We look to the Spirit for unfolding meaning because of the divine presence with and alongside the text, making it a truly living word. The Spirit, at work in the contexts of our lives, helps us grasp the divine intent of Scripture for our time. What is given is not the communication of new information but a deeper understanding of the truth that is there. Deeper understandings can be surprising, as illustrated in Acts 15 where what the Spirit was evidently doing in the world (pouring the Spirit out on the gentiles) showed the leaders how to interpret the Old Testament text in a new way. Because Scripture is spiritual, it has to be spiritually appraised (cf. 1 Cor. 2:13*b*).[17]

Donald Bloesch writes:

> It is commonly thought in lay circles more than in clerical that the surface meaning of the biblical text is sufficient and that this meaning is available to any searching person. But more often than not what first appears to be the sense of the text may not at all be the meaning that the Spirit of God is trying to impress on us through this text. It is not enough to know the words of the text: we must know the plenitude of meaning that these words carry for the community of faith at that time and for our time.[18]

There are valid concerns surrounding the idea of illumination, of course. We all fear uncontrolled subjectivity, which might simply displace biblical authority. In the evangelical family, the scholastic tendency would be more alarmed about this happening than the pietistic tendency because the latter makes more room for experience. However, there is another danger to be aware of and that is the danger of placing a fence around the Word and excluding the Spirit from the work of interpretation. After all, God gives gifts of wisdom and knowledge to help the community with its interpretation, and we must respect these gifts alongside the exegetes. The relative and oft-noted silence about illumination among evangelicals is suggestive of a certain rationalism. We have to learn to trust the Spirit-empowered Word more and not be so afraid of it.[19]

---

17. Richard B. Hays, *Echoes of Scripture in Paul* (New Haven, Conn.: Yale University Press, 1989), chap. 5. Roger Stronstad discusses Spirit-oriented pentecostal hermeneutics in his *Spirit, Scripture, and Theology: A Pentecostal Perspective* (Baguio City, Philippines: Asia-Pacific Theological Seminary Press, 1995).

18. Donald G. Bloesch, *Holy Scripture: Revelation, Inspiration, and Interpretation* (Downers Grove, Ill.: InterVarsity Press, 1994), 172. Bloesch speaks out boldly but does not provide specific examples of how his thesis works out.

19. Erickson opposes the hermeneutical rationalism he sees in Kaiser and Fuller (chaps. 1—2). Others agree, including: DeYoung and Hurty, *Beyond the Obvious*, chap. 6; Bloesch,

Illumination, even when room is made for it in evangelical interpretation, is often narrowly conceived in terms of issues of individual piety. In J. I. Packer (for example), illumination mainly serves to confirm truths of Scripture to the individual (elect) believer concerning his or her own salvation and is not thought of as applying to the larger and urgent issues of mission in our day. In contrast, the Second Vatican Council of the Roman Catholic Church sets a better example for us in "Gaudium et Spes" where it does address challenges that confront the church's mission today.[20]

GROWING AS HEARERS

The faith community needs to grow and mature as hearers of the Word of God, not approaching the Bible as a magical answer book but as an inspired witness to the love of God and the reign of God breaking through. The authority of the Bible is important, but almost equally important is the decision about the kind of text it is and how to use it. It does not generally operate on a rationalistic plane but in the context of relationship and lived experience. Bloesch speaks of Scripture as a sacrament of our encounter with God in the present day. I would add that we need to listen to Scripture, not as isolated individuals but in communities, allowing ourselves to be open to the readings of Scripture by other churches in contexts different from our own. Growing as hearers is essential because the truth of profound matters is not easily grasped and all implications are not immediately apparent. It is important to be on watch for the ways in which the Spirit is leading God's people into deeper understanding and fuller obedience. A better comprehension is always possible of a revelation that is unsurpassable and inexhaustible.[21]

History presents us with examples of future meanings that appear to

---

Holy Scripture: Revelation, Inspiration, and Interpretation, chap. 6; and Clark H. Pinnock, "The Work of the Holy Spirit in Hermeneutics," *Journal of Pentecostal Theology* 2 (1993): 3-23; idem, "The Role of the Spirit in Interpretation," *Journal of the Evangelical Theological Society* 36 (1993): 491-97; and idem, *The Scripture Principle* (San Francisco: Harper and Row, 1984), chap. 9.

20. See Samuel Koranteng-Pipim, *The Role of the Holy Spirit in Biblical Interpretation: A Study in the Writings of James I. Packer* (Ph.D. diss., Andrews University, 1998). One of the only modern social challenges that Erickson comments on is the consumption of alcoholic beverages. Ironically, he had to admit that he arrived at his position from extrabiblical influences, not from Scripture (*Evangelical Interpretation,* 75-76).

21. Postliberal theology and the Yale School are strong on the importance of a communal reading of the text and a corporate discernment of its meaning. In agreement is Simon Chan, *Spiritual Theology: A Systematic Study of the Christian Life* (Downers Grove, Ill.: InterVarsity Press, 1998), 208-10.

have been successful. Here are two examples. First, in the history of doctrine, classical Christians accept that the Spirit helped the church in the early centuries to read the biblical narrative in a trinitarian way. The community was led to see that this was the direction in which the biblical narrative was tending, and there was a growing realization of what the gospel was indicating. They discerned that Father, Son, and Spirit constituted the identifying description of God and the key to an understanding of the Bible as a whole. This doctrine of the Trinity became the conceptual framework for interpreting the whole metanarrative. The fondness for trinitarian doctrine today among classical theologians reflects the fact that the model represents a revelation-based understanding of God uncorrupted by philosophical presuppositions.[22]

Second, on an ethical matter, Christians agree that in the case of slavery the full significance of the Christian message was not completely grasped by earlier generations, but only subsequently in terms of the abolition of slavery. The direction of revelation was discerned only after many centuries and the implication recognized. Interestingly, it was those (like Hodge) who read the Bible like a rule book who argued in favor of slavery, while those who read it as the story of human liberation saw the truth of the matter more readily. The truth about slavery was inherent in the gospel from day one, but became plain at a later time, thanks to the providence of God and the illumination of the Spirit.[23]

Harder to discern are issues in our own day that are still being debated and where there is the need of further illumination. Being finite, we have difficulty understanding exactly how and where God is working in our world. Sometimes we think we know, but others caution by telling us that it is not the way they see it. There is no way to avoid risks in interpretation, and modesty is essential all round. The examples that I name inevitably reflect my own situated beliefs about how God is leading and need to be considered on a broader basis than the individual. Certainly, for a new item to enter tradition, it would have to be more than an intuition and a passing fashion. A solid scriptural basis would have to be indicated and a widespread consensus in the churches secured. These two criteria are especially good indicators that the mind of Christ is being revealed and rightly perceived.

---

22. This is the theme of Jean-Luc Marion, *God Without Being: Hors Texte* (Chicago: University of Chicago Press, 1991), and McGrath, *Passion for Truth,* 112-13.

23. Longenecker, *New Testament Social Ethics for Today,* chap. 4, and Willard M. Swartley, *Slavery, Sabbath, War, and Women* (Scottsdale, Pa.: Herald, 1983), chap. 1.

CURRENT OPENINGS OF GOD'S WORD

To provoke discussion and to share my own insights, let me indicate a few items where I discern an opening up of the Word of God in timely ways today. They are not necessarily the best or only examples of such timely interpretations, but they represent what is possible by way of fresh and fruitful interpretations of our dynamic rule, the biblical base in concert with the Spirit's ongoing ministry of illumination.

1. Universal Salvific Will of God. First, there is a strong tendency nowadays to rank the universal salvific will of God higher on the hierarchy of theological truth than was formerly the case. This biblical opening arises not from mere sentimentality, but from a better grasp of God's vast generosity. One sees this illumination in Vatican Council II, in mainline Protestantism, and among the many evangelicals who seek some form of a wider hope for lost humanity. Such thinking is on the rise and reflects less restrictive modes of biblical interpretation. It has the makings of a fresh interpretation that is gaining in strength.[24]

2. Salvation Includes Justice Issues. Second, it has become clearer to more Christians than it was before that the gospel of Christ necessarily relates to issues of social justice in the world as well as to issues that affect individuals and churches. Thus a new theological emphasis (not unprecedented) pioneered by Latin American theologians has arisen that concentrates more on the practical and social implications of theology. There is a widespread agreement now that theology must address the human struggle for justice and freedom. More than merely a humanitarian impulse, it arises from the recognition of Christ's solidarity with the poor and from the social dimensions of sin and salvation. It represents a better reading of the Bible and an enrichment of traditional theology (whatever mistakes have been made in pursuing it). At the same time, the particular model of liberation developed by the Latin Americans is not a universal norm and has not been an especially impressive option for many evangelicals. Nonetheless, the fundamental thrust and direction of political theology is not going to go into recession.[25] There is Spirit illumination in process here.

---

24. See Francis A. Sullivan, *Salvation Outside the Church? Tracing the History of the Catholic Response* (New York: Paulist, 1992), 199-204, and Richard H. Drummond, *Toward a New Age in Christian Theology* (Maryknoll, N.Y.: Orbis Books, 1985). John Sanders documents the rise of wider-hope thinking among evangelicals in his *No Other Name: An Investigation into the Destiny of the Unevangelized* (Grand Rapids: Eerdmans, 1992).

25. Simon Chan, for example, does not see the relevance of the Latin model for his Asian setting, although he agrees with the basic principle (Chan, *Spiritual Theology*, 32).

3. Concern for the Nonhuman Creation. Third, the relevance of the Bible for ecological concerns also is more widely recognized now than formerly. More and more Bible-oriented Christians are coming to see that the nonhuman creation is not just something to be exploited and that the gospel is concerned about nature as well as salvation. The spirit of St. Francis of Assisi, which was formerly the exception, is now becoming the rule. We are now seeing that the natural world is more than a stage for the divine-human drama and that the value of nonhuman creatures is intrinsic to human welfare, not merely instrumental. Modern pressure on the ecological web of life has challenged anthropocentric interpretations of the Bible and alerted us to view the creation from a more inclusive point of view.[26]

4. The Gifts and Callings of Women. Fourth, from the experience of the Sunday School and the foreign missionary movements as well as from trends in culture, God seems to be leading us into a clearer recognition and stronger support for the gifts and callings of women.[27] Although debates remain over female ordination in some church settings, the conviction is growing that both men and women share in ministry as they share in baptism. More and more serious Bible readers are asking why people would be excluded from certain ministries on the basis of gender when God calls all believers to minister and gifts them all. Although it will likely be a point of tension for some time to come, the impulse to include women in the full range of Christian ministries is likely to persist and even prevail. I think it is clear that the Spirit is pointing us to those aspects of the biblical tradition that point in the direction of affirming and not quenching the Spirit's liberating activities.[28] At the same time, one must remember that feminism as such is a product of Western liberalism and not a universal value. Any application of it in other parts of the world (e.g., Asia) will have to take account of the nature of those societies.[29]

---

26. See H. Paul Santmire, *The Travail of Nature: The Ambiguous Ecological Promise of Christian Theology* (Philadelphia: Fortress, 1985), and Jürgen Moltmann, "Ecology of the Creative Spirit," in *The Source of Life: The Holy Spirit and the Theology of Life* (Minneapolis: Fortress, 1997), 111-24.

27. I appreciate that this point, perhaps obvious to many, was made by Roger Nicole in Alvera Mickelsen, ed., *Women, Authority, and the Bible* (Downers Grove, Ill.: InterVarsity Press, 1986), 47. Nicole is a staunch paleo-Calvinist and must have taken some criticism for his observation.

28. Longenecker, *New Testament Social Ethics for Today,* chap. 5; and Swartley, *Slavery, Sabbath, War, and Women,* chap. 4.

29. Compare Chan, *Spiritual Theology,* 31.

5. Openness to the Full Range of Spiritual Gifts. Fifth, the rediscovery of the power of Pentecost in the 20th century has led to a widespread correction of the cessationist traditions of biblical interpretation. Openness to the full range of spiritual gifts as inherent in the kingdom proclamation of Jesus is now characteristic of the thinking of a large percentage of Christian people, even outside Pentecostal and charismatic circles. Again, the material was already there in the Bible but had been pushed to the side. Now the balance of interpretation has noticeably shifted to support of the proposition that charismatic experience is not a fad but intrinsic to Christian existence.[30]

6. Relational Interpretation of the Doctrine of God. Sixth, the interpretation of the doctrine of God in the Scriptures is moving in a relational direction away from the unrelational and/or deterministic motifs characteristic of Augustinianism, Thomism, and Calvinism. There is developing a more relational model of a God who sympathizes with and responds to what happens in the world. The pressure toward a more relational model comes from many quarters—from Orthodoxy, from Wesleyan-Arminian traditions, from Hendrikus Berkhof's and Karl Barth's neo-Reformed thinking, and from the social trinitarians who ground the model in a trinitarian relational ontology. It is influenced also, of course, by the modern ethos that favors more dynamic metaphysical interpretations. This has moved Thomists like Norris Clarke and Calvinists like Alvin Plantinga to question the nonrelational thinking of their own traditions. At the same time, opposition to this trend is strong in the evangelical coalition that for so long has been dominated by the paleo-Reformed impulse and can be fierce in its critique. In the newly formed Alliance of Confessing Evangelicals with its Cambridge Declaration, one sees a vigorous campaign to defend the causal categories of the conservative Reformation.[31]

7. Permanent Election of the Children of Israel. Seventh, we are seeing a rejection of the supersessionist account of the church in relation to Israel. Supersessionism refers to the theory that the church displaced and replaced Israel as the people of God. In part the shift stems from

---

30. Jon Ruthven lays out the exegetical issues forcefully in *On the Cessation of the Charismata: The Protestant Polemic on Postbiblical Miracles* (Sheffield: Sheffield Academic Press, 1993).

31. John Sanders' recent book will play a central role in this struggle: *The God Who Risks: A Theology of Providence* (Downers Grove, Ill.: InterVarsity Press, 1998). The book is of high quality, and it will be interesting to see whether the critics will be able to answer it or have to resort to questionable tactics to counter it.

events like the Holocaust and the return of the Jewish people to the land God gave to Abraham. But it also arises out of a fresh reading of Paul in Romans: "As regards the gospel they are enemies of God for your sake; but as regards election they are beloved, for the sake of their ancestors; for the gifts and the calling of God are irrevocable" (11:28-29, NRSV). Paul taught the permanent election of the children of Israel who are and remain God's "treasured possession" (Deut. 7:6). Christian theology has no right to nullify the promises of God. Israel is the root, and we Gentiles are and remain branches. There may be disagreement about what this affirmation entails and what it will mean for our Christian faith and practice. But it must surely mean at least that God loves the people Israel, even though they have rejected the gospel of their Christ. Dispensationalism gets criticized by almost everyone, so it might be opportune to say that it never endorsed supersessionism, although most of its critics did.[32]

Here then are a few contemporary interpretations that may illustrate possible directions in which God is leading us in our interpretation of Scripture today. One cannot always be certain what the timely word of the Lord is, but these are surely the kinds of issues on which growth is taking place currently in our hearing of God's Word.

CONCLUSION

When involved in mission as it always ought to be, the Christian community needs to be able to understand its message in fresh contexts, not in ways that go *beyond* biblical revelation but in ways that penetrate the biblical revelation more profoundly. It is not so much new information that we look for as it is a fresh understanding of God's Word in our new circumstances. The biblical text is quantitatively complete (that is, not requiring additions), but it can always be more deeply pondered and grasped in fuller ways. The Spirit is always able to cause what has been written to be revealed in a new light. Of course, there are always errors to overcome in interpretation and always new directions to be attempted for the sake of effective mission. Although the faith is delivered once and for all time, the church has not grasped its significance completely—nor will she until the end of time. We are on an interpretative road, not yet at the end of the journey, and we pray to the Lord for an ever more fruitful discernment of God's meaning for us and our times.

---

32. See R. Kendall Soulen, *The God of Israel and Christian Theology* (Minneapolis: Augsburg Fortress, 1996), and Bruce D. Marshall, "Christ and the Cultures: the Jewish People and Christian Theology," in *The Cambridge Companion to Christian Doctrine*, ed. Colin E. Gunton (Cambridge: Cambridge University Press, 1997), 81-100.

To use the language of theological hermeneutics, I am saying that it is fruitful in terms of fresh insight to correlate Holy Scripture with contextual factors so long as care is taken to avoid letting the context determine and not merely condition the theological reflection. Scripture should be brought into conversation with all aspects of the global situation, but in such a way that the Bible is accorded priority over contextual factors. The hermeneutical task is not a matter of reducing the meaning of Scripture to what readers want to hear but is an exercise in discerning what the Word of the Lord is for this time and place. Bloesch's distinction between correlation and confrontation is important. He is very sensitive to the fact that the gospel often finds itself in conflict with culture and at variance with worldly wisdom. Thus, for example, it would not be possible to accept an inspirational Christology or a gay theology just because of the pressures of pluralism and gender in the culture that is calling for it. The need for watchfulness and prayer in discerning the mind of Christ and the future meaning of biblical texts is very great.[33]

---

33. Donald G. Bloesch, *A Theology of Word and Spirit: Authority and Method in Theology* (Downers Grove, Ill.: InterVarsity Press, 1992), chap. 9.

Professor Thompson originally offered this chapter as a sequel to his earlier one within this collection. There he suggests, based on both practice and theory, that written texts lend themselves to a range of possible interpretations due to the reader's (or readers') role in making judgments and conclusions throughout the reading process. Linked to the role of the reader is the active role of the Holy Spirit in that process, as believers read and engage with the biblical texts as Scripture. While many persons affirm that the author's approach clarifies what one often encounters in the actual practice of believers, other persons critique the approach as opening scriptural interpretation to the unlimited subjectivity of each reader.

What the author offers here is both an elaboration and a response. On the one hand, this chapter offers an elaboration of the idea that there may be multiple readings or interpretations of biblical texts. On the other hand, this also offers a response to the appropriate critique and concern that biblical interpretation cannot merely be handed over to the subjectivity of whatever reader happens to be reading at the time. Such a response does not minimize the importance of personal Bible reading but endorses such practices. What is central to this response is its affirmation of the role of the church, both in shaping those private readings and in providing the worshiping and responsive context in which readings are clarified, validated, and embodied faithfully through holy living.

9

COMMUNITY IN CONVERSATION: MULTIPLE READINGS OF SCRIPTURE AND A WESLEYAN UNDERSTANDING OF THE CHURCH[1]

Richard P. Thompson

━━━━━━━━━━━━━◆━━━━━━━━━━━━━

In the movie *Dead Poets Society,* one scene focuses on an English class at Welton Academy, a class that was beginning the study of poetry. The teacher, John Keating (played by Robin Williams), asks a student to read part of the introduction to his textbook, written by J. Evans Pritchard. The student begins to read the opening of that introduction, which suggests that poetry is appreciated and understood if the students evaluate the artistry and importance of the poetic works before them. The teacher so vehemently rejects this mechanical approach to the study of poetry that he instructs the students to "rip" out the entire introduction from their books. "Be gone, J. Evans Pritchard, Ph.D.!" His reason? Poetry is not about learning rhyme and meter. One may ask: "How, then, *should* one study poetry?" The teacher's response points the students in a different direction: "The poem goes on, and you may contribute a verse. What will your verse be?"

The open-endedness of this approach to the study of poetry that this scene presents is similar to certain contemporary approaches to Scripture but often differs from traditional approaches to biblical study. Most of us, in our educational pursuits, were instructed that, if we used the appropriate exegetical picks and shovels and mining pans, we could eventually find in the biblical text the hidden, exegetical gold nugget—the meaning of that text—that could somehow be transferred to our contemporary life situations. We rightly noted that the text itself was written in a different time and place, to a different audience, and by an author who had ideas far different from ours. But in our noble attempts to mine truth and meaning from those texts, we seldom thought about examining the role of the ones whose hands and faces and clothes were caked with the soil of those broken texts. In our pursuit of the text's one and only meaning, we did not consider (or were unwilling to admit) that we ourselves determined in

---

1. Appeared originally in the *Wesleyan Theological Journal* 35/1 (Spring 2000). Used by permission.

varying degrees what we would and would not find. We failed to realize that our decisions to dig with those exegetical picks and shovels and even bulldozers in the search for hidden treasure often destroyed a biblical-textual landscape that itself was valuable and full of life in its wholeness and beauty. Could it be that, in some sense, beauty *is* in the eye of the beholder? Could it be that our attempts to find, *even in the biblical text,* objective meaning apart from ourselves yield results that inevitably have our fingerprints all over them? In other words, the notion that a biblical text has only one possible objective meaning is flawed since the interpreter has shaped and contributed to every step of the pursuit.[2]

This challenging proposition need not be seen as a negation of the Bible and its role within the church.[3] Positive change often occurs when challenges are most threatening. And it may well be that postmodernism has given us just that kind of challenge, thereby forcing us to reassess our readings of Scripture and our hermeneutical processes. I proposed recently that literary-critical approaches to Scripture, particularly those approaches that account for the roles of *both* the text *and* the reader (i.e., approaches that one may characterize as postmodern ones), may assist us in the Wesleyan tradition as we come to these texts *as* Scripture.[4] I suggested that such approaches are compatible with John Wesley's concerns for reading the Bible—that is, the divine-human soteriological encounter of the prayerful reader with a text that itself is the product of a divine-human encounter between God and the author. I also contended that: (1) the biblical texts alone can*not* control such encounters or readings since those texts were not and are not containers of or vehicles for meaning, and (2) the reader still must account for the textual elements and clues (including historical matters) in a way that brings consistency to that reading—textual features that limit a reader's subjective contributions. Thus, constraining a biblical text to one reading or interpretation may not only squelch the possibilities inherent in the reading process but also silence the Spirit and snatch the life out of Scripture.

Thus, I propose here to explore further the possibility of multiple readings of Scripture within the context of churches in the Wesleyan tradi-

---

2. Cf. Vernon K. Robbins, *The Tapestry of Early Christian Discourse: Rhetoric, Society, and Ideology* (New York: Routledge, 1996), 215.

3. See Edgar V. McKnight, *Postmodern Use of the Bible: The Emergence of Reader-Oriented Criticism* (Nashville: Abingdon, 1988), 61, who suggests that this postmodern challenge "should not disable us, but it should make us humble."

4. Richard P. Thompson, "Inspired Imagination: John Wesley's Concept of Inspiration and Literary-Critical Approaches to Scripture," *Wesleyan Theological Journal* 34/1 (1999): 151-76 and reprinted in this volume.

tion. What is modestly offered for consideration is the hypothesis that the possibility of multiple readings of Scripture creates, not a climate of uncontrollable subjectivism (i.e., everyone has his or her own personal reading or interpretation), but a potential reemergence of Scripture as the *living* Word for the church. In a beginning step toward fulfilling this stated proposal, what follows is in two basic parts. First, the possibility of multiple readings of Scripture is explored more directly. Second, the church is considered from a Wesleyan perspective as the context (1) in which these multiple readings of Scripture occur, (2) where such readings are discussed and amended, and (3) from which these readings evoke corporate responses of faithful, holy living.

MULTIPLE READINGS OF SCRIPTURE

As has been mentioned above, recent developments in biblical studies have affirmed that one's attempt to understand or interpret a given scriptural text *always* involves the contributions of the reader.[5] That is, as Rudolf Bultmann argued over 40 years ago in his classic essay, exegesis without presuppositions is *not* possible.[6] While historical criticism has successfully identified the historical condition of the biblical text, such approaches have generally failed to recognize the historical condition of the interpreter.[7] The biblical critic has given concentrated attention to the language and historicity of the text but typically has given little attention to the immediate world from which interpretative and exegetical decisions are made. To be sure, historical criticism has offered substantial assistance in understanding the historical dimensions of the biblical texts. But even these approaches have their own presuppositions that are not part of the biblical text itself.[8] In other words, as helpful and necessary as these approaches are, they cannot claim to focus objectively only on "what the text meant."[9]

The task of reading and interpreting Scripture cannot focus merely

---

5. "Reader" in this paper refers to the one who encounters the text in the reading process. This term will be used synonymously with "interpreter" since both designations refer to persons seeking to interpret the given text.

6. Rudolf Bultmann, "Is Exegesis Without Presuppositions Possible?" in *New Testament and Mythology and Other Basic Writings,* ed. Schubert M. Ogden (Philadelphia: Fortress, 1984), 145-53.

7 Cf. Anthony C. Thiselton, *The Two Horizons: New Testament Hermeneutics and Philosophical Description* (Grand Rapids: Eerdmans, 1980), 11.

8. See Carl Braaten, "Jesus and the Church: An Essay on Ecclesial Hermeneutics," *Ex Auditu* 10 (1994): 64-65.

9. See Krister Stendahl, "Contemporary Biblical Theology," *Interpreter's Dictionary of the Bible,* 1:418-32.

on the biblical text. As attractive as a text-centered approach may sound, the reader takes an active role in the reading and interpretation of a given text.[10] The text, to be sure, directs the reader in making certain connections and judgments during the process.[11] For instance, a narrative text offers to the reader an imaginary world that is presented creatively so that the reader may imagine that world as though being a part of it. It is not enough to say that something happened. Rather, the text presents events and characters in certain ways so that the reader's attention is directed potentially to something of importance within the narrative.[12] Such textual elements and descriptions naturally have certain expectations of the reader embedded within the text—expectations that may not be familiar to the reader but for which that person must account. Nonetheless, the reader does not have a passive role in reading and interpreting Scripture, but contributes to the process by (1) making judgments along the way, (2) building consistency with what *is* and *is not* stated,[13] and (3) revising such conclusions as necessary after subsequently encountering new textual elements in the progressive reading through the text. Such interpretative activities, whether or not conscious, bring the biblical text to life, and the text remains lifeless and meaningless without them. Thus, as Wolfgang Iser suggests, the convergence of the text and reader "brings the literary work into existence."[14] Meaning, then, is not found within the text itself but in this convergence, in which the imaginative activity of the reader seeks to create coherence while reading progressively through the imaginatively composed biblical text.[15]

What must be stressed here is that neither the biblical text nor the

---

10. See Robbins, *Tapestry of Early Christian Discourse,* 19: "Texts exist in the world, and we exist in the world. Interpreters who talk about reading texts from the perspective of a text's own internal mirrors actually bring their own view of social reality to the language in the text."

11. Wolfgang Iser, *The Implied Reader: Patterns of Communication in Prose Fiction from Bunyan to Beckett* (Baltimore: Johns Hopkins University Press, 1974), 274, 288. Cf. Wolfgang Iser, *The Act of Reading: A Theory of Aesthetic Response* (Baltimore: Johns Hopkins University Press, 1978), 112.

12. Although the text may attract the attention of the reader with certain descriptions, wording, clues, and so forth, it cannot ensure that the reader sees what that text emphasizes. For example, you can use your hands to move another person's head to see something in the sky, but that does not mean the other person will see what you are trying to point out.

13. Iser, *Act of Reading,* 163-231; and Meir Sternberg, *The Poetics of Biblical Narrative: Ideological Literature and the Drama of Reading,* Indiana Studies in Biblical Literature (Bloomington, Ind.: Indiana University Press, 1985), 235-37.

14. Iser, *Implied Reader,* 275.

15. See Thompson, "Inspired Imagination," 167-68.

reader controls this reading and interpretative process. On the one hand, the text guides, invites, and coaxes the reader along with a variety of literary elements.[16] The reader must account for the text and its elements *as written* (including historical matters), but there is no assurance that a reader will make all the necessary connections or recognize the significance of every part. On the other hand, no text provides *all* the clues and information necessary to build a consistent reading anyway, and these textual indeterminacies stimulate the reader's imaginative activity in building a consistent reading.[17] Since both the text and the reader contribute to the text's reading, one must attribute variations in reading to the readers themselves.

The work in philosophical hermeneutics by such persons as Martin Heidegger and Hans-Georg Gadamer suggests that the reader's understanding, including both conscious and subconscious decisions before and during the reading process (or any attempt to understand anything), contributes to the reader's interpretation.[18] In other words, no one can understand anything except in some relation to one's world.[19] Although one may rightly argue that the biblical text—a composed document—and its world do not change (since that world has died long ago), the worlds of the readers are still very much alive. With that aliveness comes also the constant change and variety of human existence that influence the reader's decisions throughout the reading process.[20] Thus, different readers may read the same text differently as they encounter that same text from different worlds (different experiences, different life situations, different relationships, different social status, etc.).[21]

---

16. Cf. Stephen B. Moore, "Deconstructive Criticism: The Gospel of the Mark," in *Mark and Method: New Approaches in Biblical Studies,* ed. Janice Capel Anderson and Stephen D. Moore (Minneapolis: Fortress, 1992), 93: *"The critic, while appearing to comprehend a literary text from a position outside or above it, is in fact being comprehended, being grasped, by the text.* He or she is unwittingly acting out an interpretive role that the text has scripted, even dramatized, in advance. He or she is being enveloped in the folds of the texts even while attempting to sew it up" (author's emphasis).

17. Iser, *Act of Reading,* 163-231.

18. Among other things, Heidegger speaks of understanding in relation to "Being-in-the-world" (see Martin Heidegger, *Being and Time,* trans. John Macquarrie and Edward Robinson [New York: Harper and Row, 1962], 78-224). Gadamer, of course, speaks of the "fusion" of two horizons ("the range of vision that includes everything that can be seen from a particular vantage point")—the present (i.e., the interpreter) and the past (i.e., the text). See Hans-Georg Gadamer, *Truth and Method,* 2nd ed., trans. Joel Weinsheimer and Donald G. Marshall (New York: Crossroad, 1989), 302-7.

19. Cf. Robbins, *Tapestry of Early Christian Discourse,* 24-27.

20. Cf. ibid., 213.

21. Cf. Robert C. Tannehill, *Luke,* Abingdon New Testament Commentaries (Nashville: Abingdon, 1996), 24-27, who contends that the likely diversity among the Lukan implied

Let us examine one possibility. The Lukan literary context of the parable of the so-called prodigal son (Luke 15:11-32) implies that at least three groups of people were listening to this story: Jesus' disciples, the Pharisees and scribes, and the tax collectors and sinners.[22] Traditional parable studies have stressed that a parable has only one meaning. If that is so, then what is the *one* meaning of this familiar parable? Or, let us ask a different question: What would Jesus' audience, made up of these three groups of people, or the Lukan implied audience have heard? The literary context suggests that Jesus was speaking to the Pharisees and scribes who were grumbling about Jesus' associations with "sinners" (15:2). Thus, the primary audience in that setting (and perhaps others within the Lukan implied audience) probably would have identified with the older son and would have imaginatively seen images of a son who was outside his father's house but who was also invited to join the celebration inside that house.[23] However, the tax collectors and sinners who undoubtedly were listening (and undoubtedly some within the Lukan implied audience) would have heard something much different. These persons probably would have identified with the younger son and would have wanted to celebrate with him because of his father's love and offer of restoration. And we are told nothing about the disciples' response(s). In other words, the different hearers potentially would have had different responses to the open-endedness of the parable. Similar dynamics occur in the reading process. Although readers may encounter the same biblical text and seek to build consistency with the same set of literary elements, differences among those readers of Scripture do contribute to their respective readings and open the possibility for different readings.

The potential for multiple readings of Scripture, however, is even greater when such readings truly reflect to some degree the convergence between the worlds of the text and of different readers. The reading or interpretation of a given biblical text cannot be confined to the gathering of factual information or to the mere recitation of words, verses, and ideas. Wolfhart Pannenberg states: "An external assimilating of Christian language to the thoughts and manner of speaking of the biblical writings is

---

audience suggests that different groups within that audience would have heard the Lukan gospel differently.

22. Although the Lukan author does not mention the disciples in the immediate literary context prior to Luke 15 (12:22-53 is the last mention of them), the abrupt transition from the parable to the next scene ("Now Jesus said to his disciples," 16:1) implies that the disciples were also listening.

23. Note the open-endedness of the parable that leaves the story's completion to the hearers/readers.

always an infallible sign that theology has sidestepped its own present problems, and thus has failed to accomplish what Paul or John . . . each accomplished for his own time."[24] Anthony Thiselton suggests that in Pannenberg's thought a more adequate understanding of the biblical text is apparent when the interpreter "seriously engages with the problems and thought-forms" of the interpreter's own time.[25]

Such ideas about one's reading of the biblical text emphasize that the reading process is more than merely figuring out objectively "what the text meant." When a person reads the biblical texts as Scripture,[26] the reader's imagination is stimulated to begin to think about what the text means within the reader's circumstances. On the one hand, that reader comes to the text with a set of circumstances different from what the text's implied audience would have had, yet he or she must consider those historical matters embedded within that text. On the other hand, that same reader also encounters the text with a set of circumstances different from other readers of the same text.[27] Meaning, then, is no longer something to be identified in the past or extracted mechanically from the text but is inseparable from the experience—the creative event—of the convergence between that text and the reader.

THE CHURCH IN CONVERSATION

For some, the suggestion that multiple readings of Scripture are not only possible but inevitable evokes confusion, fear, or even outrage. Confusion may be a response because it appears that no criteria exist for evaluating one's reading of Scripture. Fear may be a response because it appears that persons are given license to read almost anything out of the text that they desire.[28] Outrage may even be a response because it appears that the reader, rather than the Holy Spirit, decides ultimately what God is saying through the biblical text. And these "readings" of this suggestion raise important issues that one must address.

---

24. Wolfhart Pannenberg, *Basic Questions in Theology,* 3 vols. (London: SCM, 1970-73), 1:9.

25. Thiselton, *Two Horizons,* 99.

26. Cf. Stephen E. Fowl and L. Gregory Jones, *Reading in Communion: Scripture and Ethics in Christian Living* (Grand Rapids: Eerdmans, 1991), 20-21.

27. For example, the narrative text invites the reader into that "narrative world," but in no way does the reader leave the present world completely behind when traveling into the text's "foreign" world. The reader's participation in the narrative world, therefore, occurs to the extent that it can be related to that reader's present world.

28. This common criticism against many forms of literary-critical or reader-response approaches to the Bible, however, is not valid for those approaches that affirm the role of *both* the reader *and* the text.

The proposal here is that the role of the church may be *the* critical component that has, to this point, not been considered. If we take seriously the Wesleyan idea that Scripture is, for the church, both the foundation for Christian teachings and living and a "means of sanctifying grace,"[29] then the church and *its* encounters with Scripture must take an active role in this reading process. As George Lindbeck bluntly states, "The Bible exists for the sake of the church."[30] Such an assertion does not imply, of course, that Scripture should not be read personally, but questions and misgivings about the possibility of multiple readings of Scripture may find helpful answers and consolation in the corporate dimension of that reading process.[31]

The corporate dimension that the church offers to the reading process relates to the social nature of knowledge itself. One's perception of reality is the product of social objectivation that creates order of human experiences and encounters with other persons and puts objects or entities in their places within one's everyday life. Peter Berger and Thomas Luckmann argue that the reality of everyday life is only possible because of the objectivations that fill that life.[32] Martin Heidegger describes the "everydayness" of one's existence in terms of "Being-with others."[33] Thus, one may only speak of a personal or individual reading of the biblical text in a qualified way, since no reading is truly void of these social contributions.[34] The horizon, to use Gadamer's term, from which one reads the text overlaps with but is not identical to others' horizons. Persons live in the "same" world and in different worlds at the same time. On the one hand, they encounter the same situations and events. On the other hand, they look at that "same" world from different vantage points that others may expand and influence.

The inevitability of multiple readings of Scripture, then, arises from the natural diversity of persons who constitute the church. A Wesleyan un-

---

29. This expression is borrowed from Randy L. Maddox, *Responsible Grace: John Wesley's Practical Theology* (Nashville: Abingdon/Kingswood, 1994), 210-12.

30. George A. Lindbeck, "Atonement and the Hermeneutics of Social Embodiment," *Pro Ecclesia* 5 (Spring 1996): 150. Cf. Robert W. Wall, "The Future of Wesleyan Biblical Studies," *Wesleyan Theological Journal* 33/2 (Fall 1998): 101-4, who notes problems in transferring biblical interpretation from the ecclesial to the academic setting.

31. Cf. Luke Timothy Johnson, *Living Jesus: Learning the Heart of the Gospel* (San Francisco: HarperSanFrancisco, 1999), 75; and Fowl and Jones, *Reading in Communion*, 17.

32. Peter L. Berger and Thomas Luckmann, *The Social Construction of Reality: A Treatise in the Sociology of Knowledge* (New York: Doubleday, 1966), 35.

33. Heidegger, *Being and Time*, 149-68.

34. See Stanley Eugene Fish, *Is There a Text in This Class? The Authority of Interpretive Communities* (Cambridge: Harvard University Press, 1980), who argues that *everything* the reader sees in the text is due to that reader's "interpretive community."

derstanding of the church affirms this diversity. With the apostle Paul and John Wesley, the church is seen to be "the body of Christ" in which the many members, though different, contribute and are equally important (1 Cor. 12).[35] The focus of the church, from a Wesleyan perspective, is on its soteriological *being*, not on what one often associates with the church (e.g., institutional matters). While persons from different but overlapping worlds constitute the church, what unites them is the grace of God, who continues to reveal himself to them and who empowers them to cherish the variety among them.[36] Thus, the church reads Scripture together because, in its encounter with these texts, God reveals the divine self and salvific purposes for humanity.[37] These revealing encounters in which God speaks occur when those persons of the church hear Scripture and listen together, prayerfully expecting the Spirit to help them understand *in their worlds*. This revelation of God, through the biblical texts that are products of the Spirit's inspiring activity, is not locked within the past encounter between God and the respective text's human author. Rather, God also reveals the divine self to those of the present church who listen together for God's word in their various worlds and, more specifically, their common world.

What should be apparent here is that a tension still exists between the *multiple readings of Scripture* that will naturally occur among persons within the church and the *revelation of God* to the church through those readings. Does this suggestion mean that all these readings are valid? Are we left with each person having, to some extent, a personal reading that cannot be tested or validated? Is God revealed even in *mis*readings?[38] All these questions must be answered negatively, if one understands the church as the context (religious and social) in which Christians gather collectively to worship, to hear the story of God, and to participate in that story. If one's world—including situations, persons, and so forth—also includes the community of believers, then that group of believing persons, with all that one experiences and encounters with them, potentially shapes and influences all of that one's life: perspective and outlook on life, understanding of God, and even what one sees when reading Scripture. This influence by others, however, is not merely something that the community imposes on the individual. Rather, part of the communal dynamic

---

35. Cf. John Wesley, "Of the Church," in *Works* (Jackson ed.), 6:392-401, esp. 399.

36. See Maddox, *Responsible Grace*.

37. See John Wesley, *Explanatory Notes upon the New Testament* (London: Epworth, 1958), 794. Cf. Maddox, *Responsible Grace*, 31.

38. See Mark Allan Powell, "Expected and Unexpected Readings of Matthew," *Asbury Theological Journal* 48 (Fall 1993): 31-51, for a description of misreadings.

of the church is the mutual influence that occurs *among* persons, not *to* them, as the community converses about what they hear God saying through Scripture.

Our identification with the Wesleyan-Holiness tradition *itself* reflects some of this corporate dynamic within the church. The claim to be Wesleyan means, among other things, that there is a focus on the grace of God that enables the Christian to live faithfully in love for God and others. To be Wesleyan means that special emphasis is given to the sanctifying grace of God and the holy life as an enabled response to that grace. To be Wesleyan means that there is an identification with the universal church and Christian teachings throughout the centuries.[39] Although John Wesley undoubtedly understood Scripture to be the foundation for Christian teaching and practice, it is equally clear that he recognized the influence that other factors had on the reading of those sacred texts, namely reason, tradition, and experience.[40] The importance of tradition does not mean, of course, that tradition enslaves the reader of Scripture and thereby limits that reader's discoveries to what is already believed or affirmed. The restriction of one's reading merely to what tradition affirms would ignore other possibilities for reading the biblical text that may challenge or clarify such affirmations and would potentially destroy the life of both the tradition and Scripture.[41] Nonetheless, as Michael Lodahl states, "The traditions that surround and nurture us provide the 'lens' through which we read, understand, and ap-

---

39. Cf. Robert W. Wall, "Toward a Wesleyan Hermeneutic of Scripture," *Wesleyan Theological Journal* 30/2 (Fall 1995): 55: "While Scripture's message for the whole church will surely be distorted without its Wesleyan message, so also will its message be distorted if understood only in Wesleyan terms. The mutual criticism that engages and learns from other interpretive traditions and from the full witness of Scripture only deepens the significance of each part which makes up the whole church and its biblical canon."

40. Wesley, "On Faith (Hebrews 11:6)," in *Works* (Bicentennial ed.), 3:496. See Donald A. D. Thorsen, *The Wesleyan Quadrilateral: Scripture, Tradition, Reason, and Experience as a Model of Evangelical Theology* (Grand Rapids: Zondervan, 1990; reprint, Indianapolis: Light and Life Communications, 1997), 71; and Timothy L. Smith, "John Wesley and the Wholeness of Scripture," *Interpretation* 39 (July 1985): 248.

41. Cf. Stanley Hauerwas, *A Community of Character: Toward a Constructive Christian Social Ethic* (Notre Dame, Ind.: University of Notre Dame Press, 1981), 66. See Johnson, *Living Jesus,* 25: "The willingness to learn Jesus in the context of tradition demands a combination of loyalty and criticism, and either without the other becomes distorted. Loyalty is ideally the premise for true criticism, just as critical awareness is a necessary component of loyalty. Without critical awareness, tradition can become idolatrous, replacing the living Jesus with established formulas about Jesus or ossified interpretations of him. . . . But if loyalty without criticism becomes lifeless, so also can criticism without loyalty become mere carping and complaining."

ply the Bible."[42] The relation between tradition and an encounter with God through Scripture, then, has two dimensions. On the one hand, that encounter is shaped by a tradition that has *itself* been shaped by earlier encounters with Scripture. On the other hand, each encounter with Scripture also shapes that tradition by what is revealed about God.[43] To read Scripture in the context of the church, then, is to recognize both the contributions of and contributions to the tradition by such readings.[44] To read Scripture in the context of a church in the Wesleyan tradition is to hear, to converse, and also to tell the story of God in a way that affirms the gracious activity of a holy God who calls the church to holy living.

One must inquire, however, about who is part of this conversation within the community of believers. That is to ask, who is invited to the table to converse about what the biblical texts seem to say? Should only the scholars be invited, whose education and critical study provide them with needed abilities for clarifying what are and are not appropriate readings of Scripture in our tradition?[45] Or, should only denominational leaders and officials be invited, whose oversight provides a larger perspective of the impact of the gospel? Or, should only the pastors be invited, whose role as spiritual shepherds corresponds more closely with the Wesleyan focus on the soteriological or spiritual function of Scripture? Or, should only the laypersons be invited, who alone live in "the real world"?[46] Of course, the answer is not confined to one group; one must include all.[47] The different skills, the different vantage points, the different eyes and ears—all must be included as the community of faith converses, not only about what these different ones see and hear individually but also about what they see and hear *together* that is truly gospel for their given time, culture, and setting.[48] The conversation around the table does not seek to define what is the *only* correct meaning or what we must do to remain faithful to our Wesleyan tradition. Such a perspective reflects the same problems that contemporary thought has revealed. Both this dialogue and corporate discernment compensate for possible excesses in subjective in-

---

42. Michael Lodahl, *The Story of God: Wesleyan Theology and Biblical Narrative* (Kansas City: Beacon Hill Press of Kansas City, 1994), 25.

43. Cf. ibid., 26.

44. Cf. Wall, "Future of Wesleyan Biblical Studies," 112-14.

45. See Fowl and Jones, *Reading in Communion*, 43-44, who stress the importance of scholars to the church.

46. See George A. Lindbeck, "Scripture, Consensus, and Community," *This World* 23 (Fall 1988): 16, who warns that the scholarly elite now hold the Bible captive and make it inaccessible to "ordinary folk."

47. Cf. ibid., 23.

48. Cf. Johnson, *Living Jesus*, 78.

terpretations.[49] Maybe a better perspective is one that sees the grace of God sacramentally and continually inviting us all to *God's* table again—where we break and share the *Word* together and where we converse about what we see and hear when God offers us God's *living Word*.[50]

If the church perceives its readings of Scripture as sacramental events or as means of sanctifying grace, then in the Wesleyan tradition one must also assert that these readings (and interpretations) remain incomplete without faithful responses through holy living. If the encounter between Scripture and the church is ultimately an encounter in which God reveals the divine self, then such an experience is *not* the goal of reading Scripture. If the church's goal for reading and interpreting the biblical texts is merely to "learn more of God's Word," then one could argue that this goal is inadequate since our readings should include not only an interrogation of the text but also the text's interrogation of its readers. Having all the facts right—historically, theologically, and biblically—is not enough. Stanley Hauerwas states: "If we pay attention to the narrative and self-involving character of the Gospels, as the early disciples did, there is no way to speak of Jesus' story without its forming our own. The story it forms creates a community which corresponds to the form of his life."[51] Stephen Fowl and Gregory Jones even suggest: "Unless Christians embody their interpretation of Scripture (thus producing a certain character), their interpretation is in vain."[52] Michael Lodahl writes that an appeal to Scripture (more specifically, the story of Jesus) provides answers to these questions: "What kinds of actions and attitudes most clearly and decisively characterize the committed Christian life in this world? What sort of life helps us best understand the nature of the relationship between God and human beings, and what is it that God desires and requires?"[53] John Wesley would have agreed in principle with these statements since he correlated the use of Scripture with holy living.[54] If, in our reading of Scripture, we have heard the voice of God, can life go on as before? Or is the experience enough?

MORE THAN THE WRITTEN TEXTS

The difficulty in appropriating only historical-critical methods within the ecclesial context as the *primary* means by which to do biblical exegesis

---

49. Cf. ibid., 196-97.

50. Cf. John P. Burgess, "Scripture as Sacramental Word: Rediscovering Scripture's Compelling Power," *Interpretation* 52 (Oct. 1998): 386-87.

51. Hauerwas, *A Community of Character,* 51.

52. Fowl and Jones, *Reading in Communion,* 85.

53. Lodahl, *Story of God,* 199.

54. See, e.g., Wesley, "The Means of Grace," in *Works* (Bicentennial ed.), 1:388.

is that these so-called objective methods often bracket faith (and therefore faithful living) matters from the discussion. Historical investigation may provide essential data concerning the world in which and to which a particular biblical text was written, but such studies alone cannot bridge the obvious gap between the past and present.[55] The controversies surrounding the Jesus Seminar of the Society of Biblical Literature reflect similar difficulties for the church because, although the seminar operates *outside* the ecclesial context, the Jesus of the New Testament is separated from the risen Christ of the church.[56] The common assumption is that historical information will help the interpreter understand the text or understand what *really* happened or what Jesus *really* said. The problem with a reliance on such methods alone is that the biblical texts become objects of study and scrutiny rather than texts that the readers bring to life.[57] Robert Wall provocatively states: "It is only a slight exaggeration to say that the gaps in a more precise historical understanding about the world behind the biblical text, which are then filled by competent historical critics, typically contribute little that is essential to Scripture's performance as the Word of God."[58] Wall concludes: *"If the aim of biblical interpretation is theological understanding and not historical reconstruction . . . the test of sound interpretation is whether it makes the biblical text come alive with meaning that makes sense of and empowers a life for God today."*[59] Perhaps one criterion needed for evaluating the church's various readings of Scripture should focus on this matter of faithful or holy living. Maybe George Lindbeck provides a good beginning definition of that criterion: "When other criteria are not decisive, the interpretation which seems most likely in these particular circumstances to serve the upbuilding of the community of faith in its God-willed witness to the world is the one to be preferred."[60] If Scripture no longer comes alive in the church (i.e., in holy living), have those texts lost their revelatory character? Is there some correlation between the *Word* that comes alive within us and the *living Word* (i.e., the risen Lord)?

   In the movie *Mr. Holland's Opus,* a high school orchestra director, Glenn Holland (played by Richard Dreyfuss), is confronted by Gertrude

---

55. See Lindbeck, "Scripture, Consensus, and Community," 13, 16.
56. See, e.g., Luke Timothy Johnson, *The Real Jesus: The Misguided Quest for the Historical Jesus and the Truth of the Traditional Gospels* (San Francisco: HarperSanFrancisco, 1996); idem, *Living Jesus;* and Braaten, "Jesus and the Church," 59-71.
57. Cf. Hauerwas, *Community of Character,* 52: "A truthful telling of the story cannot be guaranteed by historical investigation, but by being the kind of people who can bear the burden of that story with joy."
58. Wall, "The Future of Wesleyan Biblical Studies," 105.
59. Ibid., author's emphasis.
60. Lindbeck, "Atonement and the Hermeneutics of Social Embodiment," 155.

Lange, a clarinet player whose frustrations have carried her to that moment of resignation and defeat. Mr. Holland asks her a simple question about playing the clarinet: "Is it any fun?" "I wanted it to be," is her quiet admission, to which Mr. Holland responds surprisingly, "Do you know what we have been doing wrong, Miss Lange? We've been playing the notes on the page." Gertrude asks: "Well, what else is there to play?" Mr. Holland replies: "There's a lot more to music than notes on the page. . . . Playing music is not about notes on a page. I could teach you notes on a page." In other words, music comes not from the penned notes but from the song that the musician brings to life.

Whatever else one may say about the reading of Scripture, it is more than just reading or mastering words or sentences on a written page, ideas, historical data, or artistic beauty. Interpreting or understanding the Bible cannot and does not occur by ravaging the text before us—by trying to find meaning contained or buried somewhere in that text. In many ways, trying to master anything, including matters of faith, as objective entities apart from ourselves is impossible. We really cannot understand the biblical texts or find meaning in them apart from ourselves and our reading community of faith. Unless our readings of Scripture allow those texts to come alive in responses of faithful and holy living that truly reflect the convergence between those texts and us, the Bible loses its character as holy Scripture.[61] Could it be that Bible reading has become boring and lifeless for so many believers because we have been looking for meaning in the wrong places (e.g., in the text)? Could it be that beauty really *is* in the eyes of the beholders—that meaning *really is* in the lives of the ones who are confronted together with the written story of God's grace?

---

61. Cf. Fowl and Jones, *Reading in Communion*, 20.

Sharon Pearson, a seminary professor of biblical studies and past president of the Wesleyan Theological Society, notes that interpretation of Scripture has been crucial to how women have been able to function in the church over the centuries. Often because of ways of reading the Bible, strict gender-based restrictions have been placed on even highly gifted women of faith. In order to clarify the issues and options, Professor Pearson identifies three approaches to reading biblical material. They are three windows through which Bible texts are viewed, yielding widely differing results. It is this author's intent in this chapter to pursue the third approach, which she calls the primacist approach. She sees reflected in this method of biblical interpretation the integrity of a Wesleyan approach to Scripture and a particular vision of faithfulness to biblical authority—with particular reference to the issue of the proper roles of women in church life.

While it is clear that women participated in the ministry of the New Testament church, definition of the parameters of this participation is disputed. It must be remembered, however, that all interpreters are working from the same limited evidence. Further, the so-called clear statements of the New Testament that seem to limit the participation of women are not very clear at all. In fact, given biblical teaching and actual practice in the earliest church, Pearson concludes that women should be welcomed equally into church life, including into its formal structures of ministry. The "new creation" in Christ has come, and old human distinctions and discriminations should end. The best reading of Scripture calls us to a new and higher vision than gender-based restrictions on Christian life and leadership.

10

WOMEN AS BIBLE READERS AND CHURCH LEADERS[1]

Sharon Clark Pearson

◆

The Wesleyan-Holiness theological tradition holds a "high view" of Scripture. In a church tradition that claims the integrity and authority of Scripture, questions of practice are taken seriously. The question of whether God ordains and blesses women in the practice of ministry (both in function and in office) is crucial to women because their personal and relational lives and their participation in the church have been defined and regulated by the interpretation of Scripture (as the lives of all of us should be). It is also a critical question for the church on many levels—if the church is serious about determining God's will, and then by the grace of God is doing it!

In the church world, answers given to the question of God's will concerning women seem to fall into three categories. Each of the three categories may be defined by its approach (perspective and procedures) to biblical material. These distinctive approaches may be observed in the questions asked of Scripture, the principles exercised in the selection and evaluation (valuing) of biblical texts, the method applied in theological synthesis, and the subsequent proposed applications of conclusions. It may be further observed that conclusions are significantly shaped by the "window" through which biblical texts are viewed.

THREE GENERAL APPROACHES TO SCRIPTURE

1. Pluralist. One of these three approaches to the issue of women in ministry begins with a disclaimer. It claims that it is inappropriate to address this question to the biblical materials since these materials are inadequate for the task now at hand. The question of women in institutionalized ministry is seen as foreign to Scripture, and/or the instruction of Scripture is determined to be of limited value in the debate (irrelevant or

---

1. Appeared originally in the *Wesleyan Theological Journal* 31/1 (Spring 1996). Used by permission. The original article was dedicated to Dr. Marie Strong, the author's mentor and model who passed into eternity January 18, 1995. As a minister of the gospel for 60 years and a Bible professor for over 30 years at Church of God (Anderson) colleges (particularly Anderson University), "Mother" Marie lived out her ministry in a church body (Church of God) that has sought to be an expression of the vision that this article represents. See also note 6.

impossibly culture bound). The "window" through which Scripture is observed is a presupposition about the value of Scripture itself or about the hermeneutic that governs the way Scripture is used. In this category, theologians may proceed with general perspectives such as the equality of women and men in creation or broad principles of social justice and equality. Such an approach is either focused on appeals to reason or general revelation (natural theology) or limited to a reductionistic existentialism. Those in the Wesleyan tradition may well critique this approach as weak in that it abandons the special revelation Scripture does offer. The presupposition of this category of thought may be defined as a *pluralist*[2] view of the authority of Scripture; Scripture is only one of several authorities to which one may appeal as equally valid in the discussion.

2. Positivist. The second and third approaches to the place of women in the church share the conviction that Scripture is the source of special revelation (revealed theology). Of these two approaches, the second may be identified by the value it attaches to biblical statements of propriety and convention, such as the station codes and the traditional statements of restriction of female participation in the church (1 Cor. 14; 1 Tim. 2). These texts are made the starting place or "window" through which other biblical materials are perceived and interpreted. While this category appeals to the authority of Scripture (and so is committed to a self-consciously "high view" of Scripture), its approach is limited by a "mechanical literalism."

Methodologically, this category is inadequate in contextual investigation (literary and historical). Theologically, this approach is weakened by a restricted understanding of revelation as propositional statements. The presupposition of this category may be identified as a *positivist* view of Scripture (not logical positivism). It interprets *sola Scriptura* to mean that Scripture is the exclusive authority for theology, with the conviction that the interpreter is capable of understanding Scripture without benefit of church tradition and free from any process of reason or personal perspective wrought by experience.[3] In this paper, biblical positivism is defined as a position that takes the Bible itself to be the given, the data or the

---

2. I thank Alan Padgett for his insight, creativity, and kindness. He helped create the three "P" terms. In the process, he helped me sharpen my statements. I also thank Susie Stanley for an initial discussion that helped direct my work.

3. I am working from R. W. Hepburn's discussion of positivism and particularly from a specific statement: "The word 'positive' (probably deriving from a usage of Francis Bacon) is here contrasted with the conjectured: it is associated with the 'given,' the data of the sciences" (*The Dictionary of Christian Theology*, 1969 ed., s.v. "Positivism" by R. W. Hepburn).

evidence, and is limited to that evidence alone as authority. In hermeneutical terms, this approach might be called monism and stands in contrast to the pluralism of the first approach.

3. Primacist. The third category of approach to the issue of women in ministry may be called *primacist*. Precisely out of its commitment to scriptural authority, it attempts to incorporate the broad range of biblical evidence. The data considered to be important to the discussion includes such material as the biblical stories of the experience of the Jesus community and the early church. These stories are seen as reflections of the circumstances and the theologies of that church. The truly revolutionary practices of Jesus in relation to women, the participation of women alongside the apostle Paul in ministry, and the evidence of women's participation (leadership) in worship services are all accepted as contributions to the dialogue. The rationale for such a program is that this evidence reflects the theological perspectives of the biblical writers. For example, the Lukan and Pauline writings present theologies of a new aeon in which social and religious barriers are superseded. Texts such as Acts 2:16-21, Galatians 3:28, and Ephesians 2 (which help define the Galatians passage) are the windows through which the biblical materials are to be perceived.

This third category is also committed to standard research into broader references that are used as sources by biblical writers. So, creation accounts and the station codes are investigated for the purpose of identifying God's will as presented in the "whole council of Scripture." This category is not only serious about inductive study of Scripture as primary authority but also sensitive to the role of reason (analysis), church tradition, and experience, *norms that are reflected in the biblical materials themselves*. The presupposition that governs this approach may be described as the primacist view of Scripture on the question of authority, which also allows the evidence of reason, the appeal of experience, and the instruction of tradition. This position has been defined in Wesleyan circles as the Wesleyan quadrilateral.[4]

---

4. The argument for the primacy of Scripture does not allow for any negation of Scripture as authority. Thorsen's summary is helpful in establishing this point: "Neither Wesley nor the quadrilateral controverts the primacy of scriptural authority. Those who use the Wesleyan quadrilateral to diminish the primary authority of Scripture misinterpret Wesley's belief and Outler's intention in coining the term "quadrilateral." But, while Scripture is viewed as primary, it should not be considered exclusive. Such an understanding would be inappropriate for Wesley as well as for Christian antiquity and the Protestant Reformation (Donald A. D. Thorsen, *The Wesleyan Quadrilateral: Scripture, Tradition, Reason, and Experience as a Model of Evangelical Theology* [Grand Rapids: Zondervan, 1990; reprint, Indianapolis: Light and Life Communications, 1997], 241).

The second and third categories reflect the tension inherent in Scripture, the tension between eschatological vision (Joel/Acts) and arguments of social propriety (1 Timothy).[5] Arguments of hierarchy and dominance/subordination stand alongside stories of revolutionary attitudes and practice in Jesus' ministry and in the participation of women in the ministry of the early church.

The following presentation on the issue of women in ministry is necessarily brief but demonstrates the method of the third approach to Scripture.[6] The synthesis derived from this work reflects the conviction that Scripture is relevant and does lend guidance and inspiration to practice in the church, in this case to the issue of women in ministry. The significance of this method is that it reflects the integrity of a Wesleyan approach to Scripture and a particular vision of faithfulness to its authority.

THE CASE FOR WOMEN IN MINISTRY

All serious (and even not so serious) Bible students interpret Scripture according to some set of principles. When any question is asked of Scripture, certain principles are exercised in the selection, evaluation (valuing), theological synthesis of those materials, and proposed application of those conclusions. All who read Scripture make choices between the instructions received therein. All decide what portion of the Scripture is timeless and always applicable and which passages are cultural expressions of some larger question. For example, though many have read the stated requirement that women wear a head covering in public worship (1 Cor. 11:2-16), there is no concern expressed in most churches that this injunction is to be obeyed by women today. It has been dismissed as time (circumstance) bound instruction that no longer applies (although the principle that governed the instruction must be interpreted and does apply). The question, then, is not whether to make such distinctions, which are in fact demanded by the nature of many of the texts in the New Testament (i.e., occasional letters), but where to draw the line in that process.

In making such a choice, two almost automatic instincts govern this writer. First, we are allowed to define an expression as limited to a particular circumstance (with a corresponding application) where we have a

---

5. Those arguments are not simply for the sake of "propriety," however. In each case the purpose for the instruction has to do with a particular situation being addressed. See the following section on house or station codes.

6. This presentation is a revision of my work "Biblical Precedents for Women in Ministry" in *Called to Minister, Empowered to Serve,* ed. Juanita Evans Leonard (Anderson, Ind.: Warner, 1989), 13-33.

clear statement of such limits from that text or another. Second, an old dictum applies: Where the text speaks, we speak (without reservation). Where Scripture is silent, we speak only with a great deal of humility.

Some of the questions we address to Scripture are foreign to it. Answers may be worked out only by implication. The question of women in ministry is not foreign to the New Testament, but it is not answered explicitly therein. While it is clear that women participated in the ministry of the New Testament church, definition of the parameters of that participation is disputed. But, it must be remembered that all interpreters are working from the same limited evidence, and more, that the so-called clear statements limiting the participation of women are not clear at all. If they were, there would be no discussion.[7]

The method of this particular presentation is to begin by reviewing the information on women in general in the New Testament. That information was written, selected, and preserved in androcentric (man-centered) societies. It is remarkable that, given the patriarchal worldview of the societies in which these documents were written, women were included in the story at all. There is enough evidence available in the various accounts of women in the New Testament to indicate that women were an integral part of the life and ministry of the early church. The story of the church could not be told without including the stories of women.

WOMEN IN THE GOSPELS

It is foolish to consider the place of women in the church without recalling Jesus' attitude and actions toward the women around him. Women as well as men were attracted to Jesus in his three short years of ministry.

---

7. Some voicing a positivist view of Scripture would claim that no discussion is necessary, not only from the vantage point of Scripture but also with appeals to church history. I was made aware that some think of the issue of women in ministry as a recent concern arising out of the social impulse to radicalism of the 1960s. While a knowledge of church history would correct such a misunderstanding, it is ironic that the issue arose primarily as a low-church phenomenon in America, and as part of a reformation reaction to institutionalized and nominalized religion (high church) from the 1860s to the turn of the next century (with the Church of God, Anderson, Indiana, coming to the strongest practical expression of that phenomenon; 32 percent of its pastors being women in 1925). As these low-church denominations gained identity and later a certain respectability, radical reform was less a concern, and institutional survival more important. What made such movements (Pentecostal, holiness, etc.) suspect to established denominations was precisely such expressions as women in ministry, racial integration of worship services, and other social justice attitudes and actions. But today it is the older denominations that ordain women, and many in the fundamentalist/evangelical perspective seek to distance themselves from such "liberal" practices. For an example of this social phenomenon, see "Women in Ministry" in *Centering on Ministry* 5/2 (Winter 1980), 1-2, published by the Center for Pastoral Studies of Anderson University.

Among Jesus' rugged band of followers were a number of women. Jeremias suggests that any occurrence of women following a teacher or rabbi was "an unprecedented happening in history of that time."[8] We know about these women from a few short references (Mark 15:40-41; Luke 8:1-3). These women are said to have supported Jesus and his disciples financially. They were women with means and so probably came from an upper echelon of society. The Markan account paints the poignant picture of these women, along with other women from Jerusalem, at the scene of Jesus' crucifixion. The three women named in that portrait visit the burial site after Sabbath to anoint their Lord's body for burial. And then, in a society where a woman's word was not allowed in court, the passion narrative presents Jesus as commissioning them to be the first to proclaim the resurrection. Nothing was more natural than their being among the 120 who waited in the Upper Room for the power that would give fire to their lives and witness. The church from its inception featured women.

Who were the women who sought Jesus out and became a part of the gospel story because of his impact upon their lives? They were the three who became known as leaders among the group of women (Mary Magdalene, Mary the mother of Joses, and Salome). They were Mary and Martha, who, contrary to social rules, invited Jesus into their home. They included the woman unclean with her feminine infirmity and the despised Samaritan woman at the well who was the first commissioned by Jesus to "spread the Word." They were the Syro-Phoenician (Gentile) woman who asked him for "the crumbs" for her demon-possessed daughter and the woman who, in a prophetic act, anointed Jesus.

A significant aspect of each one of these stories is that it was ever recorded and preserved. In a culture where women were property[9] and had no rights or privileges to call their own, these stories themselves would have opened the door of the church to criticism and contempt. But what is most significant about these stories is that, in every case, Jesus crossed all lines of propriety—religious and social. His very actions were a challenge to the cherished traditions of his own people. He went so far as to commend women as examples of faith and spiritual vitality, women who no rabbi would teach, women who were not counted in the number

---

8. Joachim Jeremias, *Jerusalem in the Time of Jesus* (Philadelphia: Fortress, 1949), 374.

9. Women were listed as property along with cattle. See Georgia Harkness, *Women in Church and Society* (Nashville: Abingdon, 1972), 42-52. In general, women did not have the right to personal property; it belonged to husband or father. Exceptions to such mores would have been restricted to the elite. See Samuel Terrien, *Till the Heart Sings* (Philadelphia: Fortress, 1985), 123.

of a synagogue, who were isolated to a separate court at the Temple, and whose religious vows could be overturned by their husbands.

Along with stories of women who accompanied Jesus and his disciples is the story of Mary and Martha. Jesus teaches Mary as he would teach any man who would follow him—an unheard of breach of religious leadership (a rabbi sat to teach while the student sat at the feet of the rabbi). One rabbi in the time of Jesus said: "Better to burn the Torah than to teach it to a woman."[10] Women were not educated in the synagogue school or at home. "He who teaches his daughter the law, teaches her lechery."[11] As if that were not enough, Jesus is recorded as having chided Martha for fulfilling her socially prescribed role instead of joining Mary (Luke 10:38-42).

The cumulative effect of such stories makes clear that Jesus broke custom in his championing of women as equally worthy of his concern and ministry. His evaluation of them far outstripped the most expansive and tolerant views of his day and continually surprised even those who knew him well. The tone of his ministry was to model a new life and relationships to and for women, not simply to reflect the status quo. He challenged the sexist standards of his world—the lustful glance of an adulterous heart (Matt. 5:27-28), the casual divorce, which was a male prerogative (19:3-9),[12] and the threat of capital punishment applied unfairly—only to the adulterous woman (John 8:1-11). The popular attitude of the day was that women were responsible for all sexual temptation and therefore sexual sin.

None of these Gospel stories would be approved, much less applauded outside of the early church that preserved them. Yet, somehow, the gospel could not be told without them. Such events were so integral to the reality of the Jesus community that they comprised a part of the gospel itself.

An anticipated response to the above review of Gospel evidence regarding women is the popular objection that none of the women following Jesus became one of his 12 disciples/apostles. None was accorded equality. It is not necessary to argue cultural expediency here. It is enough to respond that no Gentile or slave was allowed that privilege either, but

---

10. Rabbi Eliezer ben Hyrkanos, as quoted in Jeremias' *Jerusalem in the Time of Jesus,* 373.

11. Ibid.

12. "The right to divorce was exclusively the husband's" (Jeremias, *Jerusalem in the Time of Jesus,* 370). Jeremias adds that public stigma and the requirement that the financial agreement in the marriage contract be honored (the money be returned) acted as a deterrent for hasty divorce. Therefore, the Hillelite provision for capricious divorce was not necessarily fulfilled. This issue does expose the attitudes of the day, however.

that was not and is not used to exclude these disadvantaged groups from the leadership and offices of the church today.

WOMEN IN THE EARLY CHURCH

Clearly, women were an integral part of the Jesus community that awaited the empowerment of the Spirit (Acts 1:14-15). And just as clearly in the Acts account, these women were among those who received the Spirit in fulfillment of Joel's prophecy. The emphasis of Peter's sermon is the universality of the Spirit's work; those who previously were not candidates to share in proclamation—the young, the woman, the slave—were now anointed to prophesy as witnesses of the work of the Messiah (Acts 1:8; 2:1-4; Luke 24:44-49). It was incredible that women were included in the Gospel accounts; it is also a wonder that the participation of women in the early church was recorded in Acts and the Epistles. Against cultural expediency and propriety, these stories continued to be told. A brief perusal of the evidence of this participation can be listed in two categories: (1) brief references included in such incidental fashion as lists of women and (2) epistolary discussions of women's participation in ministry. We also will note (3) the household codes, (4) the argument from creation accounts, and (5) the relevance of emphasis on the eschatological age of the Spirit.

1. Lists of Women. The incidental and therefore brief references to women identified as participating in various aspects of the ministry of the church are powerful evidence of apostolic recognition of women in ministry. Why? Because at least one apostolic agenda for listing these women was to elicit recognition and support of their ministry in the church. Furthermore, these texts not only assume the role of such women but also exhort support of those women precisely in their roles as ministers. In the Book of Acts, Philip the evangelist is noted with a reference to his four daughters with the gift of the prophets (21:9; cf. 2:17-18). The apostle Paul places this spiritual gift at the top of his list as the most valuable gift for the edification of the church (1 Cor. 14:1).[13] Mentioned in several epistles in the New Testament, another character, Priscilla, evidently bore quite a reputation (Acts 18:2, 18, 26; 1 Cor. 16:19; Rom. 16:3-4; 2 Tim. 4:19). How many others were mentioned as often or in such a variety of texts? Her distinction for the purposes of this study is that she, along with Aquila, taught Apollos (Acts 18:26). Against rabbinic tradition that identi-

---

13. Paul was well aware of Old Testament stories of prophetesses: Miriam (Exod. 15:20); Deborah (Judg. 4:4); Huldah (2 Kings 22:14-16). See also Luke 2:36-38 where Anna, the prophetess, verifies the coming of the Messiah.

fied a woman as "the wife" of the man who is named, the apostle Paul recognized Priscilla as prominent enough not only to be listed along with her husband but also to be the first one of the pair mentioned more often than not (four of six times; one of these occurs in 1 Timothy, indicating her prominence as the teacher of the pair). By calling Priscilla a "fellow worker" in Christ Jesus, the apostle Paul accorded Priscilla an equal place among other such workers as Timothy (Rom. 16:21), Titus (2 Cor. 8:23), Luke (Philem. 24), Apollos, Paul himself (1 Cor. 3:9), and others.

This term applied to Priscilla, "fellow worker," was also applied to Euodia and Syntyche, feuding leaders at Philippi. Another leader, Phoebe, is explicitly called a "minister" (a term historically translated as "servant" only in the case of Phoebe). The same term was applied to the leaders Apollos (1 Cor. 3:5), Timothy (1 Tim. 4:6), and Paul (1 Cor. 3:5). Along with the references to Phoebe and Prisca (Priscilla) in Paul's closing instructions to the Romans, four other women are listed as having "worked very hard" in the Lord: Mary, Tryphena, Tryphosa, and Persis. The apostle Paul applied this same description to the ministry of other leaders in the church (1 Cor. 16:15-16; 1 Thess. 5:12; 1 Tim. 5:17). Finally, one of the two who Paul called "outstanding among the apostles" was a woman (Rom. 16:7). The name mentioned is Junias. David Scholer's review of the evidence is most helpful:

> Junias is a male name in English translations, but there is no evidence that such a male name existed in the first century A.D. Junia, a female name, was common, however. The Greek grammar of the sentence . . . means that the male and female forms of this name would be spelled identically. . . . Since Junia is the name attested in the first century and since the great church father . . . of the fourth century, John Chystostom (no friend of women in history), understood the reference to be to a woman Junia, we ought to see it that way as well. In fact, it was not until the thirteenth century that she was changed to Junias.[14]

It is obvious from these informal, uncontrived lists that women played a significant role in the early church as leaders. Their function in ministry is defined in these places by the same terms applied to the ministry of men, and no gender distinction is made in role or function in the lists. Yet, despite the power of this evidence, it is clear that the record of women in ministry was more limited than that of men. The heroes of the

---

14. David M. Scholer, "Women in Ministry," *The Covenant Companion,* Dec. 1983—Feb. 1984, 12-13.

biblical records are almost always men. It is probable also that opportunity for participation in leadership was more limited for women.

2. Evidence of Participation. One of the strongest evidences for the participation of women in the worshiping community comes from the brief discussion of 1 Corinthians 11:2-16. This text makes explicit reference to women prophesying and praying in services of worship. The reference is incidental; it does not comment on their leadership. That makes a strong case for the inclusion of women in these ministries in services of worship. Such participation by women is evidently assumed under the wide rubric of spiritual gifts and ministries that have been designated to all (regardless of religious, social, or gender distinctions) for "the common good" (12:7). Several arguments are made in this text; a brief perusal is all that the confines of this study will allow.

First Corinthians 11:2-16 has been debated at length. The breadth of the arguments are best explained as arising out of what appears to be a contradiction in the text between verses 4-7 and verses 10-12.[15] Verses 4-7 require that women submit to the norms of their culture regarding head covering: "every woman who prays or prophesies with her *kephale* (head) uncovered [the word "veil" does not occur in this text] dishonors her head . . . let her keep her head covered."[16] Verses 10-12 are Paul's corrective; women may wear a covering over their heads or may not: "For this reason the woman ought to have *exousia* (power, right, or freedom of choice, the ability to do something) over (covering) her head" (v. 10; cf. John 10:18, Acts 9:14, and Rev. 16:9 for the use of *exousia* with *echo*, and 1 Cor. 9 for

---

15. Alan Padgett provides a logical presentation of the contradiction and offers the conclusion that verses 3-7b are Paul's "description" of the Corinthian position, and verses 7c-16 are Paul's correctives ("Paul on Women in the Church: The Contradictions of Coiffure in 1 Corinthians 11:2-16," *Journal for the Study of the New Testament* 20 [1984]: 69-86). This follows a pattern common in Paul's writings and certainly occurring in 1 Cor. 6:12-17 and 8:4-13. Overviews of the debate on 1 Cor. 11:2-16 are presented by Linda Mercandante in her *From Hierarchy to Equality: A Comparison of Past and Present Interpretations of 1 Cor. 11:2-16* (Vancouver: Regent College, G-M-H Books, 1978) and by Ralph N. Schutt in his "A History of the Interpretation of 1 Corinthians 11:2-16" (M.A. thesis, Dallas Theological Seminary, 1978).

16. Ibid. *Veil* or *kalymma* does not occur at all in this passage. See Padgett's summary of the evidence in "Women in the Church." Padgett points his readers to the original work in Jerome Murphy-O'Connor, "Sex and Logic in 1 Corinthians 11:2-16," *Catholic Biblical Quarterly* 42 (1980): 483-84. He also refers his readers to James B. Hurley, "Did Paul Require Veils or the Silence of Women?" *Westminster Theological Journal* 35 (Winter 73): 190-220; Abel Isaksson, *Marriage and Ministry in the New Temple* (Lund: Gleerup, 1965), 161-66; William J. Martin, "1 Corinthians 11:2-16: An Interpretation," in *Apostolic History and the Gospel*, ed. W. Ward Gasque and Ralph P. Martin (Grand Rapids: Eerdmans, 1970), 233.

exousia).[17] The Greek term "authority" should be translated as it is—that women should have "authority" over their heads. It should not be translated a "sign of authority" or "veil."[18]

In this context, *exousia* symbolizes not only a woman's (wife's) glorification (vs. shame) of man (husband) but also her authority to play an active role in worship. "That is, her veil [sic] represents the new authority given to women under the new dispensation to do things which formerly had not been permitted."[19] Following this line of reasoning, the two verses following his statement substantiate such an interpretation. Having argued for natural differences between man and woman, Paul now lays down a new principle of mutuality and interdependence also based on creation (cf. 1 Cor. 7:3-5).

Prior to the argument of verses 4-7, a basic assertion is made that often is raised in the discussion of women in ministry: "Now, I want you to realize that the *kephale* of every man is Christ, and the *kephale* of the woman is man, and the *kephale* of Christ is God." The normal meaning of *kephale,* or the head, in the New Testament is "source of being" or "origin"; the rarer meaning is "authority, dominion." While it seems obvious that the argument is an appeal to some sort of order, the meaning and application of the statement is much less obvious. This statement is made in service of the argument about what women do with their *heads* in their exercise of ministry (public prayer and prophesying); to do so without a covering brings shame upon their *heads.*[20] Whatever Paul's statement does mean, it in no way functions in this text to limit the participation or leadership of women in public worship.

---

17. Padgett, "Paul on Women in the Church," 71-72. The translation "sign"/"symbol" of authority is disallowed syntactically and semantically and does not fit the context that makes an egalitarian appeal. See Padgett's article for in-depth and orderly discussion of this text and possible translations. The phrase *dia tous angelous* is more problematic but could mean human messengers such as Priscilla who may have visited the church in Corinth. Padgett offers this suggestion with the judgment that "this interpretation . . . [is] at least as plausible as others" (81-82). *Exousia* was a watchword at Corinth. In response to the misguided grasping for "power" of the Corinthians (or at least of some significant group in the community), as is revealed throughout this correspondence, Paul makes the statement of his own *modus operandi*—example in 1 Cor. 9.

18. As many commentators have recognized, the term is Paul's normal word for "authority," which includes the sense of active exercise (and not passive reception of it as some have claimed). See Scholer, "Women in Ministry," 17. See also C. K. Barrett, *The First Epistle to the Corinthians,* Harper's New Testament Commentaries (New York: Harper and Row, 1968), 253-54, and Morna D. Hooker, "Authority on Her Head: An Examination of 1 Corinthians 11:10, *New Testament Studies* 10 (1964): 410-16.

19. Barrett, *First Epistle to the Corinthians,* 255.

20. *Head* may be a reference to the husband of the woman here. David W. J. Gill proposes that sociological factors of status and dress (including head coverings) are behind this text ("The Importance of Roman Portraiture for Head-coverings in 1 Corinthians 11:2-16,"

The translation *origin* or *source of being,* rather than *authority* or *dominion* makes quite a different statement; when translated as "authority/dominion" or "lord," this passage has been used to promote a sort of idolatry of men by women; women owe men what men owe Christ. But, while the text appeals to the order of creation from Genesis 2:18-23, it does not go so far as a straight parallel would allow. It does not claim that woman is the "image" as well as glory of man (11:7). Woman shares the image of God and therefore is not more removed from God than man; this is a concession to Genesis 1:27 and 5:2.[21] Verse 8 restates the concept of "origin" or "source" in the order of creation.[22]

A question is raised when we are encountered by the words of 1 Corinthians 14:33*b*-36, which some have read only as a limitation of the role of women in worship—only three chapters after women are casually recognized for their participation and leadership. The apparent discontinuity between these two passages also has been explained in a variety of ways.[23] Here, the governing perspective offered is that chapter 14 is instruction to three groups of people: (1) the tongues-speakers (vv. 2, 5, 9-19, 27 ff.); (2) prophets (vv. 3, 24, 29-32); and (3) women (34-35). The regulations for each group are similar, including the explicit command to "be silent" and the basic corrective requirement of "order."[24]

It is important to recognize Paul's use of the verb *lalein,* "speak" in 1 Corinthians 14:34, which should be translated as *inspired speech* or argumentative and distracting *debate* or *questioning.* The term used is not Paul's usual term for preaching or prophesying, so there is no contradiction with the reference to women praying and prophesying in the 11th chapter. No matter what final conclusion one places upon the instruction

---

Tyndale Bulletin 41.2 [1990]: 245-60). See also Richard Oster, "When Men Wore Veils to Worship: The Historical Context of 1 Corinthians 11:4," *New Testament Studies* 34 (1988): 481-505, and Cynthia L. Thompson, "Hairstyles, Headcoverings, and St. Paul: Portraits from Roman Corinth," *Biblical Archaeologist* 51/2 (June 1988): 99-115.

21. Barrett, *First Epistle to the Corinthians,* 248-49.

22. Padgett argues that the headship statement is a reference to the position of the Corinthians Paul is attempting to correct: "Thus the debate between Paul and the Corinthians can be seen as a debate over the meaning of 'head'" ("Paul on Women in the Church," 78-81). This fits the context; verses 10-12 are egalitarian statements.

23. The summary and critique by Ralph P. Martin of a number of these attempts to explain the apparent inconsistency are helpful. See *The Spirit and the Congregation* (Grand Rapids: Eerdmans, 1984), 84-88. But some insist that the text is an interpolation and so need not be explained as Paul's instruction. It seems best to begin with the text as it appears and evaluate all possible options for making sense of the text before speculating about its possible insertion into the letter.

24. Elizabeth Schüssler Fiorenza, *In Memory of Her* (New York: Crossroad, 1983, 1994), 230.

to be silent, it cannot be that women are not allowed to *pray* or *prophesy* in public worship. Ralph Martin's argument is basic: "Paul remains committed to social egalitarianism in the gospel (Gal. 3:28), and there is the undeniable evidence of the role he accorded women colleagues (Phoebe, Prisca [Priscilla], the women of Philippi [Phil. 4:3, sic] and the several co-workers in Rom. 16). It is *prima facie* unlikely that he would state categorically, 'Let your women keep silent in worship.'"[25]

One of the proposed pictures drawn to explain this text and the larger context of this Epistle is that of women who aspired to be charismatic teachers, claiming special revelations in inspired speech that were above the usual corrections of the congregation and apostolic teaching. Their claims were so inflated that the apostle is led to sarcasm: Did the word of God originate with you? Or are you the only people it has reached? In this scenario, the heretical teaching going on in the Corinthian congregations was a gnostic sort of teaching (cf. chapters 7 and 15).[26] Whatever sociological history this text is mirroring, Paul's correctives were not aimed at the total restriction of women's participation and ministry in Corinth anymore than he forbade tongues (14:39) or the ministry of prophecy in general. Women functioned with the gift to which Paul accorded highest (and corrective) value to in that community (14:1). The Corinthian evidence displays a community in which women were participating in leadership in the community, some of whom required correction, not for that function but for the abuse of the function.

---

25. Martin, *Spirit and the Congregation,* 84-88.

26. These women could be sharing in a claim of "special knowledge" that included speculations that there was no actual resurrection of the body, but that a spiritual "resurrection" had already occurred at baptism. Such teaching could have prompted Paul's extended reply beginning with his question, "How can some of you say that there is no resurrection of the body?" (15:12). Their denial of the resurrection lay in the claim that they were raised in baptism—they were "angelic beings" (13:1) after a misapplication of the words of Jesus recorded in Luke 20:35-36. It is also apparent that Paul was responding to a belief in sacramental efficacy (11:17-34; 10:1-22). Such a concept led to confusion in the home; as resurrected beings they no longer participated in marriage obligations—they were attempting to live in a state of celibacy in marriage (7:3-5). These heretical teachers (women glossolaliacs) were to be kept "under control" as the "law" required (*nomos* meaning "principle" and here referring to Paul's teaching; cf. v. 37). The meaning of "asking their husbands at home" is a response to the challenge these women presented to their husbands in public assembly. The verb "inquire after," *eperotan,* is used in the sense of interrogation, in the same way as they challenged apostolic authority. This interpretation, offered by Martin, fits the larger portrait drawn of the Corinthian church. This portrait is supported by a parallel circumstance in 1 Tim. 2:8-15 where arrogant women have aspired to be teachers of things they know not (possibly also teaching gnostic perspectives and presuming the right understanding of the faith). See Martin, *Spirit and the Congregation,* 84-88.

The above discussions of the participation of women in public worship and lists of women who were leaders in the early church all bear evidence to the fact that women did function in ministry in the early church. While there is no claim to "office" here, there is no question that the "function" occurred. The use of the lists of women in this discussion is an appeal to at least some of the tradition and experience of the early church. Such information should be considered alongside what are seen by some as propositional instructions.

3. The Use of Household Codes. One argument against women in ministry is an appeal to the household or station codes located in the New Testament. These codes with their hierarchical order were not created by the New Testament authors but rather were drawn from the Greco-Roman culture of that day.[27] The Greek philosopher Aristotle, who predated Christ by three and a half centuries, was the source of the formal arrangement of pairings based on the dominant/subordinate hierarchical model:

The primary and smallest parts of the household are "master" and "slave," "husband" and "wife," "father" and "children." . . . Authority and subordination are conditions not only inevitable but also expedient. . . . There is always found a ruling and a subject factor . . . between the sexes, the male is *by nature* superior and the female inferior, the male ruler and the female subject.[28]

Aristotle expanded this household code to the realm of political life because in his thinking "the household was a microcosm of the state."[29] He taught the authority/subordination model in the pairing of ruler/people. He promoted his social order as necessary to stability, harmony, and political security. Any threat to this Aristotelian value system was consid-

---

27. The information about household codes is collected in the following two texts: John H. Elliott, *A Home for the Homeless: A Sociological Exegesis of 1 Peter, Its Situation and Strategy* (Philadelphia: Fortress, 1981), and David L. Balch, *Let Wives Be Submissive: The Domestic Code in 1 Peter,* Society of Biblical Literature Monograph Series 26 (Chico, Calif.: Scholars, 1981). The articles most helpful for the argument developed here are by these same two scholars: John H. Elliott, "1 Peter, Its Situation and Strategy: A Discussion with David Balch" in *Perspectives on First Peter,* ed. Charles H. Talbert (Macon, Ga.: Mercer University Press, 1986), 61-78, and David L. Balch, "Hellenization/Acculturation in 1 Peter" in the same text, 79-102. I agree with Balch on the meaning of the "household codes" in the text of 1 Peter as I have presented it here. Much of the following discussion comes from information collected by Balch in his article "Early Christian Criticism of Patriarchal Authority: 1 Peter 2:11-3:12," *Union Seminary Quarterly Review* 39/3 (1984): 161-73.

28. Emphasis added. Aristotle, *Politics* I, 1253b 7-8; 1254a 22-23, 29-31; 1254b 13-21. Unless noted, quotations from ancient Greek sources are taken from the Loeb Classical Library.

29. See the discussion of Aristotelian political philosophy in Balch, "Early Christian Criticism of Patriarchal Authority," 161-63.

ered by the Roman Empire to be a threat to such stability and security. The Roman emperor Octavian instructed his soldiers to "allow no woman to make herself equal to a man."[30] The occasion for such an instruction was Anthony and Cleopatra. David Balch reviews the problem as follows:

If democratic equality between husband and wife as it existed in Egypt were allowed to influence Roman households, the government would degenerate into a democracy; and the Romans believed this changed form of government would be morally worse than the aristocracy or monarchy which had brought them to power. The Egyptian Cleopatra's goddess Isis, who "gave women the same power as men," was perceived as a threat to continued Roman rule.[31]

The rights of the one in authority were assumed. Tyranny was not criticized as an expression of that authority in the dominant culture, as directed by Aristotle's words: "For there is no such thing as injustice in the absolute sense towards what is one's own."[32] In the same writing Aristotle assumes that, since the one owned is "as it were a part of oneself and no one chooses to harm himself, hence there can be no injustice towards them and nothing just or unjust in the political sense." He was advocating a benign tyranny based on inferior/superior natures. Yet, Seneca, the Roman Stoic, critiqued Roman treatment of slaves as "excessively haughty, cruel and insulting."[33]

This lengthy look back at Greco-Roman history is necessary for us to recover the impact of the household code as used in the New Testament. What is significant about the use of the code in the New Testament, at least in the earliest books in which it appears, is that it was not simply *adopted.* It was *adapted,* that is, changed or modified with particular qualifiers (Col. 3:18—4:1; Eph. 5:21—6:9; 1 Pet. 2:13—3:7). The early believers did not accept the Roman code as absolute but critiqued it even as they appealed to it. For example, in Colossians 3:18—4:1, the traditional pairings are each followed by an unthinkable modification, which in fact points to a higher code of ethics than the one encapsulated in the original code:

Wives be subject to husbands . . . husbands love wives.

Children obey parents . . . fathers do not provoke children.

Slaves obey masters . . . masters treat slaves justly.[34]

---

30. Cassius, *Roman History* 50.25.3, 28.3.

31. Ibid., 162-63.

32. Aristotle, *Nicomachean Ethics* V, 1134*b* 9-18.

33. Seneca, *Moral Letters* 47.1.

34. This is David Balch's organization expressing the household codes. This layout of the passage also reveals the qualification of each aspect of the code. In "Early Christian Criticism of Patriarchal Authority," 161.

Such modification would have stood out to the original readers; they would have assumed the instruction to the subordinate member of the pairings.

The injunctions of the code in Ephesians are filled with new meaning as they appear under the revolutionary paragraph heading "submit to one another," which is applied to all of the following discussion. The reason given there for submission is not an appeal to the superior or inferior created nature of the other, but rather reverence to Christ. It is impossible for the 21st-century student of the Bible to appreciate fully the newness of the relationship commanded of husbands and wives in Ephesians. Likewise, the command to Christian masters was full of the seeds of change: "treat your slaves in the same way" (i.e., by the same set of attitudes and conduct required of Christian slaves toward their masters). Such radical qualifications of the household codes were a class apart from any parallel in Greek philosophy, Stoicism, or Roman household codes of the time.[35] And the seeds of such thinking produced the fruit of the story of Paul, Onesimus, and Philemon.

First Peter also set conditions on the household codes. In a setting of persecution, submission to human authority is for the Lord's sake. Christians were suffering "unjustly" at the hands of tyrannical masters (2:19-20), husbands (3:6), and local government officials (2:14; 3:14, 17). The purpose of the code in 1 Peter was not to insist on conformity to traditional values but pragmatically to steer a prudent line. The appeal was for Christian commitment even when it involved suffering.[36] There was no question of an "inferior nature" being advanced here, for all were called to live as "servants of God" (2:16). Christ as the "Suffering Servant of God" was the model to follow (vv. 21-24). In the specific address to slaves in chapter 2, the terms used elsewhere in the codes in the New Testament for servant (doulos) and master (kurios) are not used here. Rather, the terms household servants (oiketai) and despots (despotai) are used. The reason for the shift from the traditional use of the code language is that the author had already used the term "servant" to refer to every Christian (v. 16) and "master" (or "Lord") for God (v. 15).

Roman rulers might not judge "justly" as God has ordained that they should (1 Pet. 2:13-14) and as God himself does (vv. 21-23), but they are to be submitted to for the Lord's sake. Christian wives are to submit to pagan husbands for the purpose of evangelism (3:1-2) and are not to fear them (v. 6). Christian husbands are called to a relationship with their

---

35. Ibid.

36. "Household codes" are better defined as "station codes" in 1 Peter. Submission to government is also enjoined.

wives quite different from the cultural norm. In fact, a most revolutionary concept appears here: the husband's spiritual vitality is dependent on the way he treats his wife.

The most significant critique of the husband-wife roles in the household code as in 1 Peter would be immediately obvious to the original hearers of this Epistle. And yet, without historical and cultural background, readers today all but miss it. The Christian women addressed in 1 Peter 3 were married to pagan husbands. And yet, despite the norms of the Roman (and, in fact, Jewish) culture of that time, these women were allowed the freedom of religious choice by 1 Peter; they could remain Christian! That instruction went against the typical Roman perspective, such as Plutarch expressed:

> A wife should have no friends but those of her husband; and as the gods are the first of friends it is becoming for a wife to worship and know only the gods that her husband believes in, and to shut the door tight upon all queer rituals and outlandish superstitions. For with no god do stealthy and secret rites performed by a woman find favor.[37]

Even while addressing women in this text by appealing to the social code of the day, 1 Peter assumes their religious independence from their pagan husbands (cf. 1:18; 4:3-4). These women were encouraged to keep their faith and not to fear their husbands, who likely had been expressing extreme displeasure and concern at their wives' conversions. So, when those women heard this Epistle in a service of worship, they heard a proclamation of freedom, religious responsibility, and increased personal value. Had their pagan husbands heard that same text, they would have heard insubordination and anarchy. And how would they have heard the words to their wives, "Do not give way to fear"? But, oh how differently this text is read today.

Many scholars have recognized the difference in the way the household codes were used in 1 Timothy and Titus. The predominant attitudes of the culture of that day seem to be expressed in the codes in these letters.[38] In these texts, there is no leveling instruction to the dominant members of the pairs that is comparable to the Colossian or Ephesian texts. And yet, the motivation for use of the code is telling. The concern that women and

---

37. Plutarch, "Advice to Bride and Groom," in *Moralia* 140D-E.

38. It was not too much later that misogynism developed in full form both in Jewish and Christian literature. Plato's low evaluation of women is well-documented, and the Greek culture certainly influenced these times. The Jewish law that a woman was unclean during menstruation (Lev. 15:19 ff.) and the rabbinical speculations on the special culpability of woman in the Fall were developed into negative doctrines and attitudes by some early church fathers.

slaves ought to be subject is stated in Titus as the desire for the church to win the acceptance of society. This is still not the Roman appeal to a created nature of superior or inferior. It is a pragmatic appeal not unlike the exhortation to prayer in 1 Timothy 2:1-3. The purpose for both instructions is "that we may live peaceful and quiet lives" that will provide the opportunity for salvation of all.

First Timothy 2:11-15 is the text most often quoted by those who would limit the ministry of women. In fact, it has been used by some as the defining text of the discussion of women's place in the church. It seems that the reason the passage is given such priority is that it is judged by some to be a clear statement of instruction for the church regarding women. Yet, the complexity and difficulty of the passage is mirrored in the disagreement it engenders even among conservative scholars. The two major perspectives radically affect the interpretation of this text. If the text is adopted as a propositional statement, as Paul's definitive (eternal and everywhere) word on restriction of the participation of women, then it follows that "I permit no woman to teach or to have authority over a man" (2:12) is to be taken as "clear instruction." However, once one begins literary and historical analysis, a number of serious challenges immediately arise. The text is not at all clear.

The first major challenge is that the interpretation of verse 12 depends on how one translates the verb *authentein,* which is a *hapax legomenon,* which appears only once in the New Testament. The translator must rely on other sources to determine possible meanings; four are possible, each one radically affecting the sense of the whole passage.[39] The challenge is increased by the fact that the verb *didaskein* (to teach) in 1 Timothy is always used in conjunction with another verb that qualifies its focus (e.g., 1:3-4; 4:11; 6:2-3). Therefore, in verse 12 *authentein* qualifies and so refers to the negative content of the teaching and not to the activity of teaching itself. The Kroegers have concluded:

> If the context of 1 Timothy 2:12 is neutral and refers only to the activity of teaching rather than to its positive or negative content, then it is the only time that *didaskein* is so used in the Pastorals . . . it is in keeping with the other uses of *didaskein* to find in this directive a condemnation of their heterodoxy.[40]

This interpretation is strengthened by recognition that the grammar of the sentence allows at least two interpretations: if it is an indirect statement

---

39. The technical study of the use of this verb is meticulously presented in *I Suffer Not a Woman* by Richard and Catherine Clark Kroeger (Grand Rapids: Baker, 1992), 79-104.

40. Ibid., 81.

with a repeated negative, the emphasis of the sentence would be on the content of the teaching and not on the function of teaching. The reading then would be: "I do not allow a woman to teach/proclaim herself originator or author of man."[41]

Further difficulties are presented in the verses surrounding verse 12. In verse 11, the term for *silence* is not the term used in 1 Corinthians 14 and has five possible meanings, none of which is as strong as the term used in that letter. The best interpretation of that term is *quietness* or *in a quiet demeanor,*[42] which is precisely the term's sense in the instruction just verses earlier that exhorts prayers "so that we may lead a quiet and peaceable life" (1 Tim. 2:2; cf. 2 Thess. 3:12 and 1 Thess. 4:11). The term does not mean verbal silence but an attitude of reverence or a state of peacefulness. Consistency requires that one's interpretation of "quietness" in 2:2 should be applied to 2:12. Finally, the Greek phrase translated "I do not permit" is in the present tense, indicating continuous action. It is better rendered as "I am not permitting," which then suggests specific instruction for a particular circumstance.[43]

For some, another problem in this passage is that Paul's usual term for "man" is not used in 2:8-15. In the Pauline letters, *aner* or *man* occurs 50 times, and *gyne* or *woman* occurs 54 times in 11 texts. In each case, the terms refer to husbands and wives and not male and female. This complicates the interpretation of "full submission." To whom exactly are women to be in full submission? their husbands? men in general? true Christian teachers? The grammar of the sentence does not make the answer easy. Once again, the passage is not "clear." Nevertheless, the best interpretation for the unit seems to be that these are general instructions directed to men and women. The conclusion selected here as best fitting the overall context is that women are to learn quietly or with a quiet demeanor from true Christian teachers such as Timothy.

Finally, the relationship of verse 15 to the total passage is unclear. There is no consensus about the meaning of "she will be saved."[44] Contextual and historical studies suggest that the passage is one of the several re-

---

41. See Randy Huber and John Stanley's cogent explanation in *Reclaiming the Wesleyan/Holiness Heritage of Women Clergy: Sermons, A Case Study and Resources* (Grantham, Pa.: Messiah College, Wesleyan/Holiness Women Clergy, 1999), 40.

42. Gordon D. Fee, *1 and 2 Timothy, Titus,* New International Biblical Commentary (Peabody, Mass.: Hendrickson, 1988), 72.

43. Ibid.

44. However, if one interprets the restriction on women literally, to be consistent, one must interpret this statement literally as well. See Mary Jane Evans' discussion in *Women in the Bible* (Downers Grove, Ill.: InterVarsity Press, 1983), 107.

sponses of the letter to the false teachers at Ephesus. The content of that teaching included misunderstanding of the Old Testament, speculative Jewish myths (genealogies), and asceticism. This false teaching was particularly attractive to women and to younger widows who avoided remarriage and had opened their homes to false teachers (2:9-15; 5:11-15; 2 Tim. 3:6-7). Such teaching has been identified as a "precursor to Gnosticism"[45] and as doctrines based upon "perversions of the Adam and Eve saga" with Eve as creator and spiritual illuminator of Adam and the serpent as offering "gnosis" to the world.[46] The passage is best identified as part of the correction of false teachers and teaching that is going on at Ephesus.

Given just the few of the many difficulties of 1 Timothy 2:11-15 that are listed here, it is remarkable—no—indefensible that a single verse, verse 12, would be given the status it has been given by some in the church. Even more, it is incredible that one verse would be made the basis for any doctrine, especially one so critical in its impact on the church. Whatever one finally makes of this passage, if one counts the Epistle as Pauline, one must consider the evidence that Paul allowed women in ministry and required submission to their leadership.[47] Also, if one interprets the instructions regarding women literally, integrity requires other assertions in the passage be interpreted literally as well (holy hands lifted, no braided hair, and no jewelry; women saved through childbearing [1 Tim. 2:8, 15]).

The second level of investigation that affects the interpretation of 1 Timothy 2:11-15 is to study the passage in the broad context of the station codes as used in the New Testament. The major difference between 1 Timothy 2 and the earlier appeals to the codes is that there is no reciprocity in

45. Alan Padgett presents a compelling presentation for typology as the interpretive approach governing verses 11-15. Both Eve and the Ephesian women are deceived and "saved through childbirth" recalls Gen. 3:15. Eve bears the seed that is at enmity with the serpent. Eve then is made both positive and negative type: "She is an example of deception in verses 13-14 and an example of salvation through childbirth in verse 15" ("Wealthy Women at Ephesus," *Interpretation*, 41 [1989]: 19-31).

46. Richard Clark Kroeger and Catherine Clark Kroger present a lengthy study of the cultural and historical influences behind the false teaching that include pagan goddess religions and Jewish mythologies and genealogies or origins as Gnostic developments. They then read this passage, along with Padgett and others, as a refutation of false teaching (*I Suffer Not a Woman*, 19-23, 62-66, 88-98, 103-77). See also Samuel Terrien, *Till the Heart Sings*, 191-93.

47. For example, Phoebe is called a *prostatis* (overseer, guardian; Rom. 16:1-2) which is the term used to indicate elders who *preside* (1 Tim. 5:17), *rule* (Rom. 12:8), or *hold authority over* (1 Thess. 5:12), and which occurs in short instructions to respect and honor leaders or elders.

this instruction.[48] And yet, even here in the most conservative expression of the code in the New Testament, the reason given for submission is not the nature of the creation but rather the story of the Fall. This appeal to woman's greater culpability in the Fall cannot be taken as a theological absolute. The Genesis account itself (Gen. 3) here referred to does not assign such a meaning to the woman's succumbing first to temptation (only the man who is defending himself appeals to any "priority" of guilt!); punishment is equally assigned. And the apostle Paul, when referring to the Fall, talks about Adam's sin (Rom. 5:12-14). In fact, the claim made in 1 Timothy 2:14 that Adam was not the one deceived (it was the woman who was deceived and became a sinner) cannot be equated with the Genesis or Romans references to this event. It is much more like the rabbinical speculations of that time as expressed, for example, by Philo, the apostle Paul's older contemporary: "the woman, being imperfect and deprived 'by nature,' made the beginning of sinning; but man, as being the more excellent and perfect nature, was the first to set the example of blushing and being ashamed, and indeed of every good feeling and action."[49]

Long ago, Adolph von Harnack presented his theory to explain the changes in social attitudes from Jesus' followers and the earliest expression of the church to Christianity as represented by the Pastoral Epistles (1 Timothy and Titus). He observed the following progression: (1) the radical perspectives of Jesus, (2) unconventional freedom for women in the earliest congregations, (3) conditional appeals to the cultural norms by use of the household codes, and (4) uncritical acceptance of Greco-Roman values. He called this progression a Hellenization process.[50] While Harnack's theory is simplistic and outdated, his observation may be redirected into a perspective of accommodation for the sake of evangelism or, in this case, orthodoxy in the face of heresy.

This process may be observed in a historical glance at slavery—a comparable social issue. In relationship to the institution of slavery, Jews were never to forget that they were once slaves. In fact, the central story of the

---

48. The same is true of Titus 2:1-10. David Schroeder, *Die Haustafeln des Neuen Testament* (Diss., U. Hamburg, 1959) as summarized by Alan Padgett in "The Pauline Rationale for Submission: Biblical Feminism and the *hina* Clauses of Titus 2:1-10," *Evangelical Quarterly* 59 (1987): 44. Padgett refers to the codes in the pastorals as "church codes" because they focus on relationships in the church (not the home).

49. As quoted in Balch, *Let Wives Be Submissive*, 84.

50. I am indebted also to Balch's summary of Harnack's work (*The Mission and Expansion of Christianity in the First Three Centuries*, trans. James Moffatt [New York: G. P. Putnam's Sons, 1908], 1:19, 31, 77, 314; *History of Dogma*, trans. Neil Buchanan [New York: Russell and Russell, 1958], 1:45-57, 116-28; 2:169, 174) in "Early Christian Criticism of Patriarchal Authority."

Torah is the Exodus. God freed the Hebrew slaves from their Egyptian lords. Therefore, slavery was conditioned with many protections in Israel. Slaves were to be freed after six years of service and more and were to be sent off with blessings and liberal provisions for livelihood (Exod. 21:1-6; Deut. 15:12-18). Slavery was not to become a perpetual institution. There was no elitism involved. This was quite a different expression from Aristotle's concept of a natural hierarchy. Such a historical and literary history surely influenced the thinking of the early church, but the attitudes and values of the church through time have often followed (or even led) arguments for cultural expediency and orthopraxy (or in the case of segregation of the church along racial lines, arguments for the effectiveness of evangelism).[51]

Careful study of the household codes reveals a very different usage in the New Testament than is claimed in some popular teaching today. While the codes may be expressing a "reversion to convention,"[52] the motivation demonstrated in the New Testament was pragmatic concern and was not based upon some concept of natural order by creation. The popular interpretation of these codes in some churches today is more Aristotelian than Christian and ignores the impact of the spiritual qualifications placed on them by the New Testament writers and the motivation for their use.

4. Argument from Creation Accounts. In the above examination, the arguments from the creation accounts have been referred to briefly. The creation account of Genesis 1 presents a creation in which male and female are together created in the image of God (cf. 5:1-2). The second creation account that Paul appealed to (Gen. 2) includes two aspects that have been used to promote a hierarchical model of authority/submission. First, woman is created after man and from his rib. While it might be argued that 1 Corinthians 11 suggests an order of priority on the basis of this

---

51. It was not so long ago that Paul's words in Eph. 6:5-9, Col. 3:22, and 1 Tim. 6:1-2 were used to support the institution of slavery in the United States of America and elsewhere, and that further, some church teaching included an Aristotelian philosophy of the natural inferiority of some peoples. Subordination to government has also been enjoined as an appeal to the station code texts. Martin Luther based his teaching on "Orders of Creation." This theory was behind the Lutheran support of the German state until the fall of the Hohenzollerns. As the Nazis gained power, German Christians justified the Nazi concept of the State by the same means. Karl Barth and other church leaders of the day critiqued such a use of Scripture to define a social order. See summary statement by Adam Miller in *The Role of Women in Today's World* (Anderson, Ind.: Commission on Social Concerns, 1978), 3-6.

52. This language, created by Elaine H. Pagels, is an attempt to recognize the motivations for various teachings on women. See her article, "Paul and Women: A Response to Recent Discussion," *Journal of the American Academy of Religion* 42 (Summer 1974): 546. This article comes from her presentation at the AAR annual meeting in Chicago in 1973.

text, the original text does not support the development of a model of dominance/subordination. The "rib" is the symbol of correspondence between man and woman. The man and the woman belong to each other in a qualitatively different way than they belong to the animals: "The unique closeness of her relationship to the man is underlined above all through the fact that she is created, not from the earth but out of the rib from man himself."[53] If anything, the woman is distinguished from the animals who are not suitable for relationship with the man, who are subordinate to him (Gen. 2:18-20). The woman's superiority over the animals, not her inferiority in relationship to the man, is the point of the story.

The second aspect of the text used to support the dominance of man is that woman was created to be a *helper* for man (Gen. 2:20). Yet, this term "helper" is the same term used of God in God's relationship with man (e.g., Exod. 18:4; Isa. 30:5; Ps. 146:5). With some humor, one might argue that since this term is used of the helping one who is superior (God), the woman who *helps* man is the superior party. At the very least, there is no connotation of subordination with the use of the term, only that of correspondence. The term has been misapplied when it is interpreted to mean that woman was created to be servile to man.

The concept of subordination is only first referred to in Genesis 3:16 as *a consequence of the Fall.* Domination/subordination is presented as a new reality brought into being by sin and is represented as a part of what is broken in the marriage trust. Speculation on this text that envisages women as inferior or as properly subordinate is a late development in Judaism, occurring first in the second century B.C.E. "The Old Testament [itself] does not emphasize the subordination of wives."[54] If the consequence of the Fall is the subordination of women, should that subordination be lifted up as the ideal? It seems obvious that it is a part of the fallen creation, the old order, which in the apostle Paul's mind is passing away (2 Cor. 5:17).

There is no doubt that the Jewish culture was patriarchal, especially in Jesus' day. Yet, women were generally accorded more value in the Jewish culture than in the Roman world. It is certain that misogynism (extreme devaluation of women) was a late Jewish rabbinical development that was adopted later by some of the church fathers of the second and third centuries. Such attitudes are not careful reflections on the creation accounts of Scripture but are adaptations of the biblical message that reveal the influence of Greco-Roman culture.

---

53. Hans Walter Wolff, *Anthropology of the Old Testament* (Philadelphia: Fortress, 1974), 94.
54. Balch, "Hellenization/Acculturation in 1 Peter," 97.

5. The Eschatological Age of the Spirit. Another line of reasoning in the discussion of women in ministry is that which is developed along the lines of Peter's use of Joel's prophecy on the Day of Pentecost as presented by Luke (Acts 2). The uniqueness of that event is described in the universality of the pouring out of God's Spirit. This prophecy proclaims the means behind the method in the Book of Acts; the gospel will be proclaimed across many barriers because (1:8—"to the ends of the earth") the Spirit will be poured out "on all flesh"—across all categories of the church —age (young and old), gender (male and female), and social status (slave and free).[55] The sentiment of this prophecy is also presented by the apostle Paul in his teaching on the church (Gal. 3:28), the new creation, the new Adam (Rom. 5), and a new Israel—all eschatological (end times) categories. In the line of such thinking, the apostle Paul preaches a new time in which "we are no longer under the law." It is the time now in which "faith has come" (Gal. 3:25). In the same discussion, Paul speaks of the inception of that faith and baptism into Christ; in Christ (here in the corporate sense of the church): "There is neither Jew nor Greek, slave nor free, male nor female, for you are all one in Christ Jesus" (Gal. 3:28).

The threefold distinctions excluded in Paul's pronouncement "you are all one in Christ Jesus" corresponded to popular formulas that maintained such distinctions. The morning prayer of the Jewish male included the thanksgiving that he was not created a Gentile, a slave, or a woman.[56] Against the Roman expression of distinction and division in the household codes and Jewish man's prayer, the apostle Paul proclaims the positive dissolution of all such realities. The fact that Paul is presenting more than a

---

55. Jews were more likely to have been disturbed by the inclusion of slaves as prophets than women. The Old Testament includes no stories of slaves as God's prophets. In contrast, there was a strong tradition of women as prophets (Miriam—Exod. 15:20; Deborah—Judg. 4:4; Huldah—2 Kings 22:14; the wife of Isaiah—Isa. 8:3). Rabbinical tradition refers to seven prophetesses—Sarah, Miriam, Deborah, Hannah, Abigail, Huldah, and Esther. This point is made by Knofel Staton in the paper he presented to the Open Forum of the Church of God and Christian Churches (Independent) in Lexington, Kentucky, on April 3, 1991, "The Teaching in Acts 2:17, 18 and Its Implications for Christian Unity," 7.

56. The earliest record of this prayer identified thus far is in the work of Rabbi Judah ben Elai, c. CE 150. However, the formula itself can be traced back to the Greek Thales who was grateful that he was a man and not a beast, a man and not a woman, and a Greek and not a barbarian (Diogenes Laertius, *Vitae Philosophorum* 1.33). Socrates and Plato said substantially the same thing, and Aristotle adopts their thinking. As noted earlier, Aristotle's teachings were spread (process of Hellenization) by Alexander the Great in the 300s B.C.E. His empire covered much of what would later become the Roman Empire. See expanded argument in F. F. Bruce, *The Epistle to the Galatians*, New International Greek Testament Commentary (Grand Rapids: Eerdmans, 1982), 188-91. It may be noted that the Jewish thanksgiving remains part of the orthodox Jewish expression. It occurs in the popular volume *Daily Prayers*, ed. Rabbi M. Stern (New York: Hebrew Publishing, 1928).

visionary and "spiritual" ideal is proven in that it was precisely the human structures of these distinctions that were addressed in the life and practice of the early church.

For example, the vision of Peter in Acts 10 is lived out in Caesarea and then was the motivation for inclusion of the Gentiles in Acts 11. The unity Paul preaches is to be a reality in the social experience of the church (Eph. 2). Not only does Paul insist that the church live out such a vision, but he also attempts to model it himself. That vision is the basis of his confrontation with Peter. Paul appeals to Philemon for the sake of Onesimus out of such convictions. And his practice of including Christian women as partners in his ministry was the culminating expression of his conviction that "in Christ, all things are made new" (2 Cor. 5:17). Nevertheless, "whereas Paul's ban on discrimination on racial or social grounds has been fairly widely accepted . . . there has been a tendency to restrict the degree to which 'there is no male and female.'"[57] In the text of Galatians, the context may be limited to a discussion of baptism that is open to all (as opposed to circumcision, which was the old sign of the law). Surely the denial of discrimination that is affirmed in relation to baptism holds good for the new existence "in Christ" generally. F. F. Bruce's conclusion seems to be the best, given both content and context:

> No more restriction is implied in Paul's equalizing of the status of male and female in Christ than in his equalizing status of Jew and Gentile, of slave and free person. If in ordinary life existence in Christ is manifested openly in church fellowship, then, if a Gentile may exercise spiritual leadership in church as freely as a Jew, or a slave as freely as a citizen, why not a woman as freely as a man?[58]

THEOLOGICAL SYNTHESIS

The evidence selected and analyzed above creates an argument that is cumulative in force; women should be included, not only in the life of the church but also in the function of ministry (with appropriate office) in the church. The visionary expression of Jesus' life and ministry with women implies this. The practice and expressions of mutuality of the apostle Paul indicate the same. The household codes are best thought of as cultural expressions appealed to for pragmatic concerns and in their very qualification indicate an open future. The appeals to "creation order" are not so conclusive as many would like us to believe and at any rate will not support the exclusion of women from ministry. Finally, the idealism of the es-

---

57. Bruce, *Epistle to the Galatians,* 189.
58. Ibid., 190.

chatological age, the age of the Spirit, was certainly understood to have come into being at Pentecost. The implications of the "new creation" were gradually recognized and affirmed in the life and practice of the church. The record of the New Testament is the story of that process.

The question of degrees of implementation that the evidence implies has been argued by some along the lines of function versus office. This line of thinking is that women may function in ministry but are not to be allowed the formal legitimacy of office. A derivation of this idea is that women be allowed in an office only where they would not be "over men." In this case, a woman always functions under the authority (and so supervision) of a man. Such a distinction seems artificial, especially given the history of distinctions between clergy and laity. Even the Catholic Biblical Association's committee on the Role of Women in Early Christianity makes the following observation:

The Christian priesthood as we know it began to be established no earlier than the end of the first or the beginning of the second century. In the primitive Church . . . ministries were complex and in flux, and the different services later incorporated into the priestly ministry were performed by various members of the community. . . . Thus, while Paul could speak of charisms as varying in importance . . . the NT evidence does not indicate that one group controlled or exercised all ministries in the earliest Church. Rather the responsibility for ministry, or service, was shared.[59]

Therefore, the committee recognized that all of the members of the body were understood to have been gifted for upbuilding ministries (Eph. 4:12; cf. 4:15-16; 1 Cor. 12:7, 12-31; Rom. 12:4-5). Women did perform ministry and exercise functions that were later defined by offices of ministry. Therefore, the committee concluded *against* their own church tradition that "the NT evidence, while not decisive by itself, points toward the admission of women to priestly ministry."[60]

It has already been noted that nowhere does the New Testament speak explicitly of women in church office. Only three discussions in the New Testament even touch on the participation of women in worship

---

59. "Women and Priestly Ministry: The New Testament Evidence," *Catholic Biblical Quarterly* 41 (1979): 609.

60. Ibid., 613. The whole issue of church tradition must be reviewed given the explicit and astounding new evidence of participation of women not only in ministry but also in office. Against the standard presentations of the Catholic church, Mary Ann Rossi, translating the work of Giorgio Otranto, offers summaries of archaeological findings that portray women functioning as priests and bishops in the early catholic church: (1) fresco of a woman blessing the Eucharist in the Priscilla catacomb in Rome—possibly Priscilla; (2) inscriptions

services. The basic concern of these texts is for proper conduct. The instruction in 1 Corinthians 14 cannot mean that women are not to pray and prophesy (preach) in public assembly (cf. 1 Cor. 11:3-6). And the prohibition in 1 Timothy (2:11-15) seems to run counter to the evidence of the other texts in the Scripture.

The household codes cannot be appealed to for the general supervision of all women functioning in ministry in the church. In their contexts they are applied to husbands and wives and are discussions of proper interpersonal relations in the family (and perhaps to that particular family in their experience in worship). If the apostle Paul were applying his use of the household codes to ministerial function in the church, he never would have mentioned Priscilla's name first in the lists. He was already breaking tradition to mention her name at all, and more so to list her as a teacher of Apollos.

While the early freedoms for women in the New Testament apparently were later restricted along societal conventions, the same impetus for change regarding the status of women existed in the church as for Gentiles and slaves. Participation of women in services of worship and their inclusion in ministry are evidence of that. Some of the early motivation for accepting present societal role or status was the conviction that Jesus was returning immediately (e.g., 1 Cor. 7). In later texts that motivation was replaced by the need for the tolerance of society, and harmony in mixed-religion homes with the institution about "submission."

Despite the variety in the record of the experience of early Christian communities, there is much that leads us to see the early church as self-consciously wrestling with the new realities called into being in the kingdom of God or "in Christ" when they recognized women in ministry. The best understanding of Scripture invites us to be so visionary today.[61]

---

identifying four women by name as priests; (3) a Roman mosaic picturing one of four bishops as a woman, Theodora; and (4) ninth-century correspondence from Bishop Atto confirming that women served the early church as priests and bishops, but were banned in the fourth century. Evidence such as this raises the question of official suppression of historical evidence of women's leadership in the church. Such evidence has been used for a popular argument against the Catholic hierarchy by its appearance in *Megatrends for Women* by Patricia Aburdene and John Naisbitt (New York: Random House/Villard Books, 1992), 126.

61. Two organizations that promote such a vision (and the *primacist* model) are Christians for Biblical Equality that puts out a quarterly newsletter, *Mutuality,* and hosts a biennial conference, and Wesleyan/Holiness Clergy Women (seven denominations) that has a biennial conference in the United States. Both groups produce materials and catalogues containing a wide variety of resources. CBE may be reached at 122 W. Franklin Ave., Suite 218, Minneapolis, MN, 55404; e-mail: cbe@cbeinternational.org. The W/HCW's web site is www.messiah.edu/whwc.

Diane Leclerc is a professor and historical theologian who is convinced that the Wesleyan theological tradition champions a particular way of reading and interpreting the Bible. She insists that this Wesleyan way is centered in the significance of love and naturally has affirmed the equality of women in church life. For her, Wesleyan hermeneutics is gender hermeneutics, "love hermeneutics." In this chapter, Professor Leclerc considers what John Wesley had to say about women, taking into account the interpretation of difficult biblical passages in this regard. She then considers the interpretive methods of Phoebe Palmer, the "matriarch" of the 19th-century Holiness Movement. Finally, she reflects on how such methods of Bible reading and theological vision relate to the present-day reading method of "feminists." Leclerc's conclusions center in some theological observations that she offers on Wesleyanism and gender issues.

The women of early British Methodism were afforded ministry opportunities rare to women in the 18th century. Phoebe Palmer's theology encouraged women to believe that they had equal access to Pentecostal power through the Spirit, thus having confidence to know themselves as fully devoted to God and free to be fully themselves apart from male stereotypes of them. Relating all this to biblical understanding, Palmer may have anticipated some of the interpretive nuances of today's feminist concerns and methods. Leclerc is certain that identifying a Wesleyan way of reading Scripture will rebirth the powerful affirmation of women that has been part of the historic Wesleyan tradition. Such is very much needed in our time.

11
WESLEYAN-HOLINESS-FEMINIST HERMENEUTICS: A HISTORICAL RENDERING WITH CONTEMPORARY CONSIDERATIONS[1]

Diane Leclerc

◆

A distinctly Wesleyan interpretation of Scripture reaches many conclusions with tremendous theological and practical import. One of the more significant aspects of Wesleyan hermeneutics, which has played itself out in the history of the Wesleyan-Holiness movement, is that it affirms an underlying equality of all persons, Jew or Greek, slave or free, male or female. I argue, then, that Wesleyan hermeneutics is race hermeneutics, class hermeneutics, gender hermeneutics by nature of an underpinning that could be called a *hermeneutics of love*.[2]

It is not coincidental that the Wesleyan-Holiness tradition has affirmed the equality of women from its inception. This reality has not been disjoined from biblical interpretation within the tradition, but rather strongly connected to it. Thus it is appropriate to speak of a Wesleyan-Holiness-feminist hermeneutic. It is my task here to attempt to construct such a juxtaposition. Since I stand as a historical theologian and not a biblical scholar, I will approach the topic from a historical point of view and conclude with some constructive theological reflections. I will first consider what John Wesley himself said about women, touching briefly on his interpretation of the difficult biblical passages. I will then consider the hermeneutics of the matriarch of the Holiness Movement, Phoebe Palmer. I will then consider how Wesleyan hermeneutics relate to present-day feminist hermeneutical method, concluding with some theological considerations of Wesleyanism and gender.

1. Appeared originally in the *Wesleyan Theological Journal* 36/2 (Fall 2001). Used by permission.

2. I give reference to the title of a highly influential book within the Holiness Movement. See Mildred Bangs Wynkoop, *A Theology of Love: The Dynamics of Wesleyanism* (Kansas City: Beacon Hill Press of Kansas City, 1972).

WESLEY'S HERMENEUTICAL HEDGING: WOMEN IN EARLY METHODISM

Paul Chilcote and Kent Brown are among those scholars who have provided primary evidence of John Wesley's very strong advocacy of women.[3] Such evidence is highly credible. Methodism in the second half of the 18th century, under the leadership of Wesley, reveals a growing acceptance of the giftedness of the women of the movement. This giftedness included the leadership of bands and societies, pastoral care of the sick and dying, public prayer and testimony, and eventually preaching because of the extraordinary call of many extraordinary women. Some of these women earned the name "female brethren" from Wesley and his associates. It was a name that denoted considerable respect. According to Chilcote, "In the evangelical revival under the Wesleys, the waters of reform and renewal would once again sweep through the ever-widening channel of human equality, women riding the crest of the wave."[4]

After beginning the revival in England, Wesley discovered that a high percentage of the members of the societies were women. He very quickly allowed women to lead bands, and then societies, even when men were members. Women who were otherwise disenfranchised in a world dominated by men began to develop a new sense of self-esteem and purpose.[5] In the setting of the societies, women were encouraged to pray publicly, offer personal testimony, and exhort the other members, often using Scripture as the basis for such exhortation. The steps toward public preaching were being made by numerous women across England.

We find in his journal Wesley's reaction to a woman giving public testimony. He records that this particular woman could not refrain from declaring before them all what God had done in her soul. The words that

---

3. See Paul Wesley Chilcote, *John Wesley and the Women Preachers* (Metuchen, N.J.: Scarecrow, 1991), and Earl Kent Brown, *Women of Mr. Wesley's Methodism* (Lewiston, N.Y.: Edwin Mellen, 1983). Other historic studies include: George Cole, *Heroines of Methodism: Sketches of the Mothers and Daughters of the Church* (New York: Carlton and Porter, 1857); Maldwyn Edwards, *My Dear Sister: The Story of John Wesley and the Women in His Life* (Leeds: Penwork, n.d.); Abel Stevens, *The Women of Methodism; Its Three Foundresses, Susanna Wesley, the Countess of Huntingdon, and Barbara Heck; with Sketches of Their Female Associates and Successors in the Early History of the Denomination. A Centenary Offering to the Women of American Methodism, from the America Methodist Ladies' Centenary Association* (New York: Carlton and Porter, 1866); and Zechariah Taft, *Biographical Sketches of the Lives and Public Ministry of Various Holy Women, Whose Eminent Usefulness and Successful Labours in the Church of Christ, Have Entitled Them to Be Enrolled Among the Great Benefactors of Mankind*, 2 vols. (London: Mr. Kershaw, 1825).
4. Paul Wesley Chilcote, *She Offered Them Christ* (Nashville: Abingdon, 1993), 21.
5. Ibid., 34.

came from her heart went to the heart. Reports Wesley, "I scarce ever heard such a preacher before. All were in tears round her, high and low; for there was no resisting the Spirit by which she spoke."[6]

Wesley offers an even more overtly positive view of women assuming ministerial roles. From a sermon titled "On Visiting the Sick" we find these bold words:

> Herein there is no difference; there is neither male nor female in Christ Jesus. Indeed it has long passed for the maxim with many, that women are only to be seen, not heard. And accordingly many of them are brought up in such a manner as if they were only designed for agreeable playthings! But is this doing honour to the sex? or is it a real kindness to them? No; it is the deepest unkindness; it is horrid cruelty; it is mere Turkish barbarity. And I know not how any woman of sense and spirit can submit to it. Let all you that have it in your power assert the right which God of nature has given you. Yield not to that vile bondage any longer! You, as well as men, are rational creatures. You, like them, were made in the image of God; you are equally candidates for immortality; you too are called of God. . . . Be not disobedient to the heavenly calling.[7]

By 1771 Wesley seems to have moved beyond the pragmatic benefit of women preachers and have begun to wrestle with the idea theologically, as he reflected on the whole nature of the movement called Methodism. On June 13, 1771, he writes to Sarah Crosby:

> I think the strength of the cause rests here; on your having an extraordinary call. So I am persuaded has every one of our lay preachers; otherwise, I could not countenance his preaching at all. It is plain to me, that the whole work of God termed Methodism is an extraordinary dispensation of his providence. Therefore, I do not wonder if several things occur therein which do not fall under ordinary rules of discipline. St. Paul's ordinary rule was "I permit not a woman to speak in the congregation." Yet in extraordinary cases, he made a few exceptions; at Corinth in particular.[8]

Ultimately it can be said with confidence that, compared to church leaders of his era, John Wesley stands out as an exception to the rule. The women of early British Methodism were afforded ecclesiastical opportunities rare to women in the 18th century.[9] Wesley himself made exceptions to

---

6. *Journal* (Curnock ed.), 3:250.
7. *Works* (Jackson ed.), 7:125-26.
8. Ibid., 356.
9. See Chilcote, *John Wesley and the Women Preachers*, 4-17, for a review of similar "feminist" activities just prior to Methodism's inception.

rules that prevented women preachers; he believed that God would use extraordinary means to accomplish extraordinary ends in extraordinary
times.[10] He finally even made preaching by women an official position of
Methodism (as in the case of Sarah Mallet, the first such sanctioned female
preacher).[11] While formal institutional power remained with the male
preachers who Wesley himself placed and moved at will, his class leaders—
often women—served, for all practical purposes, as the veritable pastors of
Wesley's congregations, for the male circuit preachers were rarely present.[12]

These more pastoral relationships with women do reveal Wesley's
more "feminist" impulses. But he also deeply valued his more reciprocal
friendships with women, counting them his true equals. Women such as
Sarah Ryan, Mary (Bosanquet) Fletcher, and Sarah Crosby acted the part of
Wesley's confidants; they were clearly part of his inner circle.[13] To his female correspondents "he writes with peculiar effluence of thought and
frankness of communication. He in fact unbosoms himself, on every topic
which occurs to him, as to kindred spirits, in whose sympathies he confid-
ed, and from whose re-communication he hoped for additional light."[14]
He wrote and visited them as often as he could. As they apparently were
to him, Wesley remains loyal to his women friends over the decades.
When Mary Fletcher lost her husband,[15] Wesley wrote, "Should not you
now consider me as your first human friend?"[16] He invested even more in
the relationship for the remainder of his life.

Sarah Ryan was converted out of a life of ill-repute, and Wesley took
a pastoral interest in her spiritual progress. However, he also soon found
himself depending on her for emotional support; she was often the bearer
of his burdens. This alarmed some of Wesley's colleagues. Still, in 1758 he
comments: "The conversing with you, either by speaking or writing, is an

---

10. See Letter to Mary Bosanquet (3 June 1771), in *Letters* (Telford ed.), 5:257.

11. See Chilcote, *John Wesley and the Women Preachers,* 192-218, esp. 192-98.

12. After explaining his reasons for moving a certain preacher from her society, Wesley
tells Sarah Baker to "Feed the lambs!" Letter to Sarah Baker (30 July 1785), in *Letters*
(Telford ed.), 8:275. Also see Letter to Mrs. Downes (Oct. 1776), in *Letters* (Telford ed.),
6:233, for Wesley's rationale for allowing Mrs. Downes to lead even mixed classes.

13. They were also a part of their own type of circle. Edwards alludes to an almost con-
vent-like environment in their household. See Edwards, *Dear Sister,* 87.

14. Alexander Knox, "Remarks on the Life and Character of John Wesley," in *The Life of
Wesley and the Rise and Progress of Methodism,* ed. Robert Southey, 2 vols. (London: Longman, 1846), 2:295.

15. John Fletcher can be considered John Wesley's closest male friend. Wesley appointed him as his successor in the leadership of Methodism, although in the end Wesley
outlived him (see Edwards, *Dear Sister,* 93-97).

16. Letter to Mary Fletcher (2 Oct. 1785), in *Letters* (Telford ed.), 7:295.

unspeakable blessing to me. I cannot think of you without thinking of God. Others often lead me to Him; but it is, as it were, going round about: you bring me straight into His presence. Therefore, whoever warns me against trusting you, I cannot refrain, as I am clearly convinced He calls me to it."[17]

Wesley seems to have placed himself under the spiritual direction of Sarah Crosby, a prominent female preacher. There are several examples of Crosby's "plain dealing" with Wesley. The Leytonstone society was apparently disposed to criticize Wesley's own spiritual experience. Crosby wrote a letter in which she outlined their complaints. Wesley responded that they knew nothing about his personal experience and thus had no basis for their harsh dealings with him; he added, however, that Crosby had been given access to his inner life, and she therefore had more right to judge him.

> My Dear Sister,—Last night I received yours, and was in some doubt whether to write again or no; and if I did, whether to write with reserve or without. At length I resolved upon the latter, and that for two reasons: (1) because I love you; (2) because I love myself. And if so, I ought to write and write freely; for your letters do me good. . . . I take well all that you say; and I love you the more, the more free you are. That is another total mistake, that I dislike any one for plain dealing. And of all persons living Sarah Crosby has least room to say so.[18]

In a comment reminiscent of Jerome when speaking of his male colaborers, Wesley says that "I have none like-minded."[19] But in a selected few women in his life, he found kindred spirits. These brief examples show that not only did Wesley allow for women to serve in places of leadership within his movement, but he also considered his intimate friendships with women invaluable.

Can a case be made, then, for recognizing a feminism in Wesley's exegesis?[20] Evidence can be found in Wesley's *Explanatory Notes upon the New Testament.* And yet, most notes about women further display an

---

17. Letter to Sarah Ryan (20 Jan. 1758), in *Letters* (Telford ed.), 4:4.

18. Letter to Sarah Crosby (12 Sept. 1766), in *Letters* (Telford ed.), 5:25-27.

19. Letter to Mary (Bosanquet) Fletcher (12 July 1782), in *Letters* (Telford ed.), 7:128.

20. It should be noted that one study is available that implicates Wesley as a rank misogynist and that interprets his leadership of the Methodist movement in terms of sexual seduction. See Henry Abelove, *The Evangelist of Desire* (Stanford, Calif.: Stanford University Press, 1990). Many Wesley scholars, including myself, are at great odds with Abelove's driving thesis. See the critique by Richard P. Heitzenrater, review of *The Evangelist of Desire: John Wesley and the Methodists*, by Henry Abelove, *Methodist History* 30 (1992): 118-20.

equivocalness in Wesley's exegesis. Three texts will serve as examples. First, Acts 17:4:

> Our freethinkers pique themselves upon observing that women are more religious than men; and this, in compliment both to religion and good manners, they impute to the weakness of their understandings. And indeed, as far as nature can go in imitating religion by performing outward acts of it, this picture of religion may make a fairer show in women than in men, both by reason of their more tender passions, and their modesty, which will make those actions appear to more advantage. But in the case of true religion, which always implies taking up the cross, especially in time of persecution, women lie naturally under a great disadvantage, as having less courage than men. So that their embracing the gospel was a stronger evidence of the power of Him whose strength is perfected in weakness, as a stronger assistance of the Holy Spirit was needful for them to overcome their natural fearfulness.[21]

When commenting on Paul's infamous passage that women are to keep silent in the church (1 Cor. 13:34), Wesley writes, "Be in subjection to the man whose proper office it is to lead and to instruct the congregation." But he also writes, "Let your women be silent in the churches—unless they are under an extraordinary impulse of the Spirit."[22] The first section of 1 Peter 3 deals with the subjection of wives to their husbands. Here Wesley advises men to "Dwell with the woman according to knowledge—knowing they are weak." He clarifies, "Yet do not despise them for this, but give them honour—Both in heart, in word, and in action; as those who are called to be joint-heirs of . . . eternal life."[23] In accordance with this type of exegesis, Wesley writes to one of his female preachers, "Be subject to no creature, only so far as love constrains. By this sweetest and strongest tie you are now subject to, dear Sally, Your affectionate friend and brother."[24] While Wesley maintained the typical (and misogynistic) interpretive conclusions of his day regarding women, a certain degree of ambivalence nudged his exegesis in novel directions.

THE HERMENEUTICS OF A HOLINESS HEROINE

Thomas Oden writes, "Phoebe Palmer, after having been one of the most widely known women of her time in England and America, has re-

---

21. John Wesley, *Explanatory Notes upon the New Testament* (London: Epworth, 1950), 462.

22. Ibid., 632.

23. Ibid., 881.

24. Letter to Sarah Crosby (1 July 1757), in *Letters* (Telford ed.), 3:219.

mained virtually unknown during the past hundred years." It is clear that Phoebe Palmer was considered the great heroine, even matriarch of the Holiness Movement during her own day, thus making her quick descent into obscurity a great irony and historical puzzle. Oden, among others,[25] has attempted to re-present her not only to the movement that owes her so much but also to wider Christianity. He offers his own interpretation of Palmer. "[Her] spirituality . . . is deeply rooted in classical Christianity, not on the fanatic, idiosyncratic fringe of centerless enthusiasm. She deserves to be counted among the most penetrating spiritual writers of the American tradition."[26] His anthology of her writings was published under the *Sources of American Spirituality* series by Paulist Press, which indicates that Palmer should be seen as more than an insignificant sectarian figure. And yet, despite Oden's endorsement, her immense popularity in the 19th century, and the continuation of her influence—although unattributed—on holiness theology throughout this century, Palmer is a neglected and even despised figure by some holiness scholars today.

The character of Palmer's interpretation of biblical holiness has been a matter of much interest and debate. It is beyond the scope of this study to delve extensively into the intricacies of her expansive theology. However, a bit of commentary on her commentators' interpretations is in order here. It is not my intention to defend Palmer against her various critics but rather to clarify that the many negative assessments of Palmer's theology represent only one reading of Palmer. Other readings are available. The following reading establishes Palmer's hermeneutics as a crucial foundation of her broader doctrine of holiness.

Because of Palmer's initial hesitancy to embrace the sentimentalized American appropriation of Wesley's doctrine of assurance, charges of rationalism have been leveled against her.[27] Almost exactly 100 years after Wes-

---

25. See John L. Peters, *Christian Perfection and American Methodism* (Nashville: Pierce and Washabaugh, 1956). Perhaps one of the first to call Phoebe Palmer the "founder of the holiness movement" was M. L. Haney. See M. L. Haney, *The Inheritance Restored: or Plain Truths on Bible Holiness* (Chicago: Christian Witness Co., 1904), 215. Also see Timothy L. Smith, *Revivalism and Social Reform* (Nashville: Abingdon, 1957). Smith's thesis is that the Holiness Movement preceded and anticipated the themes of the social gospel movement; he believes the Holiness Movement's social concern partly originated from Phoebe Palmer's Five Point Mission. For full-length biographies, see Harold Raser, *Phoebe Palmer: Her Life and Thought* (Lewiston, N.Y.: Edwin Mellen, 1987); and Charles E. White, *The Beauty of Holiness: Phoebe Palmer As Theologian, Revivalist, Feminist, and Humanitarian* (Grand Rapids: Zondervan/Francis Asbury, 1986).

26. Thomas Oden, "Introduction," in Phoebe Palmer, *Selected Writings*, ed. Thomas Oden (New York: Paulist, 1988), 2-3, 8.

27. I would suggest, as others, that Palmer was in fact playing out the logical conclu-

ley's own experience of assurance at Aldersgate,[28] Palmer disposed of this type of assurance as a great hindrance to many seeking heart purity. In its place she prescribed a faith independent of a specific emotional response and initiated what critics call a new rationalism that chilled the warmth of Methodism.[29] This prescription was given because of her own difficulty in attaining an assurance (or "witness of the Spirit") that precisely fit the exhortations of early 19th-century Methodist preaching. Al Truesdale has examined the Holiness Movement's "reification" of and demand for a specific type of experience in entire sanctification. According to Truesdale, "The fallacy of reification and misplaced concreteness [Alfred North Whitehead] are the same. The fallacy consists of treating an abstraction as a substantive."[30] Truesdale examines several 19th-century holiness figures and highlights how a particular type of experience of entire sanctification was demanded by such figures. But, rather than charging that Palmer was guilty with the others, he calls Palmer a creative detour from this tendency in Methodism. "Palmer did not simply correct popular Wesleyanism. In important respects

---

sion of Wesley's own scheme. Charles White agrees that "she was carrying Wesleyan doctrines to their natural conclusion; she was working out their inner logic." White continues: "If it is true that all Christians will eventually be sanctified, and if it is true that it is better to be sanctified than merely justified, and if it is true that God can sanctify the believer now just as easily as a thousand years from now, and if it is true that God gives sanctification in response to the believer's faith, then every Christian should be sanctified now. Wesley preached each of the protases, and he admitted the truth of the apodoses, but as he said, *non persuadebis etiamsi persuaderis* (you will not persuade me even though you do persuade me): he was not confident of the conclusion, no matter how logical it seemed" (White, *Beauty of Holiness,* 204). Howard elaborates: "Wesley states that one knows he is sanctified by the same means as that by which he knows he is justified, or by witness of the Spirit he hath given us. [This] statement alone [is] perfectly clear, but Wesley is equivocal, or at least confusing, in further elaboration of the evidence of the experience. In another statement he says there are times when the witness is weak or even completely withdrawn and adds that the witness is not always clear at first nor is it afterward always the same. With such statements he has implicitly contradicted his first assertion of the witness of the Spirit, or at least he has greatly weakened it." Ivan Howard, "Wesley Versus Phoebe Palmer: Extended Controversy," *Wesleyan Theological Journal* 6 (1971): 31-32.

28. For interpretations of Aldersgate, see Randy L. Maddox, ed., *Aldersgate Reconsidered* (Nashville: Abingdon, 1990). Joe Gorman has most recently argued that despite Wesley's "warm heart" of assurance, his spiritual life very soon evidenced continuing doubts and struggles. See Joe Gorman, "John Wesley and the Age of Melancholy," *Wesleyan Theological Journal* 33/2 (Fall 1999): 196-221.

29. For a very recent study that attempts to counter the tendency to see Palmer as antiemotional, see Chris R. Armstrong, "Ravished Heart or Naked Faith: The Kernel and Husk of Phoebe Palmer," presented at the Society for Pentecostal Studies (in special session with the Wesleyan Theological Society), Cleveland, Tenn., March 13, 1998.

30. Al Truesdale, "A Reification of the Experience of Entire Sanctification in the American Holiness Movement," *Wesleyan Theological Journal* 31/2 (Fall 1996): 96.

she replaced it by setting aside its reification of experience and inserting a predictable theological formula that minimized (if not negated) experience, and could not fail to deliver certainty. In the replacement, there were no experiential patterns to approximate and no hurdles to overcome."[31]

Palmer did struggle for several years to match her own experience with a dictated experience of assurance. In retrospect, she attributed much of her struggle both to the obtuse sophistication of more professional Methodist theology and to a sentimentalized ethos found among the Methodist grassroots. In an attempt to sort through her own spiritual struggle, she dismissed the theologians and the expectations of a sentimental experience and turned to the Scriptures directly. For this, she has been characterized as anti-theological and anti-Wesleyan. Paul Bassett critiques Palmer's shift away from Wesley's more balanced understanding of the theological sources, that is, the quadrilateral (although he resists this term), toward a shallow bibliocentrism and he mournfully attributes the unfortunate course of mid- to late-19th-century holiness thought to Palmer's naïveté.[32] While evidence does show that Palmer considered herself a woman of one book, she, like Wesley, respected and utilized other sources for her own thought. Besides evidence that shows she read extensively in the works of Wesley and Fletcher and even in the patristic sources themselves, by her own admission she always read the Scriptures with commentaries at her side.[33] It is also crucial to note that some scholars rightly see that Palmer read the Bible through a particular lens, through a presupposed or assumed theology. David Bundy argues that this lens and its assumed theology is specifically Eastern in origin.[34] Ultimately, what Palmer was attempting to reject through her "biblicism" was the technical theology of her day, not theology in general.[35] It could be said that Palmer refused to idolize the prescribed experiential patterns of such theology and of a more popular holiness ethos, and through such a re-

---

31. Ibid., 116-17.

32. See Paul Merritt Bassett, "The Theological Identity of the North American Holiness Movement," in *The Variety of American Evangelicalism,* ed. Donald W. Dayton and Robert K. Johnston (Downers Grove, Ill.: InterVarsity Press, 1991), 72-108.

33. See Phoebe Palmer, *Israel's Speedy Restoration and Conversion Contemplated; or Signs of the Times in Familiar Letters by Mrs. Phoebe Palmer* (New York: John A. Gray, 1854), 3.

34. See David Bundy, "Visions of Sanctification: Themes of Orthodoxy in the Methodist, Holiness and Pentecostal Traditions," unpublished paper, 1-21.

35. Oden observes that while she "constantly disavowed that she had anything original to contribute to theology," nonetheless "her powers of theological reasoning were subtle, original, biblically and classically grounded, historically aware, clear, extraordinarily influential, and spiritually vital." Oden, "Introduction," 14.

fusal, she opened up other creative pathways to the holy life. Her call to biblical holiness was anything but a naive call.

It is also important to note that when Palmer called for radical faith in the biblical promise of entire sanctification, she was not rejecting Wesley's doctrine of assurance altogether. She writes this about her own sanctification experience: "While thus glorying in being enabled to feel and know that I was now altogether the Lord's, the question, accompanied with light, power, and unquestionable assurance, came to my mind. What is this but the state of holiness which you have so long been seeking?"[36] In her own theological formation, however, Palmer greatly modifies the meaning of assurance and its means of attainment. For Wesley, the attainment of assurance was quite dependent on the Spirit's movement and required a responsive stance (i.e., dependent on God's initial action) on the part of the seeker. In Palmer's scheme, feelings of assurance would come, but only after consecration, entire devotion, and through an active faith.[37] Melvin Dieter has commented that "the newness then essentially was a change in emphasis resulting from a simple, literal Biblical faith and the prevailing mood of revivalism combined with an impatient, American pragmatism that always seeks to make a reality at the moment whatever is considered at all possible in the future."[38] There is no doubt that this pragmatism was at work in Palmer's theology.[39]

Such pragmatism can be readily found in Palmer's "altar covenant,"[40]

---

36. Palmer, "Letter X to Mrs. W.," in *Phoebe Palmer, Faith and Its Effects; or Fragments from My Portfolio* (New York: Foster and Palmer, Jr., 1867), 72.

37. Although I do not wish to contradict Palmer's reliance on grace here, it is also important to note that this human element need not be interpreted as necessarily negative. This personal spiritual "activism" can be explicated as a positive movement toward greater spiritual liberties for women. I have suggested elsewhere that such can be seen as providing women with an unmediated access to spirituality and with a means of overturning the stereotypical and damaging portrayal of woman as spiritually "passive." See Diane Leclerc, "A Woman's Way of Holiness: An Analysis of Phoebe Palmer's Theology with Reflection on Its Intrinsic Feminist Implications," paper presented at the American Society of Church History conference, Chicago, April 1996.

38. Melvin Easterday Dieter, *The Holiness Revival of the Nineteenth Century* (Metuchen, N.J.: Scarecrow, 1980), 31.

39. Harold Raser also recognizes a pragmatism in Palmer's theology: "Hers is a very practical theology which eschews strictly theoretical considerations in favor of those things which have a direct payoff in terms of bringing about the desired religious experience. One might even say that Palmer's thought constitutes in its essence a 'theology of means' pertaining to holiness, so preoccupied is she with actually getting persons to the place where they are made 'holy' and live lives of 'perfect love'. . . a kind of holy pragmatism." Raser, *Phoebe Palmer*, 150.

40. Raser sees a possible dependency on Hester Ann Rogers, a correspondent of John Wesley, for the seed of altar terminology. It is unquestionable that the life and letters of

which was a rhetorical formulation of her own experience; this phraseology is most clearly seen in her famous *The Way of Holiness*. Her motivation for this work was to help others who also had possibly struggled with a sentimentalized presentation of the doctrine of assurance. Palmer intended this "altar principle" as a source of assurance to the seeker after holiness who was following her method of attainment, and it clearly served this purpose for her and for many who embraced her teachings.[41] This altar phraseology reduced what could be a complicated and perplexing search for holiness into what she termed a "shorter way," one that offered assurance on the basis of the truth of a typology found in Exodus.[42]

Palmer is often severely criticized for this type of exegesis. What is often overlooked is that Palmer took Adam Clarke's commentary note on Exodus 29:37, which displayed the same exegetical typology, and applied

---

Rogers were immensely popular with Methodists of later generations. Raser writes, "Rogers both reflected and contributed to the development of the Wesleyan tradition on the popular level along those paths marked out by Fletcher and Clarke on the more scholarly level. In other areas, however, Rogers contributed some more or less original elements to the popular tradition, elements which were potent influences upon Phoebe Palmer" (Raser, *Phoebe Palmer*, 247). Palmer acknowledges Rogers' influence on her own spiritual journey. Although Raser goes on to list the specific ways Palmer has utilized Rogers' ideas in her own theological formation, he fails to mention among these elements the fact that part of Rogers' spiritual struggle concerned her loss of a child. I would suggest that Hester Ann Rogers perhaps represents the best link between Wesley's conceptualization of "singleness of heart" expressed in his letters to women, including Rogers, and Phoebe Palmer's own hamartiological ideas. During Palmer's travels in England, she visited Rogers' house, where she wrote, "How her vows [to God] were fulfilled, and the persecutions which followed, are known to thousands in both hemispheres. Being dead, she yet speaketh and will continue to speak as long as time endures." Phoebe Palmer, *Four Years in the Old World* (New York: Foster and Palmer, Jr., 1866), 446. Also see Hester Ann Rogers, *Autobiography of Hester Ann Rogers* (reprint, Hampton, Tenn.: Harvey and Tait, 1981), 74-5. David Bundy ("Visions of Sanctification," 15) traces the altar covenant further than Rogers to Madame Guyon.

41. Raser, *Phoebe Palmer*, 160.

42. This phraseology takes prominence in almost all of Palmer's written works. Thus, there are innumerable texts that could be used for citation. The following comes from the chapter titled "Is There Not a Shorter Way," in *The Way of Holiness*. "Over and again, previous to the time mentioned, had she endeavored to give herself away in covenant to God. But she had never, till this hour, with the solemn intention to reckon herself dead indeed to sin, but alive unto God through Jesus Christ our Lord; to account herself permanently the Lord's, and in verity no more at her own disposal, but irrevocably the Lord's property, for time and eternity. Now, in the name of the Lord Jehovah, after having deliberately counted the cost, she resolved to enter into the bonds of an everlasting covenant, with the fixed purpose to count all things loss for the excellency of the knowledge of Jesus." Phoebe Palmer, *The Way of Holiness, with Notes by the Way* (New York: W. C. Palmer, 1867), 29-30. Also see "A Covenant" from *Entire Devotion*, where Palmer takes a person through the three-step process as a type of confession/profession of entire sanctification, which the person then signs and dates (in Palmer, *Selected Writings*, 198-200).

it to the experience of sanctification. Clarke explains that in Hebrew ritual, whatever was laid upon the altar became God's possession; it was from then on to be used for sacred purposes. Clarke alludes to Christ as the altar. Palmer took Clarke's suggestion and held that the altar of sacrifice is a type, that is, a prefiguring and foreshadowing of something yet to come, the antitype, namely Jesus.[43] According to Palmer's scheme, a person who seeks entire sanctification must first and foremost consecrate everything completely to God by "placing all (all of one's being and all of one's idols) on God's altar." After this consecration is complete, the seeker must then have faith that the altar sanctifies the gift.

Because of Palmer's emphasis on the human element in this step of faith, she has been accused not only of rationalism but also of a type of Pelagianism.[44] Yet I suggest that this is a gross overreading of Palmer's point.[45] Palmer affirms that one's ability to turn from idols, consecrate everything, and believe the biblical promise is not accomplished through human ability, but rather through one's reception of God's prevenient grace. She writes often of the absolute necessity of grace: "I saw that nothing less than the omnipotence of grace could have enabled me thus to present my whole being to God."[46] She resists and rejects her own efforts as utterly fruitless, writing this to a friend: "Such a deep, piercing sense of helplessness prevailed, that it seemed as though I could not go forward until endued with power from on high."[47] Elsewhere she writes, "The idea that I can do anything myself, seems so extinct, that the enemy is not apt to tempt me in that direction."[48] Her assertion of faith is filled with language of God's prior, prevenient action, specifically through his Spirit.

Charges of Pelagianism also represent a reading that fails to take into account the rhetorical difference between *The Way of Holiness* and Palmer's description of sanctification elsewhere in her writings, particularly in her letters and diaries. When critiques of rationalism and Pelagianism are made, it is *The Way of Holiness* that is most often quoted. However,

---

43. Raser, *Phoebe Palmer*, 160.

44. E.g., Raser, *Phoebe Palmer*, 260-62. Although such charges are directed toward her supposed emphasis on human effort, they implicitly question whether Phoebe Palmer had a doctrine of original sin. This chapter quite obviously argues that she held to the doctrine, although not in its traditional Augustinian form.

45. Palmer's preference for Pentecost as the primary paradigm for entire sanctification in itself argues against any type of human or Pelagian attainment of holiness.

46. Palmer, "Letter XIII, to Mrs. W.," in *Faith and Its Effects*, 86.

47. Palmer, "Letter IX, to Mrs. W.," in ibid., 66.

48. Richard Wheatley, ed., *The Life and Letters of Mrs. Phoebe Palmer* (New York: W. C. Palmer, 1876), 83.

like Wesley, Palmer's theology takes on different nuances and emphases in her more personal works. *The Way of Holiness* is written as a testimony of Palmer's sanctification and therefore has been interpreted as if it were an exact replica of her actual experience. In my reading, producing a simple summary of her experience was not Palmer's agenda or literary motivation. Rather, this book was written for popular consumption[49] and therefore structures and formulizes its agenda so that the reader may also take specific steps to attain a similar experience. Failure to make this rhetorical distinction has skewed interpretation of Palmer's broader theology.

In Palmer's more personal works, it is more transparent that she is not resting on her own efforts in the process of reaching the crisis of entire sanctification, nor is she separating faith from devotion. While *The Way of Holiness* does portray faith as believing the promises of God as represented in the written Word, Palmer's expression of faith in her diaries and letters is deeply personal; she incisively perceives the relational and devotional aspect of faith. It is all here: "I, through the Spirit's influence, have given all for Christ, and now he hath revealed himself, and given himself to me, and become my all in all."[50] Abraham is often used as a model of faith in her letters and diaries;[51] she represents him as believing the promise of God, but also as representing a deep trust in the person of God. This type of trust enabled Abraham to place Isaac "on the altar." There is an intricate interdependency of each step in Palmer's altar formula, particularly the first two. Consecration of other potential rivals for God's proper place in one's heart opens a person to the potential of holding a faith that expresses itself as entire devotion.

Palmer is known for her typological use of imagery from Exodus. She is just as well-known for her appropriation of the biblical account of Pentecost, which more directly impacts her feminist concerns. John Fletcher, Wesley's friend and theologian of early British Methodism, was the first to link entire sanctification with "the baptism of the Holy Spirit." Asa Mahan, Phoebe Palmer's contemporary, wrote a book by that title that gave biblical and theological justification for linking the Pentecostal image with the experience of entire sanctification. Palmer took the image and popular-

---

49. This parallels the differences scholars have noted between John Wesley's journals and diaries.

50. Palmer, "Letter X to Mrs. W.," in *Faith and Its Effects,* 74.

51. E.g., see Palmer's diary entry for September 11, 1837 (in Wheatley, *The Life and Letters of Mrs. Phoebe Palmer,* 46-48). According to Oden, "The testing of Abraham in the command to sacrifice his only son would henceforth become for her a principal metaphor of her own experience" ("Introductory note to September 11, 1837," in Palmer, *Selected Writings,* 132).

ized it. What occurred in Acts 2 occurred to the disciples, to those who already believed in Christ for salvation. Their Pentecostal baptism was thus interpreted by Palmer as an instantaneous event and a "second work" of the Spirit, different from anything they had experienced previously. Later theologians would more delicately define the relationship of this second work with holiness terms such as "cleansing" and "eradication" of the carnal nature.[52] But Palmer readily adopted the Pentecostal experience as a transferable experience for all believers and preached its imperative necessity in her revivals and camp meetings and in her written works. This would greatly affect the way the doctrine of entire sanctification was expressed in the Holiness Movement; and "her popularization of Pentecostal language . . . laid a firm foundation" for later Pentecostal developments."[53]

Arising out of the conceptualization and utilization of baptism language is the linking of holiness with power. White states: "Fletcher noticed this connection but did not develop its significance. Adam Clarke devoted one sentence to the idea, but Phoebe Palmer made it a central element of her teaching."[54] "Holiness is power" is an oft-repeated phrase in Palmer's writings.[55] The disciples in Acts were empowered by the Spirit to accomplish what was impossible without divine assistance. Persons who had experienced entire sanctification also were empowered to accomplish what was beyond their own human limitations. According to Palmer, through empowerment and unhindered freedom a person was enabled to progress in his or her spiritual journey as never before and to accomplish what was

---

52. For an extensive treatment of later usage of eradication language, see Leroy E. Lindsey, Jr., "Radical Remedy: The Eradication of Sin and Related Terminology in Wesleyan-Holiness Thought, 1875-1925" (Ph.D. diss., Drew University, 1996). Also see Paul M. Bassett, "Culture and Concupiscence: The Changing Definition of Sanctity in the Wesleyan Holiness Movement, 1867-1920," *Wesleyan Theological Journal* 28 (Spring/Fall 1993): 59-127. Bassett's thesis can be summarized by the following quotation: "Wesleyan/Holiness people as a whole, in the period between the late 1860s and the late 1910s . . . re-defined some of the most critical elements in their theology. Most important were the nuances of the understandings of original sin/inherited depravity, and, by implication, of entire sanctification. More precisely, in the 1860s and 1870s, Wesleyan/Holiness people believed that original sin/inherited depravity characteristically manifests itself in 'worldliness.' By the 1880s, they began to believe that the characteristic manifestation of original sin/inherited depravity is pride. By around 1900, the grassroots of the Wesleyan/Holiness Movement, if not its theologians, had come to believe that lust is the characteristic mark" (60-61).

53. White, *Beauty of Holiness*, 158.

54. Ibid., 128.

55. During her travels in England, Palmer visited Wesley's grave and there said, "Holiness is power; and it was an apprehension of this fact that fitted the founder of Methodism for his wondrous calling, and then God thrust him out to raise a holy people" (Palmer, *Four Years in the Old World*, 33).

beyond human expectation or conventional custom. This theology was particularly significant for women's religious experience. Palmer's *The Way of Holiness,* possibly more than any other Christian book of doctrine available during the first half of the 19th century, brought the Romantic vision of inner autonomy and unlimited personal growth to middle-class women, a highly significant development.[56]

Such women began to see their own potential for ministry and usefulness in church and society and started to challenge structures that would limit them. Nancy Hardesty elaborates:

> [Palmer] affirmed that Christians were not only justified before God but were also regenerate, reborn, made new, capable of being restored to the Edenic state. For women it made possible the sweeping away of centuries of patriarchal, misogynist culture in the instant. . . . The argument that "this is the way we've always done it" holds no power for someone for whom all things have been made new.[57]

Palmer's theology contains a strong call for women to live out their new spiritual potential. Since her theology contained an idealism that made all things seem possible, limitations were determined only by one's own disobedience. As a result of this theological premise, women began to strive toward the realization of the new life they claimed. These women believed they had equal access to the Pentecostal power available through the Holy Spirit; they were equally capable of being Pentecostal witnesses to what God can do in a life that is entirely devoted. Richard Wheatley includes the following anecdote in his biography of Palmer: "In Tully [New York] Mrs. Palmer's loving instructions were blest, to the entire sanctification of a minister's wife, who was changed from a timid, shrinking, silent Christian, into a tearful, modest one, but one filled with Pentecostal power, and who afterwards spoke in public with remarkable effect."[58] To be empowered through sanctifying grace compelled women to enter the sphere of society and effect change. It often meant ministering to the physical needs of others, especially to those of a lower social position, as evidenced by Palmer's strong emphasis on mission work. But most importantly for our purposes here, sanctifying power meant empowerment to speak.

The final requisite of Palmer's three-step vision that led one through the experience of entire sanctification—formula faith, consecration, and testimony—is crucial for women. Even if a woman had surrendered every-

---

56. Theodore Hovet, "Phoebe Palmer's Altar Phraseology and the Spiritual Dimension of a Woman's Sphere," *Journal of Religion* 63 (1983): 279.

57. Nancy Hardesty, *Women Called to Witness: Evangelical Feminism in the Nineteenth Century* (Nashville: Abingdon, 1984), 83.

58. Wheatley, *Life and Letters of Mrs. Phoebe Palmer,* 66.

one and everything to God and had faith in him, if she was not willing to testify, she would lose the experience, without exception. Testimony was a verifiable performance of the fact that the domestic sphere had ceased to be absorbing and that a woman was in fact entirely devoted to God. Note this about the teaching of Palmer:

> Her emphasis on public testimony usually took the form of varying degrees of insistence that testimony was not only essential to the promulgation of Christian holiness, but even more essential to the personal retention of that grace. One had to give public testimony in order to be clear in his experience. Indeed if personal testimony lagged, it was one of the most certain signs of a lack of religious life which would finally culminate in complete apostasy.[59]

As Porterfield says, "It was better to refuse the coming of the Spirit than to refuse afterward to prophesy."[60] Palmer describes her own experience: "The Spirit then suggested: If it is a gift from God, you will be required to declare it as his gift, through our Lord Jesus Christ, ready for the acceptance of all; and this, if you would retain the blessing, will not be left to your own choice. You will be called on to profess this blessing before thousands!"[61] Because of the requisitional nature of Palmer's injunction to speak, women across the United States, in Canada, and in Great Britain began, like her, to testify in public, standing in mixed assemblies to proclaim God's sanctifying power despite the fact that it was considered undignified for a woman to speak in public at all.[62]

Charles White offers an account of the experience of a Mrs. Butler. When a certain Dr. Butler brought his wife from Vermont to New York City in 1855, he hoped to get her mind off holiness. She had made "a perfect spectacle of herself by professing sanctification . . . in the local Congregational church, pastored by her brother-in-law." Dr. Butler was apparently unaware that the author of the book that had so influenced his wife lived in

---

59. Dieter, *Holiness Revival of the Nineteenth Century,* 36.

60. Amanda Porterfield, "Phoebe Palmer," presented at Women in New Worlds Conference, Cincinnati, Ohio, February 1980, 19.

61. Palmer, *The Way of Holiness,* 39-40.

62. Such a "public" role was not only considered undignified but also considered dangerous. Deborah L. Rhode writes, "A common premise within the nineteenth-century scientific community was that individuals had limited 'vital forces' available for cognitive and reproductive tasks. Females who diverted their scarce biological reserves to intellectual endeavors could expect a host of maladies including, in some cases, permanent sterility. Rigorous education or vocational pursuits could result only in deforming, defeminizing, or eventually depleting any group of women who sought to avoid their domestic destiny" ("Theoretical Perspectives on Sexual Difference," in *Theoretical Perspective on Sexual Difference* [New Haven, Conn.: Yale University Press, 1990], 3.

New York City. She met Mrs. Palmer personally, which only fueled her desire to witness.[63] Dieter generalizes experiences such as these and states: "It was the theology of the movement and the essential nature of the place of public testimony in the holiness experience which gave many an otherwise timid woman the authority and power to speak out as the Holy Spirit led her. . . . To those who allowed the theology, the logic was irrefutable."[64]

Therefore, if a woman professed entire devotion to God and counted herself free from idols and an absorption in domestic cares, she must be willing to do what God next asked of her, even if it went against social norms or protocol. Thus, in Palmer's theology, there was an intricate connection between the requisite to surrender idols and the requisite to speak. As Nancy Hardesty shows, "Palmer declared that a person must first consecrate everything to God. Volumes of subsequent testimonials showed this to usually include one's children, spouse, material possessions and reputation; for women it often included being willing to preach."[65] Sacrifice could mean a "giving up" but also a "willingness to." While Palmer does speak in terms of freedom, her rhetoric also often identifies speech as "self-sacrifice." It is crucial to see that for Palmer self-sacrifice did not mean playing the typical, martyrlike role of the subservient wife and mother. This, if fact, would have been the easiest or widest road, in her mind. Rather, sacrifice meant being courageous in the secular sphere: it was a personal sacrifice for a woman to be considered undignified by society for overstepping her feminine boundaries. But such an undignified position, according to Palmer, was required by God. Rather than fulfilling their Christian responsibilities in the home alone, women were finding in Palmer's theology a religious imperative that necessitated a conceptual shift of women's calling and women's place. What is clear is that women in the 1840s and 1850s, "emboldened by a religiously-engendered individualism . . . were forging an autonomous self and voice. They were allowing themselves to view this self-development as part of their Christian duty, rather than something egotistical or evil."[66]

Amanda Porterfield has offered an essay that analyzes the nature of Palmer's language and her requisites of female consecration and, specifi-

---

63. White, *Beauty of Holiness,* 187-88.

64. Dieter, *Holiness Revival of the Nineteenth Century,* 42.

65. Nancy A. Hardesty, *Great Women of Faith: The Strength and Influence of Christian Women* (Grand Rapids: Baker, 1980), 90.

66. Joanna Bowen Gillespie, "The Emerging Voice of the Methodist Woman: The Ladies Repository, 1841-61," in *Perspectives on American Methodism: Interpretive Essays,* ed. Russell E. Richey, Kenneth E. Rowe, and Jean Miller Schmidt (Nashville: Abingdon/Kingswood, 1993), 255.

cally, female testimony. In Palmer's own life, "liberty meant freedom of speech, and, of course, more specifically, the freedom to prophesy—the liberty to speak in metaphors."[67] *The Promise of the Father* portrays women's call to prophesy not as a right to be won, but as a responsibility. This subtle linguistic difference had powerful consequences. Although Palmer argues that Scripture supports the imperative of speech placed on women and offers a quite sophisticated exegetical argument to that end, the greatest portion of her 400-page work is composed of verbatim accounts and summaries of women obeying God's injunction to preach. The effect of the words of women themselves is masterful. Going beyond this specific work, Porterfield illumines Palmer's overall use of language:

> Phoebe Palmer invested language with the power to structure experience. Her view of language is the key to her power as an evangelist, and the key to understanding her mysticism and theology as well. She slipped back and forth with ease between language and life itself, not with any intention to trick or confuse, but to enlighten. At the heart of her spirituality, language and life were the same. In her role as poet of such religious inspiration, Phoebe Palmer functioned as agent in the radical transformation of the feelings and behavior of thousands of persons.[68]

It could be said that theory and practice collapse into one where language and life are so tightly integrated.

Galea argues that Palmer's use of mystical language gave her an authority that bypassed traditional and conventional sites of (male) authority.[69] It was this same type of authority, unmediated and directly from God, as well as a new confidence, that Palmer challenged other women to embrace. Schneider offers a helpful summary:

> The cultivation of confidence was essential to the task [of building a more visible feminine identity]. One is tempted to call it self-confidence. The quest for holiness, however, led to a curiously convoluted sort of self-confidence. It was a confidence in calling, in duty, and ultimately in God who called a woman and who assisted her duty. It was confidence in a self that was no longer a woman's own self, but God's, and that nevertheless, felt freer and more authentic than she had ever felt simply on her own.[70]

---

67. Porterfield, "Phoebe Palmer," 23.
68. Ibid., 15.
69. See Kate Galea, "Anchored Behind the Vail: Mystical Vision as Possible Source of Authority in the Ministry of Phoebe Palmer," *Methodist History* 31 (1993): 236-47.
70. A. Gregory Schneider, *The Way of the Cross Leads Home: The Domestication of American Methodism* (Bloomington, Ind.: Indiana University Press, 1993), 182.

Palmer's religious vision provided 19th-century holiness women with a new confidence, not only to know themselves as fully devoted to God but also to be fully themselves.

Phoebe Palmer offered women access into a specifically female subjectivity, while forging particular and novel liberties under the rubric of devotion to God. In other words, Palmer regendered the Eastern and Wesleyan theories of subjectivity—which affirmed the necessity of holy women becoming symbolic males—by actually occupying the traditionally female roles of wife and mother, and thus barring a sweeping rejection of her own and other's maternal bodies. Still, she maintained the freedoms for women offered by the Eastern/Wesleyan theological framework by also rejecting an Augustinian paradigm of sin that promoted submission as virtue. Palmer accepted the basic assumption of the cult of domesticity—that women had more "natural" access to spirituality and sanctity; yet, paradoxically, this enabled her to transcend such a traditional configuration because, while women were "naturally" domestic, in Palmer's estimation they were also equally implicated in the experience of Pentecost and thus equally responsible for Christian service outside "women's sphere." They were specifically responsible to speak. Especially in light of Joel's injunction,[71] Palmer believed women to be prophesying daughters of God, not female sons. They were dignified by their calling, while simultaneously considered undignified in society for being speakers at all. Yet, for women whose only "lord" was God alone, speech could be both female and dignified. In a diary entry only a year before she died, Palmer reflects:

> Well do I, as a daughter of the Lord Almighty, remember the baptism of fire that fell upon me, over thirty years since. Not more assuringly, perhaps, did the tongues of fire fall in energizing, hallowing influences on the sons and daughters of the Almighty, when they ALL spake as the Spirit gave utterance, on the day of Pentecost, than I felt its consuming, hallowing, energizing influences fall on me, empowering me for holy activities and burning utterances.[72]

Palmer's burning utterances changed history—not only the religious history of the 19th century but also the individual histories of women who walk in Palmer's footsteps. She not only gave them an example but also gave them theologically based requisites that demanded they refuse to keep silent in the churches and in the world.

---

71. See Joel 2:28-29.
72. Wheatley, *Life and Letters of Mrs. Phoebe Palmer,* 83.

CONTEMPORARY HERMENEUTICAL CONSIDERATIONS FOR WESLEYAN WOMEN

It has been stated that Phoebe Palmer's *Promise of the Father,* a defense of women in ministry written in 1859, anticipates many of the interpretative moves of late 20th-century feminist exegetes. I would argue, however, that while Palmer reaches many of the same conclusions, her methodology could not have anticipated many of the methodological nuances of present-day feminist hermeneutics. Perhaps the most well known of the feminist exegetes is Elisabeth Schüssler Fiorenza. She has developed a hermeneutic known as the "hermeneutic of suspicion and remembrance."[73] Highly popular, this hermeneutic challenges biblical texts and patristic texts as androcentric in nature but discovers within these very texts a means subverting a misogynistic reading.

Averil Cameron has offered a deft analysis and implicit critique of specifically "feminist" readings of early Christian texts.[74] She accurately illumines the purposes and procedures of this hermeneutic, which has been enthusiastically embraced by many Christian-feminist exegetes and historians, to the detriment, it has been charged,[75] of their own objectivity. Since the Christian texts themselves are "fixed," such scholars are "bound and constrained" to deal with them in some manner; more specifically, according to Cameron, feminist scholars of early Christianity who embrace the hermeneutic of suspicion methodology cannot escape, but only manipulate[76] apparently misogynistic passages by proposing redeemed reinterpretations that make them more palatable to feminist tastes. Cameron, herself a feminist, is anxious about the potential abuses of this approach; when the feminist agenda becomes so apologetic as to force rhetoric in certain and perhaps even contrived directions, the integrity of the interpretation can be legitimately questioned.[77]

---

73. For the most conspicuous example, see Elisabeth Schüssler Fiorenza, *In Memory of Her: A Feminist Theological Reconstruction of Christian Origins* (New York: Crossroad, 1986).

74. See Averil Cameron, "Virginity as Metaphor: Women and the Rhetoric of Early Christianity," in *History as Text: The Writing of Ancient History,* ed. Averil Cameron (Chapel Hill, N.C.: University of North Carolina Press, 1989), 181-205. Cameron references biblical and patristic literature.

75. E.g., Kathleen E. Corley, "Feminist Myths of Christian Origins," in *Reimagining Christian Origins: A Colloquium Honoring Burton L. Mack,* ed. Elizabeth A. Castelli and Hal Taussig (Valley Forge, Pa.: Trinity Press International, 1996), 51-67.

76. Cameron, "Virginity as Metaphor," 187.

77. Cameron asserts that all "history is itself indeed a matter of interpretation" and emphasizes the inherently subjective stance of every interpretation. She does not, I believe, im-

Lone Fatum echoes Cameron's concern, specifically as it applies to biblical hermeneutics. It is worth quoting him at length:

What I am concerned with is the project of feminist reconstruction which seems to me to be a highly problematic attempt to achieve two different results through one analytical process, namely exposing the suppression of women by the biblical material and, at the same time, seeking the affirmation of women by the biblical material. . . . The hermeneutical consequence, it seems to me, is a faulty methodology, allowing utopian vision and wishful thinking to stop critical questioning and consistent analysis in an effort to explain away or make light of the suppressive evidence in the texts and tradition before us. . . . The result of this historical reservation in feminist exegesis is very often, I find, critical inconsistency, feminist apologetic interest allowing itself to turn a blind eye to the full and unpleasant implications of the fact that Christian faith and interpretation are rooted in androcentric structures, symbolic values, transmitted and institutionalized through patriarchal organizations. Thus Christian interpretation is androcentric interpretation, but feminist Christian exegesis cannot bear to acknowledge the full implications of this hermeneutical insight. Therefore, instead of deconstructing with critical consistency to the bitter end where androcentric values and patriarchal strategies can be fully unveiled and analytically exposed, it stops half way and chooses to (re)construct a pattern of utopian values which may serve as an affirmation of Christian women. Deconstruction becomes reconstruction and the hermeneutical difference between the two is blurred by apologetic endeavors.[78]

In Cameron's estimation, feminist exegetes, in an attempt to argue for a kind of early Christian feminism, "claim that whatever the Christian texts themselves might imply, there was once a golden age of early Christianity in which women played a role they were scarcely to enjoy again until the rise of the feminist movement."[79] This presupposition impels historical reconstruction in certain directions. Yet when faced with charges of lost historical-critical objectivity, the reply given is that (false) hopes of objective interpretations of history have faded with postmodernity and that the

---

ply that every interpretation is of equal value or legitimacy. For example, "It may be theoretically possible to recapture, or rather to postulate an unpolluted source in the Gospels, but a more sympathetic reading of, say, Jerome, is hardly in the cards" ("Virginity as Metaphor," 188).

78. Lone Fatum, "Women, Symbolic Universe and Structures of Silence. Challenges and Possibilities in Androcentric Texts," *Studia Theologica* 43 (1989): 61-62.

79. Cameron, "Virginity as Metaphor," 184.

"hermeneutic of suspicion and remembrance" should be commended for its forthrightness concerning its underlying agenda.[80] The consequent reinterpretation of early Christianity (as an institution embodying principles of feminism) is not compromised, according to the proponents, by its programmatic approach to Christian texts.[81]

At first glance, Wesleyan women who embrace an interpretation of certain scriptures that allows for full ecclesiastical leadership for women may seem programmatic and even apologetic in their (re)interpretation of problematic biblical texts. However, it is not necessary to operate under the presupposition that affirms a feminist "golden age" during the early church period. Wesleyan hermeneutics is a methodology that can read biblical androcentricism, even misogynism, for what it is, while also advocating the full equality of all persons in all functions within the church. Through a utilization of the Wesleyan hermeneutical principle of the "analogy of faith," it is possible to avoid the pitfalls of feminists such as Schüssler Fiorenza, who, not unlike Wesleyan feminists, find their historical task fueled by a desire to reach theological conclusions with feminist implications. It is not necessary to manipulate texts. It is not necessary to seek to justify, hide, or explain away the clearly difficult passages. It is not necessary to argue that biblical writers somehow meant something other than what they said, or that the message is, by necessity, strictly independent of the author's intentions. It is not necessary to assert that biblical writers are—intentionally or unintentionally—subversive "feminists" despite their own rhetoric.

The analogy of faith provides an entirely different approach that has

---

80. Cf. Bernadette J. Brooten, "Early Christian Women and Their Cultural Context: Issues of Method in Historical Reconstruction," in *Feminist Perspectives on Biblical Scholarship,* ed. Adela Yarbro Collins (Chico, Calif.: Scholars, 1985), 66.

81. Speaking of a more general category of theological biases, Castelli and Taussig declare, "The point here is not to eliminate theological convictions—an impossible task, even were one to consider it desirable. Rather, the point is to call the whole study of Christian origins to a higher level of consciousness in which those both with and without Christian convictions develop a heightened awareness of the ways that Christian presuppositions can frame and color the critical analysis of how it all began. Put more positively . . . the process of reimagining Christian origins must start with an awareness of the ways various cultural and theological forces can cause important sources and approaches to be ignored or enthroned uncritically," from Elizabeth A. Castelli and Hal Taussig, "Drawing Large and Startling Figures: Reimagining Christian Origins by Painting Like Picasso," in *Reimagining Christian Origins* (Valley Forge, Pa.: Trinity Press International, 1996), 3-22. In Castelli and Taussig's scheme, the question becomes whether a feminist hermeneutic is, in fact, honest about its subjectivity or whether it "enthrones" its methodology uncritically; and therefore it follows that it should be evaluated not on the basis of its product but on the basis of its sincerity.

the potential to yield equally positive results. It considers each biblical text in light of overarching biblical themes. As Randy Maddox explains, "For Wesley, this term referred to a 'connected chain of Scripture truths.' He highlighted four soteriological truths in particular: the corruption of sin, justification by faith, the new birth, and present inward and outward holiness. He believed that it was the shared articulation of these truths that gave the diverse components of Scripture their unity. Accordingly, he required that all passages be read in light of these truths."[82] Each of these soteriological truths, interpreted from a Wesleyan perspective, has powerful implications for women.

Scholars such as Maddox suggest that a correct interpretation of Wesley's doctrine of sin must recognize the strong influence of the Eastern fathers on Wesley at this point. This is important in two regards. First, these patristic fathers imaged sin as a disease needing healing, rather than just a forensic problem needing legal justification. This greatly influences Wesley's understanding of the new birth and sanctification. Second, the eastern patristics in general interpreted gender distinctions primarily as a result of the Fall and posited that the process of *theosis,* finally culminated in the afterlife, would produce genderless saints. It was the Western, Augustinian paradigm of sin and the Fall that argued that female subordination was God's intended design. Wesley is progressive on this point. As Maddox points out:

> In 1754 [Wesley] invoked with no qualifications the common supposition that Eve's creation subsequent to Adam demonstrated that women were originally intended to be subordinate to men. However, by 1765 he inclined more to the view that male and female were created by God to be equal in all ways, with women's subjection to men being one of the results of the Fall. . . . [This created] at least the possibility of advocating restoration of the social equality of women as one aspect of the Christian healing of the damage of the Fall.[83]

I have argued at length elsewhere that a Wesleyan understanding of sin has dramatic implications for women. Suffice it to say here that a Wesleyan hamartiology deconstructs images of the saintly woman that are directly tied to Augustine's paradigm. Wesley and Wesleyan theology and hermeneutics offer a new imago of the "holy woman." Female virtue need no longer be imaged as humility, submissiveness, complicity, and silence.

---

82. Randy L. Maddox, *Responsible Grace: John Wesley's Practical Theology* (Nashville: Abingdon/Kingswood, 1994), 38.
83. Ibid., 72-73.

Rather, Wesleyan theology allows for a reimagining of the holy woman as strong, dependent on God, free through grace, and even vocal.[84]

Related to this is Wesley's interpretation of justification and the new birth. His concept of unlimited atonement, that justifying grace is available to all who believe, presupposes the (equal) value in the eyes of God of each individual. The effects of free grace give each person *real* new birth; all are deemed new creations, the old is gone, the new has come. Righteousness is imparted, not just imputed to the graced individual. But as much as Wesley valued the individual's spiritual renewal, he was not content to leave faith as an individual matter. New creation, for Wesley, had strong social implications. A deep sense of social justice permeates the Wesleyan vision. Women are thus affected doubly by Wesley's understanding of new birth; they benefit from Wesley's optimism about grace in two ways. Individual women find new birth, and the spiritual and social equality of women (and all marginalized persons) is (or at least should be) affirmed in Wesley's analogy of faith.

Finally, Wesley's doctrine of sanctification, and the inward and outward holiness that he expected to be a present experience for his Methodists, also has "feminist" implications. Wesley strongly believed that Methodist women should be entirely devoted to God. This is a theme that was picked up and strongly emphasized in the Holiness Movement a century later. For Wesley, this level of consecration, absolutely necessary in order to be open to God's sanctifying work, at times required women to disobey family obligations in order to serve God.[85] Inward and outward holiness was conditioned on such servanthood; it was servanthood not in the home, as it has been traditionally understood, but in the bands, the societies, and in society itself.

Many women of early British Methodism performed responsibilities usually connotative of more traditionally male roles. Women of John Wesley's movement led class meetings, carried on pastoral functions, traveled itinerantly, and preached. These religious duties offered women a spiritual transcendence as well as opportunity to transcend the established social roles for women of 18th-century England. Such opportunity was afforded to these women because of an underlying theological anthropology, based firmly on Wesley's interpretation of Scripture. He held to an overarching optimistic theology that gave women equal spiritual status that overcame any "natural" essentialisms. His strong concept of prevenient, redemptive,

---

84. See Diane Leclerc, *Singleness of Heart: Gender, Sin, and Holiness in Historical Perspective* (Metuchen, N.J.: Scarecrow, 2001).

85. Again, see my book for substantiation of this strong reality within Methodism.

and sanctifying grace, as well as a strong belief in the restoration of original freedom, allowed women in particular to strive for a more transcendent existence in a spiritual context that approximated a new Eden.

This is our Wesleyan heritage. The question is whether or not we still make the connections between the Wesleyan doctrines of sin, justification, new birth, and holiness and women that were readily enacted in Wesley's day and carried on by the Holiness Movement of the 19th century. I am optimistic enough to believe that identifying a Wesleyan way of reading Scripture will rebirth the powerful affirmation of women that has been a part of our tradition, a part of our experience, and an affirmation that many can reason through quite well. It is time we said with great confidence, the Bible is on our side.

LIST OF CONTRIBUTORS

Barry L. Callen
Editor, *Wesleyan Theological Journal*
University Professor of Christian Studies
School of Theology and Department of Religious Studies
Anderson University
Anderson, Indiana

Joel B. Green
Dean of the School of Theology
Professor of New Testament Interpretation
Asbury Theological Seminary
Wilmore, Kentucky

Diane Leclerc
Professor of Historical Theology
Department of Philosophy and Religion
Northwest Nazarene University
Nampa, Idaho

Sharon Clark Pearson
Professor of New Testament
School of Theology
Anderson University
Anderson, Indiana

Clark H. Pinnock
Professor of Systematic Theology
McMaster Divinity College
McMaster University
Hamilton, Ontario, Canada

Richard P. Thompson
Professor of Greek and New Testament Studies
Department of Philosophy and Religion
Spring Arbor University
Spring Arbor, Michigan

Donald A. D. Thorsen
Professor of Theology
Haggard School of Theology
Azusa Pacific University
Azusa, California

Geoffrey Wainwright
Robert Earl Cushman Professor of Christian Theology
Duke Divinity School
Duke University
Durham, North Carolina

Robert W. Wall
Professor of the Christian Scriptures
School of Theology
Seattle Pacific University
Seattle, Washington